Stasis Leaked
Complete

The Unofficial
Behind the Scenes Guide to

RED DWARF

Elly Books

STASIS LEAKED *COMPLETE*

THE UNOFFICIAL BEHIND THE SCENES GUIDE TO

RED DWARF

by Jane Killick

Published by
Elly Books

ISBN: 978-1-908340-06-1

www.ellybooks.co.uk

Author's Note

On Sunday December 1ˢᵗ 1991, I was invited onto the set of *Red Dwarf* for the first time. The cast and crew were in a multi-storey carpark at Shepperton Studios filming the fifth series episode, *Back to Reality*, and I was reporting for *Starburst Magazine*. This was the first time I had been to watch anybody film anything and, as *Red Dwarf* was one of my favourite television shows, I was incredibly excited. It left me buzzing for days afterwards and, as the magazine liked my article, I was commissioned to do more.

So began a long association with *Red Dwarf*, writing for various magazines, most notably *Red Dwarf Magazine* (or *Smegazine*). I interviewed all members of the cast many times over, and also members of the production team. One of the things I always wanted to do was to look at the individual episodes of *Red Dwarf*, find out some of the ideas behind them and learn their behind-the-scenes secrets. Being *Red Dwarf* — a challenging show to film which starred a lively bunch of people — there were a lot of crazy anecdotes waiting to be told. I started a series of articles looking at the episodes for the *Smegazine*, but sadly the magazine folded before I got past the first series.

The stories can now, at last, be told. I have brought together all the material from the interviews I conducted over the years to tell the story of *Red Dwarf*, episode by episode. All the quotes in this book are taken from those interviews, unless otherwise stated. The book concentrates on the BBC years of the space comedy, although the more recent episodes made for digital channel Dave are also covered. I've included bonus chapters on other *Red Dwarf* projects too, such as the failed attempts to make a movie and an American series, and the original article from the filming of *Red Dwarf V* in 1991 which started it all.

Jane Killick, 2012

Contents

The Long Journey Into Space

The Story of How *Red Dwarf* Came to Be

Red Dwarf became one of the BBC's most successful comedies in the early 1990s, topping the BBC2 ratings and selling widely around the world. But, at the beginning, no one was interested in a sitcom in space. Lots of individuals said they liked the script, but the people who mattered — the BBC — most definitely did not like it. They were given several opportunities to commission *Red Dwarf* in the mid-1980s and turned it down every time.

The idea for *Red Dwarf* had come from the minds of Rob Grant and Doug Naylor, two childhood friends from Manchester with an ambition to become comedy writers. Their careers began modestly on radio, with projects like the badly-received sitcom *Wrinkles*, the popular sketch show *The News Huddlines*, and the award-winning *Son of Cliché*. It was *Cliché* which featured a recurring sketch called *Dave Hollins: Space Cadet* — about a man alone in space talking to his computer — which became the seed for *Red Dwarf*.

Following on from their radio work, Rob and Doug wrote for a series of television sketch shows, culminating in a job as lead writers on the hugely successful puppet satire programme, *Spitting Image*.

But it was while working on *Three of a Kind* that they met producer Paul Jackson and decided to send him a copy of a sitcom pilot they'd written called *Red Dwarf*. Paul Jackson liked the script, but said the science fiction element would limit its audience and make it hard to sell.

Armed with this warning, Rob and Doug did their best to make the script TV executive-friendly. They only put one model shot in the first episode (in other words, only one shot of the spaceship moving through space) so it wouldn't seem too expensive and based the humour around the characters rather than 'space stuff'. Their philosophy was to make it, not so much 'comedy *Star Trek*', but more '*The Odd Couple* or *Steptoe & Son* in space'. It didn't seem to help. TV executives at the BBC in London rejected the script three times.

It was at this point that Paul Jackson had a bit of luck. In 1985, he'd produced a series called *Happy Families* starring Dawn French and Jennifer Saunders for BBC Manchester. When BBC Manchester worked out their production budgets for the following year, they simply pencilled in another series of *Happy Families*, even though French and Saunders had no intention of doing more. Suddenly it meant there was a comedy slot available with Paul Jackson's name on it. Paul's next move was to send a copy of the *Red Dwarf* script northwards, where it landed on the desk of commissioning editor Peter Risdale-Scott.

Peter Risdale-Scott had a system when it came to reading scripts. He would gather up a pile of them and read them on the train as he travelled from Manchester to London. When he arrived at Euston Station, he would simply post the scripts back to his office so he didn't have to carry them anymore. But things were a little different when he picked up a well-thumbed copy of *Red Dwarf*. "For the first time for a very long time on that train ride I laughed out loud," he said. "That's always embarrassing on a train because everyone looks at you as if you've gone mad! That was one script that wasn't sent back at Euston, I re-read it on the way back. And then I found myself regaling the office the next week with stories of the bits of *Red Dwarf* that I'd read. They thought I was mad, but they got the point that I'd got *Red Dwarf* under my skin."

Peter took the project to his bosses who agreed to go ahead, partly because they trusted him and partly because of the reputation of *Red Dwarf*'s producer Paul Jackson, who had also produced the cult comedy hit *The Young Ones*. Not that his colleagues in London approved. "They thought we were potty, absolutely nuts!" said Peter. "They remembered *Red Dwarf* and said 'oh we know what you're doing, it'll never work!' There was a lot of eyes to the ceiling. 'Why do you think that's going to work? We've read it, it isn't funny. How can something with a cat and two other people trapped in space ever develop? There are no women in it, where are you going to go for your sex interest, your glamour?' [I said] 'it's not like that. This is about characters stuck together and they've got to make a go of it and through that we'll get comedy'. The very famous story is that someone in London said 'but there isn't a set of French windows or a settee in sight, so how can it be funny?' But I knew it would work if you put it on BBC2 because it was very oddball indeed and there was an audience there waiting for something like that."

The next person to be approached was director Ed Bye. Paul Jackson asked him to come on board as they had worked together on both *Three of a Kind* and *The Young Ones*. He read the script and knew immediately he wanted to do it. "It was a science fiction script that actually dealt with the interesting ideas of science fiction," said Ed Bye. "It was about a man who's been in suspended animation for hundreds and hundreds of years and all the characters are severely flawed in one way or another — there's no obvious heroes here. I just thought it was great." It didn't seem to matter that it was a new and untested form of comedy that some people thought wouldn't work. "I've always worked on programmes like that," said Ed. "[People would say] 'oh God, you're not doing that are you? You'll get into so much trouble!'"

Deciding who would play the main roles in *Red Dwarf* involved the usual audition process. Writers Rob Grant and Doug Naylor were keen to cast traditional actors in the parts, but saw a mix of people in the auditions, including comedy performers who hadn't been to drama school. Chris Barrie — later to be cast as Rimmer — was one of them. "I always knew they were working on this project they kept pretty quiet," said Chris. "I always thought they were thinking of another actor for it, for the main Lister part, who I thought was Nick Wilton at the time. When I worked with Nick Wilton on *Carrott's Lib*, he kept saying things like, 'there's a project I might be doing with Rob and Doug' — so the only thing it could be, presumably, is *Red Dwarf*. So I didn't know anything about it at all. I went along to the auditions, like many people that they'd worked with, because they knew us and it might be a good place to start auditioning people, with people that you know."

Chris Barrie had worked extensively with Rob and Doug on *Carrott's Lib*, *Son of Cliché* and on *Spitting Image* where he had provided the voices for many of the famous people of the day, from American President Ronald Reagan to sports commentator David Coleman. But, sadly, he failed to get a part in *Red Dwarf* and Alfred Molina — a traditional actor with a drama school background — was cast as Rimmer.

This decision was something Rob Grant and Doug Naylor came to regret. They'd cast the part in isolation, for one thing, with no idea at that point who was going to play Lister; and they needed to find two actors who had the right chemistry. There was also a feeling that Alfred Molina didn't quite 'get' the concept and was asking things like how long he would have to be a hologram. It was decided it would be better if they went their separate ways and Chris Barrie received a call to ask if he would be interested in playing Rimmer after all.

It was only later that Chris Barrie realised all the drama which had been happening behind the scenes. "I heard Alfred Molina had been offered my part at one point," he said. "It would have been interesting if it had been cast with 'luvvies' — you know, traditional 'luvvies' — and not the smegheads that eventually took the roles!"

The 'smeghead' who was offered the part of Lister also came from a non-acting background. Craig Charles had made a name for himself as a stand-up poet, reciting often hard-hitting poems about issues of the day. His big break came when he was asked to appear as a regular on the TV chat show *Wogan*, where he toned down his subject matter for the early-evening audience. Craig had heard about *Red Dwarf* because Paul Jackson sent him a copy of the script to get his opinion on whether the Cat was a racist part. He got back in touch to say there was no problem with the Cat and, by the way, could he play Lister?

Casting the Cat was the easiest decision to make as Danny John-Jules blew everyone away at his audition. The trained dancer with a background in musicals — including Andrew Lloyd Webber's *Cats* — knew how to create an impression. "The door opened and he didn't *walk* in, he *leapt* in like a cat," said Peter Risdale-Scott. "The other thing about Danny John-Jules that morning is he had dressed the part. He was totally dressed in black, he'd got all the right jewellery for a cat, all the right sparkly things and he was just 'Cat'. There was no doubt in anybody's mind that he was top of the list. He was stunning."

Danny dressed for his audition in his father's black demob suit, the style of which was later copied for the Cat's pink suit, seen in the first series. While his moves were based on some of his heroes. "I thought the best way to get this Cat to move — he had to move like somebody — so I thought: James Brown. The look is really kind of Little Richard; y'know — that kind of attitude was kind of the Cat, puts everybody down — Little Richard, nobody can sit next to, right? Then you had Richard Pryor, which is kind of the facial expressions."

Norman Lovett also auditioned, but for the part of Rimmer. "I thought I was very good," said Norman. "I probably didn't look right for that sort of character. Chris is perfect for it really, that person that strives for perfection and is a prat. I can do the prat part, but probably didn't look officer-type material."

But he must have impressed at the audition because he caused the writers to change their plans when it came to finding someone to play Holly. "Holly was originally meant to be a woman," said Rob Grant. "We saw Norman Lovett and thought he wasn't right for Rimmer, who he'd auditioned for, but he'd make a great Holly and give an interesting twist to it."

Older than the rest of the main cast, Norman was a late-comer to showbiz, having turned to stand-up comedy in his thirties. At the time, there were no plans for Holly to appear on screen and he wasn't sure whether to accept the part. "I'd just done Ruby Wax [the Channel 4 show *Don't Miss Wax*] and I'd been a minor cult hit in that as the floor manager and just doing a voice-over seemed like stepping backwards," he said. But he eventually agreed to do it and later badgered the production team until they agreed to show his face. "It wasn't until the third episode that they went back and had to re-film me doing the lines again."

So, what started out as a quest to find traditional actors to fill the roles on *Red Dwarf* had ended with casting a poet, an impressionist, a dancer and a comedian. They, perhaps rather naively, joined the writers for their first sitcom to discover some of the production values at BBC Manchester, with sets painted grey, were not quite as they would have liked. But, in the end, it seemed to turn out for the best.

"The choice we made at the beginning was a brave choice and sometimes we forget it," said writer Doug Naylor. "The choice is we could have gone for big star actors, and with big star actors they would have said 'we're not doing it in this stupid grey set' and that would have given voice to that whole complaint. It would have been fixed and much better, a far far better series, but probably they wouldn't have been around for series two or series three.

"And casting it the way we did, we knew... I mean, in Craig's case he was 21, hardly just been born! Obviously, there's going to be lots of things he's going to learn and Chris had never really done a sustained character, but because of that they've all kind of grown up together on *Red Dwarf* and now we've reaped the benefits of it. It's probably now been far more successful than it would have been if we'd have cast it with the big star-name actors that we could have done."

Red Dwarf I

Written by... Rob Grant & Doug Naylor
Produced & Directed by... Ed Bye
Executive Producer... Paul Jackson

Rimmer... Chris Barrie
Lister... Craig Charles
Cat... Danny John-Jules
Holly... Norman Lovett

Recorded: September-November 1987
First broadcast: February-March 1988

For a long six-week period in 1987, many people thought *Red Dwarf* would never see the light of day. Technicians at the BBC were on strike and, without the technicians, nothing could be filmed. "We would rehearse each show and then the show would get cancelled," said writer Doug Naylor. "We went through the whole series like this, not making a show and the whole thing got cancelled."

It was a frustrating time for everybody. Peter Risdale-Scott, as commissioning editor for the BBC, remembered hoping the strike would be over and *Red Dwarf* would get made. "We actually rehearsed every week, every one of the episodes up to pitch, but we never went in the studio," he said. "On Mondays, the cast — who were absolutely wonderful, they weren't demoralized or anything — just picked up the next script and said 'right, this may be the week we have to do it'. On the Thursday I was the one who had to go in and say 'no we're not doing it, but will you please keep going, we will do it eventually'. Because I was hoping against hope that we would get one or two done of that series because once we'd got one or two done they would find us the room to do the other four. But luck wasn't with us and we went through the entire series and never did it."

There was a feeling within the BBC that *Red Dwarf* had already been done. Even though it had never been given a chance in front of an audience, up to eighty per cent of the first series' £1.1 million budget had been spent. Writer Rob Grant remembered thinking it was the end. "Everybody thought at the time that they wouldn't bother remounting it because it's an expensive business, they had to pay for just about everything again. And there were other series around [and we] were first-timers. We were quite lucky to get re-mounted, I think."

According to Peter Risdale-Scott, the decision to re-commission was partly due to him and producer Paul Jackson inviting some important people from London to see the original rehearsals. "I think that did a lot," said Peter. "The confidence grew that if this was sufficiently outrageous, innovative, risky, it could actually be a success. I think that allowed us to re-mount it. We were very lucky, it could have so easily faded away!"

Later that year, everyone — including the technicians — returned to try again. There was a certain amount of excitement when the show was finally going to go in front of the cameras. "The first thing I remember when we walked into the BBC Manchester studios," said Rob Grant, "was these four people in these uniforms which said *Red Dwarf* on them and *Jupiter Mining Corporation* on the lapels and we got into the lift with them and I was thinking 'God, I invented you, you wouldn't exist without me.'"

The show, although filmed in Manchester, was rehearsed at the BBC Rehearsal Rooms in Acton. This was standard procedure for sitcoms as it meant spending limited time in the expensive studio space. It was a lively atmosphere, by all accounts, with lots of clowning around by the all-male cast. "That's what I liked about it," said Norman Lovett, who played Holly. "Normally in a sitcom you've got actors sitting around reading their *Guardians* with their glasses hanging on the end of their noses and smoking away… Whereas with *Red Dwarf* we were always having fun and playing jokes. We used to play football at break time in the rehearsal rooms and this little assistant floor manager, Dona [DiStefano], she confiscated the ball once. It was a little leather football and I said, 'I'm not doing any work until I get my ball back'. It was very childish. There's a man of 40 saying 'I want my ball back otherwise I'm not doing any more lines'. I mean it's disgusting behaviour, really, but it was good fun."

Such behaviour wasn't confined to the rehearsal rooms. Craig Charles liked to go clubbing and tales have since emerged of him and Danny John-Jules going out for a night on the town while they were working on *Red Dwarf*. One member of the crew once saw a furious Paul Jackson take Craig Charles aside for a severe telling off one morning when he arrived late, only for Craig to re-appear with his T-shirt all crumpled after the producer held him up against a wall and told him not to do it again.

Away from the antics of the actors, the production team were trying to work out how to achieve some of the more unusual aspects of the *Red Dwarf* scenario. Top of the list was making Rimmer appear as a hologram. Rob Grant and Doug Naylor had wanted him to be black and white, but this was too technically difficult, and they ended up sticking an 'H' on his forehead. "I would have loved to have employed a technique that wherever he walked he was slightly transparent," said director Ed Bye. "But you couldn't do it without awful restrictions on his performance, like he'd have to be acting in another room somewhere, which would have been impossible. There was an idea where I was going to try and make him black and white and everything else colour. But in order to do that he'd have to have been painted bright green from head to toe! I decided not to use that method. It's bad enough pouring one man's face into rubber all his life [with Kryten later on], I just don't think I could have turned another man green at the same time!"

Colour, it turned out, was another issue which plagued the first series — or rather, the lack of it. Everything was painted grey. Not just the sets, but some of the objects in the sets — including some bizarre things like cans of beer and popcorn boxes. There's even a scene where Lister has made a cake which is topped with grey icing.

"As soon as we opened the door and looked at the set we knew we were in big trouble," said Doug Naylor. "The one thing we'd said 'til we were blue in the face was 'the set has to be credible, it mustn't look like some terrible BBC science fiction TV series, because it won't survive, people won't buy it', and of course that's precisely what it looked like."

"We tried our best — because [we had] no experience of set design — to go over ideas with the set designer," said Rob Grant. "The idea was to make it a kind of submariney kind of look, which we thought at least would give a kind of consistent feel to it, but it didn't look much like a submarine that would float to me."

"The idea was to make it so it wouldn't look high-tech, it would look low-tech and it would look like a submarine," said Doug. "But that just meant painting all the walls grey and it even had some flowers which were painted grey. And there was a joke that the set designer's brother owned a grey paint factory and he was just trying to get rid of all this grey paint!"

The writers were much happier with the model shots, which were created by Peter Wragg and his colleagues at the BBC Special Effects Department. Peter was very experienced, having worked on programmes like *Thunderbirds* and *Doctor Who*, and therefore knew how to film spaceships. A limited number of shots of Red Dwarf in space were filmed for the first series, keeping the special effects budget at a modest level.

"It came about through discussions with Rob and Doug as to what they wanted," said Peter Wragg of the design of Red Dwarf. "It had a ram scoop on the front which was like a hoover and collected debris from space. And then we added on things as we went along, feeling that maybe a meteorite had hit it at some stage… One of the shots I did like was the end closing credits where you move into the front of it, then up over the top, then run along the top of it, then over the end of it and it makes it look as if it's going on for quite a long way."

The opening credit sequence was also devised by Peter Wragg, and has Craig Charles as Lister painting the outside of the ship. The shot then pulls back to reveal he is painting the 'F' of the words 'Red Dwarf' written on the side. "It was something that was ambitious, but something we tried very hard to do," said Peter. "Unfortunately, I was never happy with the way it turned out because it wasn't quite as successful as it actually could have been. The original intention was a pull-back from the frame of red, Craig Charles painting, pulling back, pulling back, pulling back until you see eventually the whole spaceship and it moves off, which we initially intended to try and do as one shot. Unfortunately, we weren't able to do it, so we had to do a mix in between, but we sort of got half way there and very nearly achieved it."

Red Dwarf finally made it onto television screens in 1988 and the audience was treated to something a little bit different which, for some viewers, took a bit of getting used to. Even the production was trying to get a handle on what worked and what didn't, with some episodes centring around science fiction ideas, like *Future Echoes* and *Confidence and Paranoia*, while others featured more pedestrian plots, like *Balance of Power*. "At the beginning we were floundering around a bit trying to find our feet," said director Ed Bye. "[We were] trying to decide if everything should be really funny or everything should be really science fiction-y or everything should be really dramatic. In the end we realised it should be all of those things."

Peter Risdale-Scott had been in charge of preparing trailers for broadcast and sending out press releases, but by the time the show was on air, all he could do was cross his fingers. "Nobody knew what that first series was going to be like," he said. "I'll never forget the relief when I was coming down to a meeting called *The Programme Review* in London. The department heads sit around a table on a Wednesday and review all the week's programmes and because *Red Dwarf* was on that week I came down from Manchester, biting my nails. I'll never forget that on that train journey I was reading *The Times* which had the top ten BBC1 programmes and the top ten BBC2 programmes. I just ripped to the back and I couldn't believe it — *Red Dwarf* was number four in its first week! And in a sense that assured its success."

Episode One: The End

GUEST CAST
Chen… Paul Bradley
Selby… David Gillespie
Captain Hollister… Mac McDonald
McIntyre… Robert McCulley
Petersen… Mark Williams
Kochanski… C.P. Grogan

Story

Arnold Rimmer and Dave Lister are ill-matched colleagues forced to work and bunk together aboard the Jupiter Mining Corporation ship, Red Dwarf. They spend their working days arguing with each other and carrying out vital technical duties, such as unblocking the chicken soup nozzle of vending machines, but dream of better things. Rimmer aims to work his way up the promotion ladder, while Lister dreams of becoming a farmer on the island of Fiji with his pregnant cat. When the ship's captain finds the cat on board, Lister is punished by being locked in stasis and frozen in time.

Three million years later, Lister is revived by the ship's computer, Holly. The rest of the crew have been wiped out — killed by a radiation leak — including Rimmer who is now a hologram. Together, they discover they share the ship with a creature who evolved from Lister's cat.

Funniest Moment (arguably)

Norman Lovett's exquisitely deadpan delivery of the "everybody's dead, Dave" speech.

Behind The Scenes

The first episode of *Red Dwarf* was finally filmed on the 27th of

September 1987. Rather than start with a dramatic moment in space, as other science fiction programmes might have, it began with two lowly technicians cleaning out the chicken soup nozzle of a vending machine.

"We thought a lot of TV science fiction didn't have good characters," said writer Rob Grant. "It was basically all about the ideas rather than characters, and very rarely did it have characters to relate to. You can relate to character much more easily if it's someone at the bottom of the heap, as opposed to a captain of a spaceship.

"You are supposed to write about what you know and we certainly knew about having dull, ordinary jobs," added Rob. "It was modelled on when we were working the night-shift at a mail order company, loading paper into computers and taking it out again... We were on different shifts, actually. We took the job to try and get some time to write together and found ourselves on different shifts, so one of us had just got up and the other was just going to bed whenever we had a chance to write."

The first episode is very different to those that followed because the crew are still alive for much of the episode. Indeed, the audience could be forgiven for thinking it was going to be a series about a fully-manned spaceship. That, said co-writer Doug Naylor, was originally going to be their central joke: "An idea at one point was to populate the entire crew with really famous actors, so it looks like 'here is this series in space with all these famous people'. And it's going to be, whoever, Mel Smith and Ronnie Barker who were in it and we wipe them all out, and at the end of the episode we're left with 'who are these guys?' And we thought we'd do that for quite a while, but obviously it was too expensive."

"I think also people would have been pretty pissed-off," Rob laughed. "They'd say '*that* would've been a good series!'"

As part of the characterisation for Lister and Rimmer, the writers gave them goals. Lister's goal is to save up to buy a farm on Fiji where he'll have a sheep and a cow and breed horses (with horses and horses, obviously). He also plans to take with him his pregnant cat, Frankenstein. "He's really dreaming of an advert," said Rob.

The cat which played Frankenstein was later to make a star performance on what became known as the 'Smeg-Ups', as take after take, it refused to do what it was supposed to. "They always say don't do science fiction, don't work with animals and don't work with children and we had all three with Craig in the first show!" said Rob. "The cat just refused to behave, didn't it? It's funny because when we did the American show [a pilot which failed to become a series] the cat was just — I don't know what kind of hallucinogenics they were pumping into it — but it was an absolute dream-boat, it just performed beautifully."

The cat even ran away at one point and they thought they wouldn't be able to catch it! But it was Lister's underwear, not the cat, that caused Craig Charles the most embarrassment. "If you look closely, you can actually see my testicles hanging out of the side of my pants!" said Craig. "It was weird because we did that take so many times and I was all nervous. People thought that it was supposed to be Lister spilling the milk all over the floor, but the milk came out so quickly. It kind of worked for Lister's character, but I remember at the time, I was nervous as hell and the cat wouldn't look at the photograph [of Fiji] and the cat kept scratching my leg. I got scratches all over my thighs."

According to Rob and Doug, they considered covering "Craig's family jewels" electronically, but instead went for an inferior take.

Rimmer's goal is to make something of himself, to become an officer, a role to which he is clearly unsuited. He can't even manage to sit the exam. He passes out and is removed from the exam hall on a stretcher. This was based on personal experience of "our own horror of exams and the way that there are people who do actually freeze up in them," said Rob. "But the idea of a guy actually being carried out of an exam, that actually happened at our school."

Rimmer, as becomes evident, will never become an officer because he dies before the end of the episode. But death isn't the handicap it used to be and he is revived as a hologram. All of which might have been a bit confusing if it hadn't been for George McIntyre.

George is the first hologram to appear in *Red Dwarf*. After his funeral, he is guest of honour at a welcome reception in front of all of the crew. During the reception, Captain Hollister explains George can't touch anything and has an 'H' on his forehead so people know he's a hologram and won't walk through him. George responds by giving a speech which was deliberately modelled on a best man's wedding speech.

But it didn't look much like a wedding or welcome back reception to Doug Naylor. "We had terrible problems because all the chairs in the canteen were red and I remember running around going 'this looks so, so horrific — we've got this set that looks like it's going to fall down any second and these horrible red chairs'. It just made it look so ghastly and there was no time to change the red chairs or paint them and so they had jackets hung over the backs of most of them to disguise this."

(Curiously, the version of the episode which made it to air clearly shows the chairs to be silver-coloured metal.)

Nick Maloney was originally cast as George and he was going to play the character as Australian. But, after the technicians strike, he wasn't available and was replaced by Robert McCulley who decided to play the character as Welsh. "That's an actors' thing," said Rob. "Sometimes they think putting on an accent makes the character and that annoys me a lot. He was meant to be Australian in fact, because we wanted it to be an international vessel. We wanted to give the idea that it wasn't just white Anglo-Saxons who survived. We wanted to make it as multi-national as possible."

By the end of the episode, all the people who appear at George's reception are dead. Except for Lister. In the original radio sketch which inspired the series, *Dave Hollins: Space Cadet*, Dave shut himself away in suspended animation while the rest of the crew were eaten by a monster. In *Red Dwarf*, the killer became radiation and the concept of suspended animation was called 'stasis'. "I thought it was quite a neat idea," said Rob. "I didn't know the word 'stasis' existed, but I've seen it since in earlier works. Maybe it went in subconsciously, I don't know — Asimov used it, I think, and Harry Harrison. It wasn't a deliberate copy, but we did think through the science of it — that basically it froze time and we'd been doing a lot of reading about quantum physics that previous summer. We had an horrendous time with that complex speech of Todhunter's. Poor old Bob Bathurst trying to walk down the corridor and spout all this, you know — I think we did about eighteen takes of that in the end."

That wasn't the only speech that caused trouble for the actors, as Doug explained. "Craig gave a really sad speech that was cut in the edit about Kochanski and how much he felt about her and how she was dead and all this. He was supposed to put the ashes of the deceased into this tube which shot the remains out into space. And what we had was actually a kitchen bin, just a swingy kitchen bin, and so you had this tube thing and you dropped it into the swingy kitchen bin which was painted grey, and then there was this horrible thud as it dropped down. Then he would hold up the next casket lovingly and drop this thing in the kitchen bin, and of course he just couldn't get his head around this sad speech while he was dropping things through this kitchen bin — I mean, no one could. So it was cut in the end."

The characters went through a lot of changes from conception to the finished product. But changes were still being made to Holly's character during filming. "Holly didn't go loopy in the original pilot script, [he was] just a normal straight computer," said Rob. "For the first two shows, I think, we didn't have Holly in vision. Norman was just reading the lines and then he created such a fuss, [he'd say] 'you've wasted my assets'. He was quite right, so we then had to re-do a couple of scenes from the original to put him in vision. For some reason we were going to do seven shows in the first series and then they cut it back to only six. They only wanted to air six, but we still had this seventh studio day available, so we were able to go back and re-record whole swathes of the opening pilot, which is when we dropped Norman into it. And because the cast had grown into the parts over the run of the first series, they were able to go back. Some of the opening scene, I seem to remember, we re-recorded. And the 'everybody's dead' stuff, I remember doing that. And, I think, the end as well."

It took Rob and Doug three years from writing the draft script of *The End* to getting it filmed. It was an opportunity, at last, to get it in front of a live studio audience and to hear them laugh — if only people had turned up. "We didn't get them in," remembered Rob Grant. "I mean, the first show was hopelessly under-populated and Doug actually went out to some local pubs and tried to drag people in!"

For Craig Charles, who had performed live and been on programmes like *Wogan*, it was a bit of a shock to see such a small crowd. "There was no laughs," said Craig. "There was very few laughs because, I don't know — I think the guys [Rob and Doug] thought they could do a comedy series without any jokes, through character laughs. But obviously the characters hadn't been established, no one knew what the character traits were, so they weren't getting it."

It was also a bit of a disappointment to the writers. "The reaction to the original script was very good and probably we believed them too much," said Doug. "Alan Rickman and various other people had read it and said it really was a good piece of writing. And when we started to make it, it got worse and worse and ultimately I don't think the pilot is a good show at all."

Episode Two: Future Echoes

GUEST CAST
Toaster… John Lenahan
Dispensing Machine… Tony Hawks
Jim & Bexley as babies… Remi Brocks & Jordan Russell (uncredited)

Story

When Red Dwarf accelerates to light speed, the crew see glimpses of their future which Holly calls 'Future Echoes'. Rimmer sees what he believes to be Lister's death and present-day Lister tries to stop the inevitable from happening.

Funniest Moment (arguably)

Lister has a nonsensical conversion with a future-echo Rimmer moments before present-day Rimmer walks in and says exactly the same things — except, this time, it makes a bizarre kind of sense.

Behind The Scenes

Writer Rob Grant says if it wasn't for *Future Echoes*, the show may not have survived much beyond the first series. It was the fourth episode of *Red Dwarf* to be recorded, and worked so well that it was brought forward in the broadcast order to second. Up until that point, the show had been struggling to get laughs from the audience and the science fiction element had been pushed into the background on the advice of sceptical TV people.

"I think we sat down and said 'look, let's do this really proper science fiction-y one," said Rob. "We thought, 'why not?'"

"That was clever," said Chris Barrie, Rimmer. "I like that stuff. That was easily my favourite of the first series when we did it."

The crew of Red Dwarf, on their way back to earth, accelerate to beyond the speed of light, and see glimpses of the future. The moment where Cat runs down the corridor crying about his broken tooth is merely a future echo, meaning that the event that caused his dental problem hasn't yet happened.

"I remember it was a very difficult show to write, *Future Echoes*," said Rob. "It looks a lot more straightforward than it is when it's in script form and we were trying to work it out, we had diagrams all over the place."

But the episode didn't begin in such a complicated way. The opening jokes have very little to do with the effects of light speed. In one of the opening scenes, Rimmer asks Holly to give him a short haircut, but Rimmer has been so rude to Holly, that the computer gives him a large beehive hairdo instead. "That was an attempt in the beginning just to get some cheap laughs because we were so worried by the middle," said Doug Naylor. "That wasn't in the original script, it [the original] was much more classier than that."

The script confused a lot of people. Doug said even director Ed Bye was sceptical. "I remember Ed reading it in that — what's that club? — *The Zanzibar*. He read it, he didn't smile, let alone laugh, completely baffled — I mean, you could see! That was the first draft as well, and a lot of it was just incomprehensible. He just went, 'well yes' and had to remain incredibly optimistic."

"He would never criticise, he was such a nice bloke," added Rob. "I remember lying on the floor in rehearsals trying to wrap our heads around it."

In one scene, Lister has a whole conversation with a future echo of Rimmer, but because Rimmer can't hear him, the conversation makes no sense. Seconds later, Rimmer comes in to the room again and says exactly the same words to Lister, but this time he is in the present and everything begins to come together.

"We call that the double scene," said Rob. "That was a nightmare to write, we spent about two days writing that one scene."

"That's the scene that reads like a piece of nonsense, but looks so simple on TV," added Doug. "But just working that out was so, so hard. In the read-through, it was just 'this is in Japanese!'" It was only when Ed Bye suggested working out all the actors' movements in the scene that they began to understand it.

"We thought the entire first half of this scene is just going to play to nothing because the audience is going to be just totally baffled," said Rob. "And then you will get the laughs in the second half, probably halfway through, when they finally realise what's happening. So it was a bit of a dodgy scene to be doing."

But for Craig Charles, Lister, it was one of the highlights: "I thought that was a great scene, a really funny scene. It was good fun to film and the audience seemed to get it straight away. The audience got it before any of the actors did. That was quite good because the audience were well ahead of it."

Later in the episode, Rimmer sees a future echo of what he believes to be Lister's death. Lister thinks he can prevent it, but Rimmer tells him it's unpreventable because he's already seen it. He explains this by the use of some invented future grammar: 'It will be happened. It shall be going to be happening. It will be was an event that could will have been taken place in the future. Simple as that!'

Rob remembered confusing everyone with that line. "I think that was the point where everyone was throwing the script down on the floor, thinking 'well I don't know who this is meant to appeal to!' We had fun with that."

Lister doesn't believe his fate is sealed by the future echo Rimmer. He thinks, if he can stop Cat from breaking his tooth, it will prove he can change the future and stop his own death. Lister suspects the Cat hurt himself while trying to eat one of his robot goldfish, but as Lister attempts to stop him getting to the fish, the Cat breaks his tooth.

It seems Lister cannot escape death and this brings a bit of pathos to *Future Echoes*.

A lot of the early episodes included some sad moments, often to do with Rimmer being dead and being three million years into deep space. It was a theme which they gradually left behind as the series progressed. "We intended that there would be far more of that," said Doug Naylor. "It's back to that really sad Kochanski speech that Craig had and had to be cut out [in the first episode]. We thought there'd be much more drama, there wouldn't just be comedy, but it's very hard for the thing to be taken seriously when [the set] looks as bad as it does. It just looks pretentious and rather silly when you're trying to go 'oh, this is extremely sad', or 'oh this is extremely exciting' and so that stuff was kind of cut and we put in more jokes in a bad way, slightly forced all the time; like the beehive thing was a panic measure to get 'humour' into the episode."

It seems Lister's time has come when Red Dwarf has problems navigating at light speed and Holly asks him to connect the navi-comp in the drive room — the same place where Rimmer has seen Lister die. Sparks fly everywhere as Lister makes the connections. This was achieved on set with the help of Peter Wragg and his team. "We positioned the pyrotechnic sparks all around and in rehearsals we do a few, and say to Craig, 'okay are you happy with that?' And Craig being Craig was 'yeah, go on, more of those, go for it!' Then we gradually increased the number [of pyrotechnics], but obviously always making sure there was still an element of safety there. But nothing was ever actually dangerous, although there were actually sparks flying all over the place."

Lister is amazed he is not blown up. It turns out that the person Rimmer saw die was Lister's son, Bexley. This is all revealed by a future echo of Lister, aged 171, who arrives in his bunk and tells him that he will have two sons. "It was just me with a gravelly voice, moving a little bit more slowly," said Craig Charles. "It was just great fun getting the make-up and getting those really long grey dreadlocks and things like that. I had a robot arm as well, I opened a can of beer with it. It was just nice to see Lister drinking wicked-strength lager at 170."

Anyone who keeps track of continuity will notice a contradiction over what happens to Bexley. In *Future Echoes*, old Lister says he will die in the drive room, but in the scrolling information that appears at the beginning of the third series, it says he grows up and leaves Red Dwarf very much alive. "Doug made this point all the time and I kept on telling him to shut up!" said Rob Grant.

"It's not really a great resolution that your son dies," he added. "Frankly, it's nothing to be punching the air and doing a toe-shoe shuffle about, is it? Let's face it. I mean, it's partly because I wasn't a father at the time and you don't quite realise the impact of it. So we tried to remove it as far as possible in the books [making it Lister's grandson who meets an untimely death] but even so it's not very satisfactory."

Lister's baby sons, Jim and Bexley, make a brief appearance as a future echo at the end of the episode. The two young boys were brought into the studio for the filming, but didn't sound happy to be there. Craig Charles had to hold both of them while they cried their heads off. "They were really difficult to give birth to!" joked Craig. "I had them delivered caesarean, you know what I mean! They wouldn't shut up, so we changed the line — 'stop crying, say cheese boys!' — because they wouldn't shut up and we stitched little dreadlocks on them and all that which was good fun."

Future Echoes turned out to be one of the best — if not *the* best — episode of the first series. A bit of a surprise for a script which baffled everyone. "We thought chances are it won't work, but it worked better than any of the other previous ones," said Rob. "It was the most important show of the first series for me. We were suddenly liberated and we could do all these new, different ideas. Using time during a popular sitcom was a first to my knowledge and we thought 'oh this really can be something different'. It may not be good, but it will be different! I think it changed our approach to the rest of the shows."

"We were freer after that point," said Doug. "[There had been a] cloud over the show because it was a script that had been rejected three times. We seriously expected the BBC Comedy Police to come in and arrest us all and go 'out of the building, this has been rejected three times, why are you up in Manchester secretly making this show? You know we don't like it'. And we were expecting it to be put in the can and not used, all those kind of things. Because we thought how can a script that has been rejected three times ever be made? And of course people were furious in various places, but they couldn't stop it after it had got going. So there was an element of fear about the whole thing, of 'let's creep on, be as well-behaved as possible, then after it's established a little bit we'll open out', and *Future Echoes* was really us opening out."

Episode Three: Balance of Power

GUEST CAST
Trout a la Crème & Chef… Rupert Bates
Chen… Paul Bradley
Selby… David Gillespie
Petersen… Mark Williams
Kochanski… C.P. Grogan

Story

Lister is tired of Rimmer thinking he can order him about all the time, so he decides to sit the officer's exam. Lister believes, as a superior officer, he'll be able to order Holly to turn off Rimmer's hologram and replace it with a hologram of his dream girl, Kristine Kochanski.

Funniest Moment (arguably)

In a flashback, Rimmer has taken learning drugs to help him revise for an exam, but ends up memorising a trivial conversation with Lister instead.

Behind The Scenes

The second episode to be filmed (but the third to be transmitted), *Balance of Power*, features a scene where Lister remembers Saturday night in the ship's disco. The set for the disco looked similar to the rest of the ship in one important respect, as Doug Naylor remembered: "It was just a running joke of Rob going 'okay, I've just seen the disco'; and I'm going 'what's it like, what's it like?'; and he's going 'guess what colour it is — you can only have three guesses'; and I'm going 'pink?'; and he's going 'no'; 'yellow?', 'no'; 'it's not grey is it?'; 'it is.'"

"I remember we were furiously going around trying to prop it up and putting like books in just to give it a bit of colour," said Rob.

"There were no props also," added Doug. "We had a huge problem in the first series of there being no one to put props in the set. And we were going 'people are supposed to live here' and it was like there were two shirts and one book and you go 'this just isn't credible'... I think they were so kind of scared of 'oh well, it's the future and we don't know precisely what they'll have.'"

Balance of Power is one of the few episodes that included flashbacks to the Red Dwarf of the past. Lister remembers partying with his friends Petersen, Chen and Selby in the disco on a Saturday night. When his memories fade to reality, he realises he is very much alone. It was, according to Doug, "to give the whole thing reality, and dimension and all that".

"We planned to do that a lot more, we planned to go back to the past," said Rob.

"And have him half-living in this twilight dream world of how the ship used to be," said Doug.

It was part of their *Likely Lads*-in-space philosophy: a normal-style sitcom that just happened to be set in space. For Craig Charles as Lister it gave him the chance to reunite with some of the actors from the first episode who played his drinking pals: "They were great. It was good because we'd only just finished dealing with them in the first episode, so they just had a week off and came back. We were having a little posse vibe, but unfortunately they all died!"

Balance of Power also sees the return of Clare Grogan as Kochanski, a part which had been played by Alexandra Pigg in the original rehearsals. She was unavailable when they came to do it again, and so Clare was offered the role. At this point in her career, she was best known for being in the film *Gregory's Girl* and for having several hits as the lead singer of *Altered Images*. Although widely known as Clare, she is credited on *Red Dwarf* as C.P. Grogan because of acting union Equity rules. "There's already a Clare Grogan who's an actress and she got there first," said Clare. "She got her Equity card before I did, so I have to be C.P. and she gets to be Clare Grogan… If I call myself Clare Grogan, she gets very upset about it and sends me stroppy letters."

Some years later, the other Clare Grogan left Equity, allowing C.P. Grogan to drop her initials and be credited using her full first name. All of which is a bit confusing. "The first time I did a *Red Dwarf*, I arrived in the make-up room of the BBC in Manchester and they actually had a photograph of the *other* Clare Grogan on their mirror!" said Clare. "I sat down and everything, and I said to the girl, 'you may or may not notice, but I look quite different from that photograph'. She went, 'you look really different', and I went 'that's actually because that's not me!' So I thought that was quite funny."

The plot for *Balance of Power* has Lister being bossed about by Rimmer while trying to find ways to get a date with the hologram of Kristine Kochanski. It is a tussle for supremacy for both of them. And one that was hard to achieve, considering Rimmer's status as a hologram.

"That was a problem we addressed," said Rob. "We thought 'Well now, he [Rimmer] can't touch him [Lister] or anything, how's he going to exert any power? We've written ourselves into a hole here.' In the end we just settled for Rimmer being horribly frustrated and doing whatever he could whenever he could to exert his power."

One of the things that allowed Rimmer to use his power was to hide the ship's supply of cigarettes from Lister. "We decided that if Rimmer ransomed him for his cigarettes and then rationed him according to whether he behaved or not, that would make Lister under his thumb," said Doug. "But we wanted to drop the whole idea of Lister smoking. Craig really smokes. The fact that Lister smokes meant that Craig would smoke in every take in every shot, in every scene. Of course, it looks like, when you put it all together, like he was smoking about sixty fags a day — he actually probably was, so that was why everyone got extremely agitated."

"Actually, in [the film] *Alien* they smoke, don't they? *Alien* makes it look real and credible," said Rob. "We did toy with the idea of doing non-addictive cigarettes or something like that, but then we thought that's just sending out the wrong signals."

Of course it goes without saying that all the cigarette boxes were painted grey. "If it moved it was painted grey, basically!" laughed Doug. "In later series, we said we don't want anything grey, we want some colours in this damn series and we said we don't want these grey beer cans. We went 'surely we can design our own lager can' and we had *Leopard Lager* and we made all these *Leopard Lager* things and they were all stuck on to the cans and they absorbed about a third of the graphics budget. [It was] phenomenally expensive to have these things specially designed and it was just a bit of dressing, but how many did we use in the series? About twenty-one to thirty cans of this stuff where they got crunched up or drunk or whatever."

Rimmer continues to exert power over Lister's life by refusing to allow himself to be turned off so Lister can go out with Kochanski's hologram. The idea behind Lister's infatuation with Kochanski was to make Lister more romantic than the type of person that just drinks lager and eats curries! It was an idea that disappeared from later series.

The basic plot of *Balance of Power* also has a lot less science fiction than later episodes. "It's a much more sitcom plot," said Doug. "Like 'I want to go out with this girl and I can't unless you do this and you turn off and then I can go on my date', and it's kind of like *The Odd Couple*-in-space plot, one of the first ones we did."

As Lister tries to gain the balance of power over Rimmer by taking the chef's exam to become an officer, strange things start to happen to Rimmer. He wakes up one morning with Petersen's arm. It really looks as if the arm is an add-on and doesn't belong to Chris Barrie at all. "It does," said Rob. "It was very good make-up, and somebody spent ages putting a tattoo on that."

It leads him to realise he doesn't have to walk around in his own holographic image. He could look like somebody else. Somebody like Lister's dream date, Kristine Kochanski.

It all leads up to what the writers hoped would be a *tour de force* ending when Kochanski interrupts Lister in the middle of his chef's exam, only to be unmasked as Rimmer in disguise. "Of course that didn't work at all," said Doug. "So the whole thing is very very flat indeed... I thought it [the episode] had good bits, but ultimately it didn't work."

Episode Four: Waiting for God

GUEST CAST
Cat Priest… Noel Coleman
Toaster… John Lenahan

Story

Rimmer is excited at the discovery of an unidentified object in space. When Holly brings it on board, Rimmer is convinced the pod comes from aliens. Meanwhile, Lister investigates what happened to the Cat People and discovers he's the model for their God, Cloister.

Funniest Moment (arguably)

Lister is gripped by an alien pathogen and throws himself up against the glass of the quarantine area, gasping for air as he sinks to his death — oh no, just kidding.

Behind The Scenes

In the fourth episode of *Red Dwarf's* first series, the God of the Cat People finally visits one of the Cat priests aboard Red Dwarf. The only slight drawback is that their God is Lister.

"It was good fun," said Craig Charles Lister. "It's quite ironic really that Lister is God to a whole race of people, him being a complete and utter slob."

"The idea was that Lister was the ultimate atheist who turns out to be God himself," said writer Rob Grant. "That was the joke — God likes vindaloo curries!"

This is the episode where we learn more about the Cat race and how Lister (or Cloister, as the Cats know him) became part of their mythology. All the answers lie inside the Cat's holy book, which can be read by sniffing the pages. It reveals how Lister's idea of setting up a doughnut diner on Fiji became the Cat idea of heaven, and how most of them died in holy wars fighting over what colour hats they should wear in the promised land. One old, blind Cat is still living in a temple inside the ship, where Lister finds him dying.

It is this scene that seems to tarnish the episode in the memories of some of the people involved in making it. For writer Doug Naylor, it is the set that really lets it down: "When you look at it you think, this doesn't look real, it doesn't smell real. This is supposed to be a Cat temple, he's supposed to have lived here for [years]... That was when you realised we should have been on film or OB [outside broadcast] for that, I mean... you thought you were still in a studio here and it looked like the pillars were going to fall down any minute."

The scene took a long time to film. Some of it was re-written at the last minute and Noel Coleman, who played the Cat Priest, couldn't remember his new lines.

"That was my least favourite episode," said Craig Charles. "The stale doughnuts and the golden sausage and all that. I just thought it was not my kind of comedy. And Noel Coleman took an age to do his lines. In the end we had them written in big letters and he still couldn't see them. [He's a] great old actor. I think the guy who was running the floor at the time was getting really tetchy with him, and I was thinking don't get tetchy with him, he's a 'great', the guy's a 'great'. It was just kind of sad to see him at the end of his career, not being able to know his lines."

In the end, Lister, who was initially horrified at the thought of being God, pretends he is Cloister so he can bring happiness to the Cat Priest. "To give the guy redemption and fulfilment and become what the guy wanted him to be," said Doug. "That was supposed to be a tremendously profound and interesting and moving end. Instead we're thinking, 'well this [is a] set here.'"

"We wanted to do religious satire, which we thought was another non-*Terry and June*ism of the show, but we did it better later, I think," said Rob. "It's what we call wallpaper science fiction, Aunt Sally's science fiction, where you're only knocking down your own icons, really, and we were trying to explore the mythos of the series which lasted for two shows precisely and it didn't really work."

The sub-plot of *Waiting for God* concerns Rimmer. He doesn't believe in God; he believes in aliens. The discovery of a mysterious pod floating in space fuels his imagination.

"That's the first show we started up Rimmer's obsession with aliens, which I thought was good for him," said Rob. "That was the one when the scutters came into their own, really. It was the first sort of really scutter-y episode where they actually performed a plot function and they were helping Rimmer decode the pod inscription."

The scutters themselves were radio-controlled creations of Peter Wragg and his effects team, as Peter remembered: "The line of the script was: 'The scutter appears. The scutter is something the size of a shoe box with an arm and a clawed hand'. [It was a case of] working from there and deciding what size it was going to be to fit everything in that one wanted to fit into it, and trying to create as many different movements as possible. It was extremely difficult. I have to say that Andy Bowman, one of our assistants who actually put the mechanics together, did a wonderful job."

Despite suggestions in later years that the scutters weren't very versatile machines, Peter Wragg remembered them working quite well… most of the time! "They had their moments using radio control in a studio environment, where you've got a lot of metal work around in the studio, you've got cameras etc., you've got an awful lot of interference and we had our moments when scutters went merrily on their own way, doing their own thing and Ed [Bye, the director] was saying 'I told you to cut!'"

Rob remembered it was *Waiting For God* where, in the middle of a scene in front of the audience, one of the scutters decided to attack Chris Barrie: "The scutter started going for him round the knees and chopping at his groin with its beak. Everyone was looking at the operator and he was holding his hands up — 'it's not me'. And apparently it was some taxi signals on the shortwave radio that were passing."

Despite that, Chris Barrie, Rimmer, had fond memories of the scutters. "They were quite a laugh, but God they took time," he said. "They were like a bad racing car set, they had minds of their own, really unpredictable. You'd get the classic thing of Ed Bye saying: 'Now Pete, will this scutter do this? Will it go over there, get the note and deliver it onto the chair? Can it do that?' Peter's going 'yeah, well it did that many times in the store room, so there's no reason why it shouldn't do it here'. And lo and behold the scutter goes [berserk], all the smoke starts to come through. Very funny."

Another creation of the special effects department was the Talkie Toaster, which had an integrated flashing light to indicate when it was speaking. It was voiced by magician and comedian, John Lenahan, who was originally going to be *Red Dwarf*'s warm-up man. "I had this kind of droll idea for the Toaster's voice," remembered John. "It was very funny at the audition, but when we got in to actually do it, it was very similar to what Norman Lovett was doing as Holly. So that's why they put my voice through a synthesizer. At some point in time the Toaster was actually going to become a bigger character than it ended up. At one point in time there was talk of the Toaster taking over the ship."

Sadly, it was not to be. Apart from a guest appearance in the third series (when it was voiced by Tony Hawks), the Toaster was written out. "When we cut him out of the series we had all these letters going, 'why did you get rid of the Toaster, it was the best thing in it?'" said Doug. "In fact Ed, as I remember, was particularly in love with the Toaster and was constantly saying, 'I met yet another person who said what on earth happened to the Toaster in Series two?'"

Doug Naylor described the idea behind *Waiting for God* as trying to show that "most creatures need a God and a religion", and they'll get it where they can. It's reflected in all the plot threads, from Rimmer's belief in aliens, to the Toaster's wish for something better.

But that belief is shown to be false in every case. The Cat Priest eventually receives salvation from Cloister, but it is only Lister acting out the role of God. And the mysterious pod that Rimmer had dreamed was the product of some alien race, turns out to be an old Red Dwarf garbage pod. Lister's statement at the beginning of the episode, that the only things in the Universe are 'you, me, the Cat and a load of smegging, floating rocks', is confirmed at the end.

Rimmer only realises the truth about the pod as the credits starts to roll. This wasn't in the original script and was an idea Doug Naylor had in post-production, to stop the end titles and dub Rimmer's voice over them: 'It's a garbage pod, a smegging garbage pod!'

"That was the first time we started doing a re-thinking of the titles," said Rob. "We'd already done it on *Son of Cliché*, and on *Spitting Image* we used to mess about with the titles. It's so boring running the same old titles every week. You often make a cup of tea.

"I don't think I was pleased with anything in that show, to be honest with you," he continued. "I liked the script, but then I liked it less and less as the days wore on. I never thought it came over, really, on the television."

Talkie Toaster John Lenahan had better memories: "It was always good stuff and it made us laugh… My favourite of them all, of course, was Norman Lovett, he's just the funniest man who ever walked the face of the earth. I had good times working on it. We were all up in Manchester in a nice hotel and filming was good fun. It was well worth doing. I wouldn't have minded doing it again."

Episode Five: Confidence and Paranoia

GUEST CAST
Paranoia... Lee Cornes
Confidence... Craig Ferguson

Story

Lister catches a mutated form of pneumonia which makes his hallucinations become real. It rains fish, the Mayor of Warsaw spontaneously combusts, and then Lister's Confidence and Paranoia appear on the ship as real people.

Funniest Moment (arguably)

Rimmer calls out to the scutter approaching Paranoia with a loaded syringe: "Stab him! Stab him!" Paranoia turns and sees what the scutter's up to. "Ahh, you haven't met Stabbim," says Rimmer. "Stabbim, meet Lister's Paranoia; Lister's Paranoia, this is Stabbim."

Behind The Scenes

Confidence and Paranoia was the fifth episode and everyone who worked on *Red Dwarf* was becoming more comfortable with the show. Unfortunately, the audience who came in to watch the recording and provide the laugh-track were new every week and needed a few things explained to them.

"At the beginning of each show, it was: 'has anybody seen this show? Been before?' No. 'Okay, here's the situation, da-da-da, etc.' for ten minutes," remembered writer Doug Naylor. "The audience would just go, 'eh?' Just bored them rigid. [We should have said] 'he's a Cat — it doesn't matter why; he's a hologram — don't worry about it; he's the last human being alive; the computer's nuts.' That would have been far better, but for some reason everyone thought we had to do, 'it started off as this ship and then this guy got put into stasis, which is kind of like suspended animation, and when he came out…'"

Nevertheless, the series was getting into its stride and the stories were starting to branch out. The science fiction element was becoming more important and the show was experimenting with new characters who weren't part of the dead crew or the ship's machinery.

In *Confidence and Paranoia*, Lister ventures down to the officers' quarters to watch Kristine Kochanski's dream recorder. But the Officers' quarters have not been de-contaminated and Lister contracts a mutated virus which brings two parts of his personality to life — his Confidence and his Paranoia. Like many of the early episodes, the idea came from exploring the sitcom tradition of starting from a very straightforward plot base.

"What we were doing was still treating it very much as a sitcom in an unusual place," explained Doug. "We were just looking at the plot where one of the people gets ill, which is a real staple. Then we obviously said ours wouldn't get ill in the way that a normal sitcom character would be ill, it would be some kind of space disease. And then it was 'what kind of space disease could it be?' and 'what would be the repercussions because it won't just be flu?'. And so it just came from that really, and we kind of re-visited that with space mumps in [the fourth series episode] *Justice*."

But Lister's Confidence and Paranoia don't appear in the episode until sixteen minutes in. The story begins in a more leisurely way, with Holly asking Lister to erase all references to Agatha Christie from his memory banks so he can read her novels all over again. Doug says they were working under the theory that you can do anything you want in the first five minutes of an episode. "You can use that to establish life on board the ship, what they're doing, get a few laughs, establish character, and then the plot kicks in after that. And we used to do that all the time then, and now I think we're just as wrong now where we hardly do it at all and people hate us for that because they kind of quite like that stuff, the more low-key, as opposed to screaming straight in to an adventure in the first scene."

Lister's mutated pneumonia sends him into a raging fever. He begins to dream about raining fish and it actually happens — inside Red Dwarf! This meant they had to fill the studio with buckets of fish.

"It was revolting," remembered Doug Naylor.

"It was," added Rob Grant. "The stink…"

"Also, people were incredibly worried that we'd get a lot of letters about cruelty to fish," said Doug. "I remember [executive producer] Paul Jackson saying to the audience at the time, 'notice, all these fish are alive, and we haven't killed one'. So basically all the fish were happy and loving. It was an appalling smell, as you can imagine. It was just 'oh my God!' They were all in this big net above the actors. People were hanging on the tops of the sets, emptying buckets of these fish all over the place."

Doug insisted that the live fish weren't dropped from a great height, but laid on afterwards. "That was the thing about 'we can't drop live fish, it's too cruel'. So pour the dead ones in and then get the live ones, and none of the live ones died."

Rimmer steps out of the sleeping quarters to avoid the raining fish, but instead confronts Lister's hallucination of the Mayor of Warsaw, who spontaneously combusts in front of him. This was filmed using the split screen technique where Chris Barrie played Rimmer in one half of the screen and the Mayor of Warsaw burst into flames in the other half. The two pieces of video were later brought together.

The Mayor's spontaneous combustion was created by special effects designer, Peter Wragg: "We did a flame effect where the Mayor of Warsaw would have been and then dropped clothes at the same time," said Peter. "So you get the feeling of flames and clothes dropping and Chris reacting. Although, because it was a split screen, Chris wasn't actually there at the time that the flame effect went off."

It was necessary to keep the actors out of the way of the explosion, otherwise they might have got singed. "It was pretty big," remembered

Peter. "The flame probably went up to a good two foot, and it's set off electrically, it's a pyrotechnic that burns with a rush of flame and then disappears."

Lister's two final hallucinations are much harder to get rid of. Paranoia, played by Lee Cornes, is a withdrawn, nagging individual dressed in a black suit; while Confidence, played by Craig Ferguson, is an extrovert 'medallion man', wearing an Hawaiian shirt and sporting brilliant white teeth. "They painted them with special paint so they glowed, it was luminous," said Doug.

It is Confidence who plays the greater role in the episode. "In terms of the script, we liked Paranoia just as well as Confidence," said Rob, "but he wasn't in as much of the final script. Simply we ran out of time, I think. We had a lot of stuff where Paranoia was just following Lister around and screwing up his life, really, and arranging things for him to trip over, and accurate measurements so he would stand in the dog poo and things like that. But we just didn't get time to use it. He was very good, Lee Cornes."

It was the first time that characters other than the dead crew appeared on the show and it brought a kind of freshness to the episode. "It was nice to have other people around who could talk and touch something," said Rob. "It was a nice change and something we wanted to pursue. It was good having them around in the rehearsal period, because it was like it was only us there, and it was like being on Red Dwarf, really wasn't it? I remember they brought relief to the place."

Rimmer tries to tell Lister that Confidence and Paranoia are just symptoms of his pneumonia, like the spots in chickenpox, and that he won't be better until they go. Lister ignores him because he's too busy listening to Confidence. Confidence persuades Lister that he can ask Kochanski for a date by bringing back her hologram. With the non-essential systems on Red Dwarf closed down, Holly thinks he can sustain both Rimmer and Kochanski holograms. And with Confidence's help, Lister works out where Rimmer must have hidden the personality disks — behind the solar panel outside their sleeping quarters.

Lister and Confidence put on space suits and venture outside to retrieve the hologram disks. While walking on the outside of the ship, Confidence confesses to smashing up the medical unit and killing Paranoia to ensure Lister stays sick and the two of them can stay together.

This makes Lister feel uncomfortable and Confidence tells him he can relieve his claustrophobia by taking off his helmet. Confidence is so confident he takes off his own helmet, and as soon as his body is exposed to the vacuum, he explodes.

"I really loved Peter Wragg's special effect explosion of Confidence at the end," said Rob. "That was the first time we thought 'oh my God, we can really do spectacular stuff, here'. It really does look good."

Peter explained how it was done. "It was created by making an inflatable, just like an inflatable castle, that sort of thing, a rubber inflatable of the person and double-skinning it. So we had two skins, and that was inflated so it matched the size of Craig Ferguson [Confidence]. Then a second skin that we then inflated by injecting a lot of air into it, so the whole thing became that much larger. And then we had a thing at the back called a woofer, which is basically an air discharger, so it's an air cylinder that you're pressurising with a lot of air up to 120 pounds psi [per square inch] pressure, and then you've got a quick release valve so you're releasing that pressure in one go. So once we'd inflated the figure so that it became big, we let the air mortar fire, then it just blasted the rubber suit right over camera with lots of debris floating around as well."

This effect was achieved with Craig Charles standing right next to it. "That explosion was brilliant, wasn't it?" said Craig. "It looked like I was hit, because all the crew came up to me at the end and went, 'Are you okay? Are you okay? Are you okay?' and I went 'yeah, I'm acting' because they actually thought I was hurt by the explosion. It was a great explosion, though."

With Lister's Confidence and Paranoia dead, he is cured. He has also retrieved Kochanski's personality disk. It shows that a lot can be achieved if you listen to your confidence. "There was a point to be made," said Rob, "but the idea was you're also supposed to have your Paranoia as well, otherwise you do crazy things like take your helmet off in space."

Lister sets up a second hologram projection unit and places the disk in the slot. But Rimmer wasn't so stupid as to leave Kochanski's disk in Kochanski's box and the hologram that comes out of the projection box is another Rimmer!

The original idea was to have a hologram of Kochanski revived at this point and this would have provided a cliffhanger for a possible second series. But Rob Grant and Doug Naylor decided to re-think the idea after the BBC strike that disrupted the first attempt to record the series. "*Confidence and Paranoia* was originally going to be the last show of the first series," explained Rob. "But after the strike we came back and suggested the idea of doing a different sixth episode where Rimmer brings himself back and we immediately scrapped the other show and wrote a new one — for free!"

Episode Six: Me²

GUEST CAST
Captain Hollister... Mac McDonald

Story

When a second hologram of Rimmer is created, both Rimmers decide to move in together. As their relationship descends into bitter one-upmanship and arguments, Lister discovers a video of Rimmer's death. The tape reveals his last words to have been "gazpacho soup". When the bickering between Rimmer and Rimmer becomes too much, it's agreed one of them will be wiped — but not until Lister has found out the story behind gazpacho soup.

Funniest Moment (arguably)

Lister uses the rhyme, *Ippy dippy, my spaceshippy,* to decide which Rimmer to wipe. Knowing that his fate is sealed, the losing Rimmer sits down and sighs: "I've been ippy dippied to death."

Behind The Scenes

When *Red Dwarf* first went into rehearsal, *Me²* didn't exist at all. It was originally planned that *Confidence and Paranoia* would be the last episode, but after a BBC strike disrupted production, the writers suggested a new story to finish off the series. They discarded one of the middle episodes — about Rimmer trying to steal bits of Lister to build a new body for himself — and wrote *Me²*.

In *Me²*, Rimmer thinks he's found his ideal friend — himself! His second hologram, created at the end of the fifth episode, joins the first Rimmer hologram and they get on like a house on fire. They move out of Lister's quarters and set up home in the bunkroom next door. Writers Rob Grant and Doug Naylor liked this new script much better, but executive producer Paul Jackson took one look at it and knew it would be difficult to film.

"When we handed the script in, Paul, I remember, went spare," said Rob. "He said, 'look, you can only have two scenes with him playing against himself' and we said, 'we can't do the story with just two scenes'. He said, 'look, how are you supposed to play this in front of the audience?' We didn't much care at the time, but I think we cut out a couple of the scenes with him together and got it down to three… I think, for instance, when we had the first scene when they were loading up Rimmer's things into boxes, both the Rimmers were in that originally so we had to get rid of one of them, and he just popped his head in at the end or something."

Rimmer is, of course, delighted to be able to live with his ideal companion. The other Rimmer has all the same interests, the same goals and understands him. However, each Rimmer wants to be that bit better than his partner. When the two Rimmers exercise in their quarters, they scorn each other if one stops while the other is still leaping up and down.

The sequence was filmed using split screen, so Chris Barrie had to exercise in one half of the screen as Rimmer, then run round the other side and do it all over again: "It was quite exhausting," said Chris, "but I'd rehearsed it thoroughly and Ed [Bye, the director] knew what the cameras were doing, and we executed that scene really quickly."

"This is certainly one of Chris's great strengths," said Rob Grant. "I think he plays against those split screen things very very well; he's got a great sense of timing when it comes to that. He does all kind of neat little tricks, like he does interplay between himself, and then goes and does it on the other side."

Chris explains it was all done by the clever use of monitors: "I think they put a monitor up around the cameras so I could see basically what I was doing. So for the dialogue my eye-line was with the monitor there, so we did him first, sprang up and down, then me again. I watched it recently and I was quite impressed with the way it all worked. It was a joy to see it all come off."

"I do think when they're both exercising it's very funny," said Doug Naylor.

"Very hard to do," added Rob. "And Chris, who was in great condition really, was absolutely jiggered after eight takes of that."

Craig Charles, however, described living with two Rimmers as "Hell!" Playing Lister meant he had to appear in several scenes with both Rimmers, but that's quite difficult when you can only see one of them. "There's one scene when you can actually see me leaning to get within the edge of camera so the other Rimmer can come in," said Craig. "I'm leaning and looking one way all the time, but I should have been moving my head between the conversations. And I did that, moved my head between the conversations on one take, but as with all technical stuff, I got to the edge of frame at one stage, so they used the take where I wasn't. It's really bad news sometimes, suffering for the special effects. Performances sometimes go out of the window because the special effect worked in one scene and, because they're so complicated and difficult, you go with the special effect."

For Rimmer, the novelty of living with himself soon wears off. He begins to be irritated by his own habits and niggling foibles. They start to row and the first Rimmer moves back in with Lister.

But the row merely continues when the second Rimmer joins his other self in the cinema. He looks around at the rows of empty seats and decides to sit directly in front of the first Rimmer. The first Rimmer, who now can't see the cartoon (are you following this?), gets up and sits in the seat directly in front of the other Rimmer. The two Rimmers continue doing this until they run out of seats.

"It's just what two petty-minded guys would do to one another," said Doug. "It's just so childish and so, so hard to shoot. And we had all sorts of problems with things like cinema seats because you could say a hologram hovers just minutely above a chair, but then how do you get a cinema seat down?"

The cartoon they are watching in the cinema is Mugs Murphy. This was to be Lister's favourite cartoon character and it was made especially for the show, even though it is only glimpsed in the episode. Originally, Mugs Murphy was going to become a semi-regular in *Red Dwarf*. "We thought if we could get a decent cartoon character it would be interesting for maybe he comes to life or something in the future," said Rob. "We didn't want to use any contemporary stuff, we didn't want to use Wilma Flintstone and that kind of thing, we wanted to create our own icons. We didn't want to be using Marilyn Monroe, we wanted to be using Chelsea Brown — who you've never seen — and things like that. But in the end, sometimes you've just got to have that shorthand of using something people know."

The cinema scene is where Lister finally decides he has had enough of Rimmer arguing with himself and one of them has to go. This gives Lister the chance to find out the truth about gazpacho soup.

'Gazpacho soup' were Rimmer's last words, recorded for posterity in his death video. When Lister discovers the videotape among Rimmer's things, he cannot resist watching it. It shows Rimmer's death among the final moments of the crew as they are wiped out by a lethal radiation leak. The explosion was created by Peter Wragg's special effects team, but they were squeezed for time and it wasn't as spectacular as it might have been. "Effects sequences tend to be a bit more complicated, I mean they can use up time," said Peter. "Obviously what directors want to do is try and get all the other stuff done first, but invariably time eats away at the other things and you've got five minutes left to do the effects sequences, or something like that. I agree, it wasn't particularly spectacular, it was what we could achieve there and then."

As Rimmer is thrown backwards by the blast, he gasps 'gazpacho soup'. "It was an air mortar and we had Chris [Barrie] on a jerk wire," says Peter Wragg. "So we jerked Chris back at the same time as we fired a load of glitter and dust out of the air mortar."

Eventually, Lister persuades Rimmer to tell him the story behind gazpacho soup. It was the greatest night of his life, Rimmer explains, when he was invited to the Captain's table. They were served with a starter of gazpacho soup, a soup which is meant to be served cold. But Rimmer didn't know this and sent it back to the kitchen to be heated up. "It actually happened to us, I think," said Rob. "We were working at Thames TV very early on, and we went in the Thames board room and they brought the soup in and it was cold. Something in the back of my head said 'oh, there's this soup that you're supposed to have cold, and this is supposed to be it'. I remember clocking it then. I didn't actually send it back!"

Rimmer puts his whole dead-end career and dead-end life down to that one moment which made the Captain regard him as a fool. "The idea of that episode was to make the audience feel sorry for Rimmer," explained Doug. "It was the start really of us beginning to give him three dimensions. The idea was there was this key incident in his life that really really screwed him up."

"And in the end it wasn't really anything, because he's screwed up himself," said Rob.

Rob Grant and Doug Naylor see *Me²* as one of the successes of the first series. They were able to approach the episode afresh, having already seen the earlier ones in rehearsal: it gives an unprecedented depth to Rimmer's character and it's a strong idea.

"It's one of my favourite shows," said Rob. "I think the story sort of goes a bit in the middle, but the idea I think is great — would you get on with yourself, if you met yourself?"

"I also do think it's an interesting idea," said Doug. "It's not about 'would you get on with yourself?' It's 'you *wouldn't* get on with yourself', because you have all the same irritating habits that when you perceive them, when you're able to look at yourself, you'd be appalled. Because you'd think 'I'm so much better than that, am I really that small-minded, that petty, that idiotic?' — especially writ-large with

Rimmer. One of the key scenes was 'what time shall we get up in the morning?' where they constantly top one another so it'll be earlier and earlier and earlier, so they would hardly be going to bed."

And so, the first series came to an end. It was a bumpy start to what became a hugely successful programme which changed almost beyond recognition as the years went on.

Red Dwarf II

Written by... Rob Grant & Doug Naylor
Produced & Directed by... Ed Bye
Executive Producer... Paul Jackson

Rimmer... Chris Barrie
Lister... Craig Charles
Cat... Danny John-Jules
Holly... Norman Lovett

Recorded: May-July 1988
First broadcast: September-October 1988

Following the difficulty *Red Dwarf* had in getting commissioned in the first place, the BBC asked for a second series remarkably quickly. Only a matter of months after being introduced to the world of *Red Dwarf*, audiences were sitting down to watch new episodes.

It allowed the production to put into practice the lessons they had learnt in the first series. They said farewell to insular stories such as *Balance of Power* and embraced the possibility of doing more science fiction-style plots, such as *Thanks for the Memory* and *Better Than Life*. They realised that guest characters could bring something new to the episodes, and wrote scripts such as *Kryten* and *Queeg*. The writers had also watched the main cast play their parts for a whole series and were able to incorporate what they had seen into the scripts. The pixellation of Norman Lovett's face as computer Holly was dropped, allowing the performer to be seen in all his glory.

There was a bit more money floating around for the second series, as sets were already built and the basic model shots of Red Dwarf in space already existed, freeing up funds for other things. So they were able to film on location for several episodes, and Peter Wragg and his special effects team were asked to provide new model shots such as the second series' shuttlecraft, Blue Midget.

Although stuck with the much-maligned grey sets, the production team was able to address the problem of the look of the series by adding colour wherever they could. Lighting director John Pomphrey put coloured lights around the set at every opportunity, while more props were thrown into the mix and computer screens with coloured displays were put into some of the scenes.

The second series was therefore able to build on the success of the first, not only in terms of the production, but also in terms of the audience. The first series wasn't repeated on the BBC for several years and so, for many people, the second series was the first they saw of *Red Dwarf*, which helped to ensure its popularity.

Episode One: Kryten

GUEST CAST
Kryten… David Ross
The Esperanto Woman… Johanna Hargreaves
The Android Actor… Tony Slattery

Story

Holly picks up a signal from a stranded ship being looked after by an android called Kryten. Rimmer, Lister and Cat spruce themselves up to go aboard and meet the all-female crew. But when they get there, it turns out the crew are all dead, merely skeletons being served by Kryten, who is a slave to his programming. Back on Red Dwarf, Lister teaches Kryten that his old life is over and he should rebel like Marlon Brando in the classic film *The Wild One*.

Funniest Moment (arguably)

After a big build up, lots of excitement and getting ready to meet the women on the distressed ship Nova 5; Lister, Rimmer and Cat arrive to find they're all dead.

Behind The Scenes

Kryten was the fourth episode to be recorded, but turned out to be one of the best of the run and was brought forward to launch series two of *Red Dwarf*. More straightforward than some of the later episodes, it's a great introduction for people who haven't seen the show before.

The episode begins with 'Androids', a space-age soap opera of everyday mechanical folk, which takes a not-too-subtle dig at *Neighbours*, the Australian soap opera which became a surprise hit in the 1980s in Britain. The theme tune, produced and sung by *Red Dwarf* regular composer Howard Goodall, just about gets away with copyright violations while being not dissimilar to the *Neighbours* theme. Eagle-eyed viewers will spot that, as well as the tacky dialogue, a boom microphone gets into shot as Brook the Android stands up, completing the soap opera parody.

It's a great scene which has the audience laughing from the outset. They keep laughing through the end credits which list the cast as played by numbered androids (Android 14762IE etc.). The credits also reveal Androids was produced and directed by Kylie Gwenlyn, believed to be a reference to BBC Head of Comedy Gareth Gwenlan who — legend has it — rejected the original script for *Red Dwarf* because it didn't have a sofa. The production was, of course, by Groovy Channel 27, which makes a welcome return to the *Red Dwarf* universe after Rimmer dismissed it as 'Groovy, Funky Channel 27' in the first series episode, *Future Echoes*.

Meanwhile, back on the Red Dwarf ship, it's another mundane day for Lister and Rimmer. Rimmer is attempting to learn Esperanto, but is so terrible at it that Lister and Holly beat him without even trying. Esperanto, an invented language aimed at bringing together different cultures, was championed by science fiction writer Harry Harrison who used it as the universal language in his popular *Stainless Steel Rat* books. In the late eighties, it made sense for an international spaceship to use the language. "It was supposed to be a French ship originally and we were going to have all the signs up in French, but we settled for Esperanto in the end," said writer Rob Grant.

A few of the signs can be seen in the background in some of the scenes, most notably 'Nivelo' (level) which makes repeat appearances in the corridors. "We had to have this Esperanto guy come round and translate all the signs for us," said Rob. "In fact, he was such a boring person that we dropped the whole Esperanto idea."

Rimmer's Esperanto lesson is interrupted by Holly who has picked up a signal from another spaceship. Rimmer instantly assumes it's aliens, as he assumes everything is aliens. It is, in fact, a ship from

Earth with three women on board, according to the ship's mechanoid Kryten. They embark on a rescue mission and even though Lister claims they are 'not on the pull', they spruce themselves up to the best of their ability.

Lister dresses in his 'least-smeggy things', Rimmer produces an over the top 'Clive of India' uniform replete with medals, Cat vies for best costume of the series with an amazing gold lamé spacesuit and even Holly dons a toupée for the occasion. Rimmer requests he be referred to as Ace, the nickname boys at school never called him no matter how many times he let them beat him up (shades of Ace Rimmer, the heroic version of Arnold set to feature in the series four episode, *Dimension Jump*).

The build-up sets the scene for the payoff as the crew arrive on Kryten's ship — to find the women are all dead and Kryten is serving a group of skeletons. This is the point when Chris Barrie, playing Rimmer, remembered realising the audience were finally getting the character jokes which typified the show. Each joke in that scene gets a long laugh with the actors having to wait to deliver their next lines, which hadn't been the case at the beginning. "I think they [the writers] may have over-estimated the strength of character jokes in a first series of something," said Chris. "It does take a couple of series for the audience to build up and know the characters, to laugh at the character gags. Eventually the characters started to work better in the second series."

The scene caused some trouble during the recording, however, as the set was supposed to be kept secret from the audience by a black cloth which was mistakenly removed too early by the stage-hands.

Much of the success of the episode has to be down to the central character of Kryten, played for this episode by David Ross. The stage and screen actor was known to writers Rob Grant and Doug Naylor from a role he played in their early 1980s radio sitcom, *Wrinkles*, about an old people's home. He was invited to be a guest on *Red*

Dwarf because they knew he was a talented comic actor who worked supremely well in front of audiences. All of this can be seen in his performance. David Ross played Kryten as a fussy, flighty servant because the script called for his character to develop —he rebels Marlon Brando-style at the end — and he wanted to make the change as marked as possible. It is very different from how Robert Llewellyn would later play Kryten when the character returned the following year, but worked well for the episode.

Series two was off to a great start.

Episode Two: Better Than Life

GUEST CAST
Rimmer's Dad... John Abineri
Marilyn Monroe... Debbie Ash
Rathbone... Jeremy Austin
The Captain... Nigel Carrivick
The Guide... Tony Hawks
McGruder... Judy Hawkins
The Newsreader... Tina Jenkins
The Taxman... Ron Pember
Gordon... Gordon Salkilld

Story

A post pod from Earth catches up with Red Dwarf, bringing a letter from Rimmer's mum to say his father has died. But, to lighten the load, it also contains Better Than Life, a total immersion video game that detects all desires and makes them come true. As Rimmer, Lister and Cat enjoy living out their fantasies, Rimmer's brain rebels and refuses to let anything nice happen to him, until he's laden with seven kids and is tracked down by the man from Outland Revenue.

Funniest Moment (arguably)

As Rimmer laments the death of his father, Cat bounds in saying he's hungry. "Shh," says Lister, "Rimmer's Dad's died." The Cat isn't interested: "I'd rather have chicken," he says.

Behind The Scenes

The abiding memory of everyone involved in the making of *Red Dwarf* when it comes to the episode *Better Than Life* is of being cold. A little bit of money had been put aside in the budget for location filming and, when the script called for the crew to go to paradise in the total immersion videogame, Better Than Life, it was time to go on the road. The original idea was for a tropical beach, something akin to Hawaii, but unfortunately the budget could only stretch to Rhyl in Wales. Although Rhyl is probably lovely in summer, the weather wasn't smiling down when the *Red Dwarf* team came to town. Guest actor Tony Hawks, who played the game guide, perhaps put it most succinctly. "It seems to be the law that whenever you do outside filming it's in the winter and it's miserable," he said. "It was miserably cold if I remember rightly, but we all kept each other warm with our anecdotes."

It was so cold, in fact, that the cast couldn't say their lines for shivering in one scene. Valiant attempts were made to get through the dialogue as Lister and the Cat sat in vest tops and Hawaiian shirts, but it was no good: the skies were grey, the wind was strong and they had to abandon filming.

"Rhyl beach, unless it's been like the weather's been last week [very sunny], doesn't actually look like Hawaii," said director Ed Bye. "So there were a few problems with that, but I think a lot of good ideas came out of it and I think we got away with it because there were some very funny bits in it. They opened a door coming off a golf course straight onto a beach and somehow that effect worked much better than I'd anticipated, it got huge laugh... The trouble for me is when I look at something that was shot on location I grind my teeth in anxiety because it could have been a lot better."

Things were much warmer at the beginning of the episode, which starts with traditional bunkroom banter, in the aftermath of a fairly disastrous meal which Rimmer had prepared and Lister and the Cat had eaten. The meal scene had actually been written into the first draft of the script, but was later cut and just reported in dialogue.

Indigestion is soon forgotten with the arrival of the post pod, which has caught up with Red Dwarf after three million years. Among the piles of junk mail is a letter from Rimmer's mother informing him that his father has died. In a moment of pathos for Rimmer, he reflects on his father's passing up in the observation dome, a new set for the second series which was half special effect and half set. The original idea from Rob Grant and Doug Naylor was for a room where it was possible to see space outside the ship, somewhat like *Star Trek: The Next Generation*'s Ten Forward, a bar and social area with outer space going past the windows. The result was, for them, a disappointment.

It was one of the reasons the observation dome didn't become a regular feature on the series. While it was used sparingly, it gave a chance for Rimmer and Lister to talk to each other without the bickering which characterised their bunkroom banter. Chris Barrie and Craig Charles give moving performances as they talk about their dead relatives back home, despite a couple of stumbles in the dialogue. In fact, the performances and audience reaction from that first take were strong enough that, in the edit, it was decided to go with the performances and keep the mistakes in.

This scene ends with a wonderful moment from the Cat, bounding in and yelping about being hungry. It allows what was a moving scene to end on a laugh in typical Cat fashion, with a couple of lines which steal the show. "A lot of people say you've only got a few lines to do," said Danny John-Jules, the Cat, "but you try and keep that intensity when you've got to click your fingers and have it there, there's no slow build up. That's the hard part."

It's only after this that the plot really kicks in with the introduction of the total immersion videogame, explained in a news programme that also arrived in the post pod. Once again, Groovy Channel 27 makes an appearance which, as Lister said back in *Future Echoes*, has a hologram reading the news. The woman who played her, Tina Jenkins, was a real newsreader on Thames News at the time, which explains why she is so good at it.

So Lister, Rimmer, the Cat and Holly enter Better Than Life, the game where the players' fantasies become reality. All starts off well for Rimmer as he gets off with sexy former shipmate Yvonne McGruder and they drive off the beach in an expensive car (a nod to Chris Barrie's real-life obsession with classic cars). It wasn't going so well for the production team, however, who discovered that cars and beaches don't mix. The car in question got stuck and had to be pulled out by a Land Rover, while all the time they were watching the incoming tide with trepidation. Cameras also don't much like sand either. The scene where the rear wheel of Lister's motorbike sprays sand out behind it caused the camera lens to get scratched.

Things get even worse for Rimmer as his imagination fails to cope with nice things happening to him and the game turns against him. He ends up marrying McGruder and having seven kids within a day. This little scene led to one of the classic outtakes from the series when actress Judy Hawkins — playing a pregnant McGruder with a prosthetic lump inside her dress — stopped filming by shouting 'my pregnancy's fallen out!'

Such is Rimmer's warped imagination that all of them end up buried neck deep in sand with jam smeared over their faces, about to be eaten alive by killer ants. "Rimmer does have a very nasty streak in him, as indeed do all the *Red Dwarf* characters," said Chris Barrie. "To try and make Rimmer funny was always going to be a challenge because he's such an unpleasant git. Totally without any sympathy at all."

To create the effect of burying the cast in sand without actually doing so was achieved by digging a hole in the beach, having the actors kneel inside, placing boards over the top and dressing them with sand. So, while it looked like they were buried, they were actually kneeling in a hollow. Apart from Holly, whose monitor was partially buried while actor Norman Lovett was sitting in the back of a truck.

"That wasn't much fun," said Norman. "I thought that was a bit pointless, actually. I didn't mind going to Rhyl in Wales for a few days, but there was a lot of hanging about. I just thought they could have filmed my parts and played it in to the actors. I really did feel they could do that, but they chose not to do that, so I went to Rhyl and had a few days in the sand."

Despite all the problems, the episode turned out reasonably successfully, even if it packed quite a lot of plot into the half hour.

Episode Three: Thanks for the Memory

GUEST CAST
Lise Yates... Sabra Williams

Story

The crew of Red Dwarf celebrate the anniversary of Rimmer's death with a drunken party on a planet with an atmosphere. It causes Rimmer to reflect on what a useless life he had and to confess that his only sexual liaison was a one-time quickie with Yvonne McGruder. The next morning, Lister and the Cat wake up with a broken leg each, someone has fiddled with Holly's star charts, a jigsaw has mysteriously completed itself and no one can remember a thing about the last four days. What could have happened? Could it be — as Rimmer suspects — aliens?

Funniest Moment (no argument)

While looking back at the flight recorder to see how Lister and Cat got a broken leg, they see themselves struggling to carry a gravestone which will commemorate the memory of Lise Yates. The gravestone is so heavy, they drop it on their feet — and everything suddenly makes sense.

Behind The Scenes

The confidence in the writing and performances shine in this episode. Following the success of *Future Echoes* in the first year, Rob Grant and Doug Naylor realised they could do science fiction plots and do them well. The story is, essentially, a mystery of four missing days and what happened to cause Lister and the Cat to break their legs. Rimmer's assertion that it could have been aliens seems like it could actually be true this time.

It begins with the celebration of Rimmer's 'death day' on a planet with an atmosphere. This is the first time *Red Dwarf* set foot on an alien world and broke one of the original rules the writers had made at the beginning. It was, after all, supposed to be a series akin to *The Odd Couple* or *Porridge* in space, with two opposing characters trapped in a situation together. It was not supposed to be about boldly going to alien planets *à la Star Trek*. Apart from anything else, it's difficult to make a location or a set look alien on a limited budget. Director Ed Bye remembered: "one of the things we'd said we'd never do is go to quarries and things like that where it's very obvious it's not Vesuvius or Venus or some asteroid belt. However, we did."

The trick to making it look spectacular was filming at night, so it looked nothing like a quarry, with atmospheric lighting to make it other worldly. The scene was completed with a few composite shots showing the planet against the backdrop of stars with Blue Midget parked nearby and Red Dwarf in orbit above. It looked great, but the reality was not very pleasant. The site seemed fine when it was discovered in the daytime by production manager Mike Agnew and assistant floor manager Dona DiStefano, but it turned out to be reclaimed land on top of what used to be a landfill site and, as the night went on, the smell got worse. "It was a rubbish dump," said Norman Lovett. "We did a night shoot there... and it was a really hard shoot. Holly was on location then. I used to be in a van with a cameraman filming me."

It was also a very special night for Craig Charles — because he became a Dad. "While we were filming this, my ex-wife was in labour," he told a DVD commentary. "There was a limo waiting for me to take me from this flint quarry in Wales to a hospital in north London where my son was born. I got to the hospital twenty minutes late and he was just handed to me. It was quite amazing really."

Fortunately, all his dialogue scenes had already been shot and, for the remaining scenes, Mike Agnew stood in wearing Lister's spacesuit and helmet. Craig Charles' voice was added in post-production. All the scenes where Lister's face is obscured by his helmet are actually a production manager in disguise.

One of the anecdotes often repeated about this night was that, in the confusion, Mike Agnew put the plastercast on the wrong leg. A close examination of the video reveals, however, that when the cast appears, it is always on the left leg. There is one scene — where Cat and Lister are examining the 'giant footprint' on the planet's surface — which shows Lister without a plastercast at all. Mike later revealed that it was too painful to wear a cast the wrong size for him and he simply left it off in the hope no one would notice.

This was the first and last time the Hologram Replication Cage appeared on the programme. Writers Rob Grant and Doug Naylor soon realised this was not a good solution for getting Rimmer off the ship and later invented the concept of the lightbee, which buzzes around inside him to create his holographic image. But then, they had never imagined taking Rimmer off the ship in the first place. It was only with the success of episodes like *Thanks for the Memory* that they realised they had the potential to tell much bigger stories; stories that would mean Rimmer leaving the ship more often.

Thanks for the Memory was a triumph for *Red Dwarf* and, for many people, it is the best episode of the second series. The mystery of the broken legs and the jigsaw adds a bit of drama to the episode, while it's full of classic humour. From the drunken scenes on the planet, to Rimmer claiming aliens must have wiped their memories and done a jigsaw, to the superb moment where Cat and Lister drop the gravestone.

The re-mastered version of *Thanks for the Memory* put together for a DVD release featured a new CGI version of Blue Midget, the shuttlecraft later to be displaced by Starbug. Doug Naylor, who was executive producer of the new version, defensively explained at the time of the launch. "It is able to walk around on planets. It's got two walker legs and the sequence in *Thanks for the Memory* where they're all drunk, they now walk in this drunken fashion in this new ship… There will be certain fans who go 'sacrilege, how dare you change anything!'… But different people like different aspects of the show and so you have to, in the end, do what you believe and hope people like it."

Episode Four: Stasis Leak

<u>GUEST CAST</u>
Lift Hostess... Morwenna Banks
Kochanski's Roommate... Sophie Doherty
Kochanski... C.P. Grogan
The Medical Orderly... Richard Hainsworth
The Suitcase... Tony Hawks
Captain Hollister... Mac McDonald
Petersen... Mark Williams

Story

The crew find a stasis leak on floor sixteen, which provides them with a door to the past. They can't stay because, in three weeks' time, the crew get wiped out by a radiation leak and they can't bring anybody back because they would crumble into powder. But, if they can persuade someone to go into stasis, they will survive the accident and be revived three million years later, alongside Lister. The only problem is there is only one spare stasis pod. So, who will they save — Kochanski or Rimmer?

Funniest Moment (arguably)

At the end, events conspire to bring three Listers into the same room, along with living Rimmer, hologram Rimmer and the Rimmer from the double-double future. After that, things get a little confusing.

Behind The Scenes

Confusion seems to be the abiding memory of people behind the scenes on *Stasis Leak*. Chris Barrie, for one, didn't understand it. "I never quite got the hang of that back in the second series, nor did a few people... I don't know what it is, maybe one of these days I'll ask Doug to explain that one to me."

Even on the day of recording, there were questions being asked as people tried to figure out how time paradoxes worked. This led to an angry rant by executive producer Paul Jackson who, by that point, realised there was no time to re-think anything. If they still hadn't made sense of it after a week of rehearsal and some location filming, then there was nothing for it but to put what they had in front of the cameras.

It all came together in the edit, of course, but the studio audience didn't have the advantage of seeing the finished version; they had to rely on a member of the crew to talk them through it. "At one stage, six Rimmers were wandering around the same room," said director Ed Bye (although there were actually three Listers and three Rimmers — see how confusing it is?) "The rational explanation why six Rimmers were walking round the room was so complicated that you would have had to have written a separate book to describe it! I remember the production manager Mike Agnew trying to remind people of the plot and you could just feel the audience desperately trying to keep up with him."

The stasis leak preserves a shower room from Red Dwarf three weeks before the crew were wiped out, and the second time Lister and Cat enter the shower room, they encounter a naked man. This was originally filmed with a man sent from the extras agency who was too shy to be naked in front of the film crew. The surviving footage from this first attempt shows him wearing a 'modesty stocking' (a pair of flesh-coloured tights). The scene had to be re-shot and this time included a man who was quite happy for his buttocks to appear on television.

A trip into the past meant a chance to revisit some of the crew from the first series. Olaf Petersen gets a scene, played by Mark Williams (later to find comedy fame in *The Fast Show*), while Mac McDonald returns as Captain Hollister. He gets a nice little scene doing Captain-y things before dressing up as a chicken for the ship's fancy dress party. "It was huge and stiff and my head poked out of the neck of it," said Mac. "The chicken's head was over my head and I think I was partially concealed by the wattles of the chicken."

When the Captain confronts Rimmer, Rimmer assumes he's an hallucination and throws a bucket of green paint over him. Mac remembers it being pretty horrible, but still had to engage his acting skills to get the right reaction. "It *is* acting," he said. "Because you know when you're going to get hit and you've got to not anticipate it because if you see the thing going back and you flinch, it blows the comedy. You've got to really play it that you don't know it's going to happen… It was plaster and water, or flour and water, with green food colouring in it, it was urgh. Anything like that you just want to do it once and get it finished with, it's not particularly pleasant getting hit in the face. Also, any time you get hit in the face with anything, you run the risk of getting it in your eyes or up your nose. In fact, I did get that up my nose, that green stuff. It goes up your nose, down the back of your throat; particularly horrible."

Other scenes in the past were filmed on location at The Midland Hotel in Manchester, the same place where the crew stayed during the filming. The film crew, however, were unable to take over the hotel completely and had to make do with a few bits of set dressing and a passing android waiter to suggest it was the 23rd century. In the reception scenes, it's possible to see some confused members of the public and a member of staff in the background. Look out for the genuine hotel receptionist, and two men in suits having a cup of tea, while the Cat attacks a woman wearing a fox fur.

Also making an appearance in the hotel reception is the ever-versatile Tony Hawks, this time playing the voice of a suitcase. Tony got the job because he was also *Red Dwarf's* warm-up man at the time. "To begin with there were a lot of little voice-over parts that needed doing," he explained. "We got on well and they did it partly to say thank you to me for doing the warm-up… I was never terribly keen on doing the warm-ups, so whenever I was asked to do them I would say 'yeah, okay I'll do it, but if there's anything coming along in it, can you think of me?'"

The hotel corridor and room were filmed upstairs at The Midland where Clare (C.P.) Grogan returned to play Kochanski. "We were in Manchester in a hotel room where I'd just married Craig Charles," she said. "I married *Lister*, obviously I didn't marry Craig Charles!... I think Kochanski was one of those characters that was in the first couple of series as a bit of a tease to Lister. It's always only been a very small part, it's never been a big part, but for whatever reason, it's stuck in people's minds. I don't know why, I really don't."

Present-day Lister discovers she has actually married his future self, so it means he will find a way to go back some day and they will get together. The scene called for two Listers to appear at the same time, which was achieved using a technique called split screen. The two Listers are filmed at separate times, the picture is then split, so one half (or third or fifth or whatever) includes the first Lister and the rest has the second Lister on it.

All of which was overseen by director Ed Bye. "I knew the special effects department quite well because of all the work we'd been doing with them over the years, particularly in *The Young Ones*," he said. "And the better ones like Peter Wragg have a strong knowledge of video effects, so that worked out quite well. The difficulty with it is that effects always take a long time and in a comedy show they don't normally give you a long time. Somebody coming in and breaking a cup would be the greatest piece of trauma in a regular sit-corn, whereas this is people being blown up, wandering around in differ-ent parallel universes and on board spaceships. But we managed to do it — God knows how!"

All of which didn't seem to bother the actors, according to Clare Grogan. "It was really straightforward, whatever technical things were going on, they really didn't get in the way. I think we just had a good time. It was just quite funny, I mean, Craig is really really good fun, so that always relieves the pressure a bit, and the tension, when he starts mucking about."

Kochanski also appears in the last scene of the episode, as she enters the bunkroom with future-Lister, but look at the scene carefully and it's possible to see it's not actually Clare Grogan hanging onto Lister's arm. According to one version of the story, this was because a member of the crew sent her home at the end of the location shoot by mistake. Another version has it that she wasn't available for the studio recording because she had a prior commitment. Either way, on the night it was production assistant Dona DiStefano who was asked to stand in for Kochanski, and hid her face with the help of a large floppy hat.

So the episode concludes with three Listers, three Rimmers, a Cat and Kochanski all in the one set. With actors playing multiple versions of their characters, it demanded a multitude of split screens, with the additional headache of two of the Rimmers being holograms. One of them was a disembodied head coming out of a table which was keyed in using the blue screen technique: Chris Barrie was recorded against blue in a separate part of the studio and matted in to the finished picture. The other hologram Rimmer — the Rimmer from the double-double future — had to emerge from the wash basin because the set was so full, there was nowhere else to put him.

It was a great end to the episode, even if it did confuse a lot of people.

Episode Five: Queeg

GUEST CAST
Queeg... Charles Augins

Story

After more than three million years in deep space, Holly is getting a bit flaky. When he detects an approaching meteor, but forgets to tell anybody about it, backup computer Queeg 500 decides it's time to take over. He's welcomed by the crew who are glad that things are being run efficiently, but change their minds when they realise Queeg wants them to run efficiently too. He refuses to feed the living members unless they scrub the floor, and he puts Rimmer through a punishing exercise regime. There's only one thing for it — to restore Holly to his rightful place. But Queeg won't give up control without a fight — and the scene is set for a showdown.

Funniest Moment (arguably)

Holly tells Lister how to mend the ship by explaining how to connect the various cables. When he suggests connecting one of the leads to the white cable, it causes an explosion that sends Lister flying. "Or is it the yellow cable?" says Holly.

Behind The Scenes

Red Dwarf's backup computer, Queeg 500, was played by Charles Augins who had been Danny John-Jules' mentor in the dance world. At the end of the first series, he was Danny's guest at a post-production meal where he was introduced to writers Rob Grant and Doug Naylor. Which is how he came to be invited to be on *Red Dwarf*.

At the time, he was best known to the wider public from the Babycham advert where he says the immortal line; 'I'd love a Babycham'. It's that same tough guy tone that he brings to Queeg, a hyper-intelligent authoritarian computer who is completely different to Holly. "I was Danny's dance teacher, aside from being good friends," said Charles. "As a teacher I scream a lot and I'm strict, I'm very disciplined and that's what the part called for. So immediately when they said 'that's the character', Danny said 'Charles'... I enjoyed it very much. I loved the show, so when I was asked to come and do it I jumped at the chance."

The role required Queeg to be filmed in a blacked out booth, like Holly, wearing a black polo neck jumper so only his head would appear on screen. For a dancer, that was somewhat unusual. "You didn't do anything, you couldn't move," said Charles Augins. "It was very straight ahead, it was all facial. So that was interesting, that was different for me. Usually I'm moving or my arms are moving or something, but in this one it was just your face."

It was the pinnacle episode for Holly whose character had grown considerably over the first two series. Originally conceived as a voiceover part, Norman Lovett had first pestered to get his face seen on screen, then for it to be seen without the pixellation of the first series, and still he asked Rob Grant and Doug Naylor for more. "I remember they'd said they'd written a Holly episode and I thought, 'Crikey that's good,'" said Norman. "I was very pleased about that, I was very chuffed and excited about it. And also that it turned out to be one of the more popular episodes as well, so I'm very pleased about that, very pleased."

In *Queeg*, Norman Lovett's Holly gets a lot of great lines, and a lot of laughs from the audience. As a stand-up comedian, he consciously played to the audience, which helped him judge his timing and deliver a brilliant comedy performance. "When I filmed Holly I would be in a corner and I would get them to face me towards the audience, but there'd be a camera in front of me and everything so I could actually play it out to the audience. I found that easy, being the stand-up comic in the cast."

He would only go into his own little blacked-out corner during the filming. During rehearsals, he would join the cast on the floor and stand in the place where Holly's screen would be. "So the actor would know where to look. If Craig's talking to Holly, he's got to know that the screen's going to be about here and so he can talk to him. And I just had to be there going, 'Yeah, all right, what do you want Dave?' I just found it so easy to do him. Well, it's Norman Lovett isn't it, really? But I added a little bit, a bit of nodding."

The imposition of Queeg 500 to replace Holly as ship's computer follows damage caused by a meteor. It disrupts the workings of the hologram simulation suite which causes Rimmer to lose his legs and then to behave like other members of the crew. It was a chance to employ the talents of Chris Barrie, who was known for doing impressions of famous people like Ronald Reagan and Kenneth Williams, and for impersonating the *Red Dwarf* cast. His Lister, Holly and Cat are superb, and he also impersonates the ship's psychiatrist. This, too, was based on a real person — the 'the shuttle was late' speech is a take-off of commissioning editor Peter Risdale-Scott. "Chris is one of the most marvellous mimics of all time," said Peter. "At the end of series parties, Chris used to do a piece that just mimicked everybody. He always mimicked me as a psychiatrist. I don't know why, there's obviously some secret there I don't know about!"

In order to fix Rimmer and get him back to normal, Lister has to re-connect some cables. This is when Holly gets the white cable muddled up with the yellow cable and Lister ends up causing an explosion when he connects the wrong leads. Lister is catapulted over the console and lands on the other side of the desk. Craig Charles performed his own stunt by running at a trampette and leaping over the console while pyrotechnics created a hail of sparks. It was one of the show's few early stunts and, with an added bit of slow motion, worked extremely well.

It's after this that Queeg arrives with his draconian regime, including an exercise routine for Rimmer which he had to complete, even if he passed out. For actor Chris Barrie, this meant running round the set with his eyes closed which was not easy, and resulted in at least one collision with a table. The sweat which can be seen on Rimmer in those scenes is the genuine article.

As the episode moves on, and Queeg maintains his grip on the ship, it seems Holly's future is doomed. Although Holly tries to fight back to the last, Queeg's choice of a battle-to-the-death chess match seals his fate. The script works so well, it seems as if Holly could really be gone and they could be stuck with Queeg.

This might have been because the writers didn't know how they were going to get Holly out of the mess they had written him into. After a lot of thought, they gave up and went to the pub, which is where they had the epiphany of how to end the episode. The whole thing was a practical joke, staged by Holly to encourage the others to appreciate what they've got 'because, basically,' he says, 'I'm fantastic'.

It meant Queeg was gone and it was farewell to Charles Augins. "I enjoyed it," he said of his appearance on *Red Dwarf*. "A lot of people saw it, a lot of people remember it. People keep saying, 'You did Queeg, didn't you?' That and Babycham — it'll probably be on my tombstone!"

Episode Six: Parallel Universe

GUEST CAST
Ms Rimmer... Suzanne Bertish
Ms Lister... Angela Bruce
The Dog... Matthew Devitt
Hilly... Hattie Hayridge

Story

Holly has invented the Holly Hop Drive, capable of taking Red Dwarf back to Earth. But engaging the device propels them into a parallel universe instead. There, they find an exact double of Red Dwarf, but with female opposites of the crew — apart from the Cat's opposite, who is a flea-bitten dog. With seventeen hours until Holly can get them back to their own universe, how will they get on with themselves in female form?

Funniest Moment (arguably)

Rimmer's glee when he finds out Lister might be pregnant.

Behind The Scenes

The episode opens without the usual titles, but with a dance number instead. It features Danny John-Jules as the Cat strutting his stuff with Chris Barrie as Rimmer and Craig Charles as Lister doing their best to keep up as backing singers. This little number was choreographed by Charles Augins, known best to *Red Dwarf* viewers as Queeg from the previous episode. *Parallel Universe* was actually recorded before *Queeg*, so this was his first job on the show.

"They worked very hard at it," said Charles of Chris and Craig. "I knew they weren't dancers. I also had four or five girl dancers. So when you know people are not dancers you try and do things that they can do to make them look good. Since Danny had the lead they didn't all have to do the same thing, so that made a difference... I think we did it in two days. I was up there at the beginning of the week and the girls came back later. So I worked with the boys for a couple of days and I had to rehearse the girls in London... It was nice working with them because it all worked together and there was a very close friendly family ambience."

There were grumbles, however, that practicing for the dance routine rather overtook the rehearsal time, not leaving enough time to rehearse the rest of the show. Further grumbles have been expressed over the song itself. The lyrics were written by Rob Grant and Doug Naylor and were an adaptation of a song they had written for their radio sketch show *Son of Cliché*. But, by the time Danny John-Jules had put his spin on it for the recording, they felt it wasn't as funny as it might have been.

Nevertheless, it was a big hit with the fans, as Danny John-Jules recalled: "Ever since I did it, most of the letters I ever got, nearly every letter asked about *Tongue Tied* or they ask a specific line: 'what's the line that comes after 'gud-arble diggle may'?... Basically, the line that everyone wanted to know was 'digestive system, baby.'"

Yet more grumbles came with the casting. Suzanne Bertish put on a strong performance as Arlene Rimmer on the night, but this wasn't apparent in rehearsal, leading to some jitters among the regular cast and production staff that it was all going to go horribly wrong. It turned out she used that rehearsal time to study Chris Barrie's Rimmer to get the tone and mannerisms right and pulled her performance out of the bag in front of the audience.

Perhaps it has something to do with a general dissatisfaction with the episode as a whole. As a polemic about the way men treat women and how perverse it seems when those attitudes are reversed, it was "unspeakably simplistic" according to Doug Naylor. He told a DVD documentary: "the way we did it was like written by two twelve-year-old earnest schoolboys."

There were no such sexual politics for Holly and his female opposite, Hilly. It was simple sexual attraction, albeit of the computer variety. Judging by the number of lipstick marks on Holly, it was quite a successful one at that.

Hattie Hayridge, the comedian who played Hilly, would later join *Red Dwarf* as a full-time cast member. But, at this point in 1988, she was expected to join for just one episode. She got the role after the executive producer saw her stand-up routine on television. "Paul Jackson had apparently seen me on *Friday Night Live*. When they wanted a female version of Norman's Holly, he said 'you've got to have Hattie.'"

She wasn't familiar with *Red Dwarf* at all and decided to do some homework. "I hadn't seen all the episodes before and Norman lent me all his videos to watch."

When Hattie subsequently became a regular member of the cast, she would learn her lines like any other actor. But, for her debut performance, life was made a little easier. "For that Hilly thing they [the lines] were on autocue because I suppose they didn't quite know if I was going to pass out at the actual recording and suddenly go 'oh I can't remember anything!' They didn't really know me, so they put it on autocue."

The final female opposite to appear on screen was a pink version of a scutter who had a very sexy wink for her grey parallel universe counterpart. She was made by simply removing grey panels from the second scutter and replacing them with new pink body parts. The result was a litter of baby scutters, who were able to travel behind mum and dad because they were attached by a thin nylon line which was invisible to the cameras.

Chris Barrie remembered them with fondness. "They were not best behaved at the best of times, but they were fun when you did get the scutters, like on the old series where you got the scutters with lots of little scutters. That was quite fun."

It turns out the scutters weren't the only ones procreating with each other. The Listers had a bit of a wild and drunken night too, resulting in the possibility that Dave Lister could be pregnant. It refers back to *Future Echoes* in the first series where Lister was seen to emerge from the delivery room with twin boys. As his test turns red and confirms Lister is pregnant, it seems that future is coming to pass. Which is an excellent hook to get people coming back for the third series.

Red Dwarf III

Written & Produced by... Rob Grant & Doug Naylor
Directed & Produced by... Ed Bye
Executive Producer... Paul Jackson

Rimmer... Chris Barrie
Lister... Craig Charles
Cat... Danny John-Jules
Kryten... Robert Llewellyn
Holly... Hattie Hayridge

Recorded: September-October 1989
First broadcast: November-December 1989

The third series of *Red Dwarf* arrived at the end of 1989 and immediately audiences knew things had changed. Gone was the majestic opening music over pictures of the spaceship moving through space, and in its place was Howard Goodall's fast-paced guitar theme and a montage of some of the best visuals of the series. The sets were brighter, the whole look of the show was more interesting and there were a lot more ambitious effects. The third series also received the honour of Roman numerals for the first time — and was called *Red Dwarf III*.

Accompanying a change in production values was a change in the cast. Norman Lovett's Holly was replaced by Hattie Hayridge's Holly, a decision forced on the show after Norman left following a disagreement with executive producer Paul Jackson. "It was money in the end," said Norman. "The management just halved my fee. I'd just met my wife and I'd moved to Edinburgh and I didn't want to come down for rehearsal. I always felt I was just sitting around in the rehearsal room doing nothing really. And I thought, 'I'm going to cut down on my days, I'll learn my lines at home and come in and do the stuff'. They said, 'okay, we'll cut down the filming time and the rehearsal time' and my fee was halved! I just thought, hang on, I'm still going to have the same amount of screen time and you're halving my fee? It's not on. And they said, 'Oh it is according to this', so I said, 'well it's not according to me', so I left. But I wish I hadn't now. In retrospect, I wish I hadn't."

From an audience's point of view, it might have looked as if Norman was simply replaced with Hattie, as she had already proved herself capable as Hilly in the final episode of the second series, *Parallel Universe*. But that wasn't quite how it happened. "It wasn't just a case of 'we've had her, we'll have her again,'" said Hattie. "I auditioned with other people. Janine Davitski auditioned, men and women — no animals as far as I know! They basically gave you a sheet of the script to do. It was the bit from *Backwards* where they land back on Earth and it was: 'where are we?', 'about a quarter to one'; 'what year is it?', 'a calendar would be helpful', things like that. Basically, if you made Rob and Doug laugh when you said it, then you got it. Luckily they did. I suppose I probably did have an advantage because I knew what the character was, whereas some people had auditioned and had no idea of the series."

It was a big break for the stand-up comedian who, up to that point, had mainly been working on the comedy circuit and had the occasional stand-up slot on television. "It was like leaping in the air, it was brilliant," she said. "Not just to be on TV, but to do that. Because some things, some sitcoms, you'd think if you got the part 'oh God, I don't know if I really want this', but with that I just wanted to do it so much."

Also joining *Red Dwarf* was Robert Llewellyn as Kryten. The character had already appeared at the beginning of the second series in the one-off episode, *Kryten*, which broke the writers' 'no robots' rule. It was one of a series of rules Rob Grant and Doug Naylor had invented to stop themselves falling into the standard science fiction clichés: they were to have no aliens, no monsters of the week and definitely no funny robots. But when they saw David Ross as Kryten, and how the audience reacted, they changed their minds. The fact that Kryten had left Red Dwarf five episodes earlier was something they decided to ignore. "We made that decision," said Rob Grant. "You can get so tied up with this continuity business, saying, 'oh no, we can't do that', but if it makes the show better, you just accept that you made a mistake in earlier shows, and plough on and get on with it."

"Basically we change continuity all the time," said Doug Naylor, "which amuses me because it drives everyone nuts."

Director Ed Bye wasn't worried about continuity, he just saw adding Kryten into the mix as an improvement. "It made a lot of difference," said Ed. "One of the good things about it was he could carry a lot of plot in exposition because he was the logical explanation for everything that happened. So whenever they say, 'why is this thing happening to us?', instead of us having to have some tortuous route to find out why something's happening to them, Kryten can go, 'ah, if my memory banks serve me...' and help us out. Also he was great for one-liners and he's funny: a robot with a servile comedic attitude is funny. He fitted in nicely, I liked him a lot."

The original plan was to bring David Ross back for the role, but the actor wasn't available and so the producers went searching for someone else. The person they found was Robert Llewellyn, who already had a history playing robots. "I was actually on stage at the end of the [Edinburgh Fringe] Festival doing a play called *Mammon, Robot Born of Woman* where I did lots of silly walks and funny voices," said Robert. "A man called Paul Jackson came to see that play and a year later I walked into a seedy basement in Denmark Street [to audition] and met these three totally unscrupulous scruffy little gits and talked about doing silly robot walks and silly voices. At that time I was actually involved in developing a series for Channel 4 about a robot and I said to them 'I don't really want to be the guy who does robots and I don't want to be recognised'. They said, 'don't worry Bobby, you won't be recognised.'"

This was because Robert's head was to be totally encased in rubber. The look, although similar to David Ross's original, was totally redesigned for the new series. It was notoriously hot and, in those early days, took many hours to apply. "It is vile," said Robert. "It is vile wearing that rubber suit, there is no doubt about it, it is extremely unpleasant. But… it's a great privilege to be in the show. It is a very peculiar job and it's a peculiar job in that particular role of being an unknown with that head on which suits me fine."

By this point, Rob Grant and Doug Naylor had got themselves promoted to producers and had a bit more control to do things the way they wanted. This meant finally being able to get rid of the grey sets they had been so unhappy about. Fortunately, a new production designer, Mel Bibby, was on hand to help. But he still had to work within the bounds of what had already been established. "The logic was: after the crew had died, the few surviving members would go off in search of better quarters, which were the officers' quarters," said Mel. "That's when the more hi-tech, the more clean look came in. It was then developed with corridors and other areas. It was just a transition. They were a bit tired of the grey look after two years, so they went a little bit more exciting."

Mel was a member of BBC staff who had trained at Rochdale Art College and spent his early career in interior design and designing for exhibitions. When it came to spaceships, he had to approach things from a different perspective. "Anything goes," he said. "There's a company that I use in Manchester which do plastic mouldings for the Ministry of Defence or for Honda or for Ford and they're just great big sheets of plastic moulded material that the engineering parts would be put into. So before each series I go up there and see what's on the run and buy a hundred of this and a hundred of that. And a lot of the moulding is actually architectural moulding, but used out of context. There's a lot of junction boxes in there which are all from B&Q, there's a lot of plumbing devices which are stuck on the set, then you spray it all in and it looks like a mouldy mess."

Complementing the set design were the new-look special effects. Peter Wragg and his team had already shown what they could do, with things like Confidence exploding in outer space in *Confidence and Paranoia* and Lister being blown across the drive room by an explosion in *Queeg*. The writers realised effects could be a great asset to the show and so wrote more of them into the scripts. This included a lot of model shots, many of which were more ambitious than those which had gone before, with scenes such as Starbug colliding with a fiery meteor.

Starbug was the replacement shuttlecraft for Red Dwarf, brought in because Blue Midget was so cramped and about the only thing you could do in it was sit down. The new ship was supposed to be called White Midget, but was changed during the course of the design process. The man who designed the Starbug model was Alan Marshall, known to everyone on the crew as 'Rocky'. "One of the scripts that featured it contained a crash in the snow on an ice planet," said Rocky. "So I said to Pete, 'because it's white, if it crashes in the snow you'll never see it, so it would be nice if we could make it a colour."

The insect-like design was actually picked out from several possible designs which Peter Wragg had presented to Rob Grant and Doug Naylor. It was then down to Rocky, in consultation with special effects colleague Mike Tucker, to realise the shuttlecraft. "I was not only fed up with white spaceships, I was fed up with things that were clearly just made out of flat sheets of plastic," said Rocky. "Mike said 'oh, I thought you would be doing something very blobby, they're not as blobby as I thought, they're not as rounded'. And I said, 'what do you mean?' and he said 'well, I thought you'd have a sphere for the front, the middle and the back sort of thing'. So he suggested the use of spheres, so I went away and drew up a drawing based on that. When they saw it, they thought it looked something like a bug. Now a bug, or the term Starbug, had never been mentioned at this point, it was a White Midget... When it came to the second drafting of the scripts they had changed the name of it from White Midget to Starbug. So the design came first and the name came second, which is extremely unusual."

It was from this model design that the sets for Starbug evolved, an unusual thing for production designer Mel Bibby to be faced with. "It's usually the other way around because models are often constructed or designed after we've shot the series," he said. "On this, the model was there, the parameters were there. Obviously you had a round cockpit, but from a cost point of view, to make every interior a sphere was totally out of the question. We assume that the curve is on the exterior of the squared-off room — well I do, I don't know about anybody else!"

With all the new elements in place, *Red Dwarf* was ready to launch into its most ambitious and popular series yet.

Episode One: Backwards

GUEST CAST
Waitress... Maria Friedman
Compere... Tony Hawks
Customer in Café... Anna Palmer
Pub Manager... Arthur Smith

Story

While Kryten and Rimmer are out on a flying lesson in Starbug, they encounter a time hole. It takes them to an Earth where time is going backwards. Realising they are stuck until rescued by the rest of the crew, they get jobs as a novelty act that does everything forwards. They like it so much, they want to stay — until Lister and the Cat find them and start a fight by un-eating a man's pie.

Funniest Moment (arguably)

Just before leaving, the Cat goes into the bushes — realising too late that, in this world, even bodily functions are backwards.

Behind The Scenes

The end of the second series left *Red Dwarf* with a bit of a cliff-hanger. Lister was pregnant and due to have twins. It was expected the third series would start with an episode called *Dad* where Lister copes with pregnancy and fatherhood. But writing the episode was tough going for Rob Grant and Doug Naylor who eventually realised it wasn't going to work and abandoned it. The replacement episode didn't resolve the cliffhanger, explain why Kryten had returned or why Holly was suddenly a woman. Rob decided not to worry about it, while Doug continued to feel it was a problem until the edit when he had the idea of the *Star Wars*-type scroll up the screen.

The scroll reveals that Lister gave birth to twin boys, Jim and

Bexley, who experienced accelerated growth rates and were eighteen within three days. In order to save their lives, he took them to the same parallel universe where they were conceived. Kryten re-joined the crew after he was discovered in pieces and reassembled following a space-bike crash. And Holly gave himself a face change operation by basing his new self on Hilly, the computer he once fell in love with.

With all that sorted out, it was time to get on with the new stories.

The episode *Backwards* is based on a really simple idea, that filming people and playing it backwards is pretty funny. But the spark for the idea was actually far more intellectual and came from Doug Naylor's reading of *A Brief History of Time*, the famous book about the nature of the universe from noted astrophysicist Stephen Hawking. In his book, Hawking suggests that after the universe has finished expanding from the energy of the big bang, it could start to contract, causing the universe to run backwards. Hawking's theory makes it into the script as part of Holly's dialogue.

The first scenes to be filmed of *Backwards* — and, indeed, of *Red Dwarf III* as a whole — involve the crew arriving on the backwards version Earth at a location near a lake. None of the scenes which involve Kryten in this location actually feature Robert Llewellyn in the rubber mask as he was still finishing work another job, so every shot of him is actually a stand-in wearing Robert's costume. It was, however, the genuine Craig Charles who had to walk backwards into the lake so, when the film was reversed, he appeared to walk dry out of the water. For this, he had to have weights on his body, including in his pockets so his clothes wouldn't float up in the water. There were a few worried moments for Craig when he thought he might be stuck in the silt at the bottom of the lake, but he lived to tell the tale.

Other snippets of Earth were filmed in a street in Manchester and feature a couple of members of the crew. The man smoking a cigarette is writer Rob Grant and the man who collects a newspaper from a rubbish bin is production assistant Mike Agnew. The shot of Rimmer and Kryten walking down the street was achieved with them walking backwards while members of the public carried on with their normal business going forwards — none of whom seemed to blink an eye. Perhaps holograms in green outfits and mechanoids walking backwards are a normal occurrence in Manchester.

More backwards fun took place in the club where Kryten and Rimmer are performing. Casting for the compere was easy as the role went to 'Fifth Dwarfer' Tony Hawks, their former warm-up man making his umpteenth appearance on the show. The production saved a little bit of money on the costume budget by asking him to wear the same green suit he wore in his act at the time. "It didn't seem to matter what you actually said because it was all played in backwards afterwards," he said. "I think if you're able to translate what Arthur Smith [the pub manager] said in that episode, if you could rig up your video recorder so you could play it backwards, you discover that what he said was very very filthy indeed. It was quite odd because it obviously had to be recorded forwards. I think my bit wasn't done in front of a live audience, my bit was done in the afternoon, but Arthur's bit was done in the evening in front of the audience and then the idea was they filmed it forward and then played it back. So he just came on and cursed and the audience didn't know why!"

A study of the tape reveals Arthur Smith is yelling about 'the one prat in the country' who bothered to reverse the video to find out what he was really saying. Although, these days, people can just buy the DVD where, in a bonus feature, the nice producers have reversed the tape for them.

The backwards scene of the fight in the club was very complicated and caused a lot of headaches for a lot of people. It took a long time to film with all the stunt work and people trying to work out when Lister should lose his black eye and when the man had his tooth knocked back in again. A complicated job for continuity at the best of times, let alone when the whole thing is wrapped in *Red Dwarf* backwards logic. For Craig Charles — who described himself as "the Bruce Willis of Liverpool" — it was the chance to do more stunts as he was pushed along a bar full of beer glasses and thrown out of a window. "I kind of do like it a bit," he confessed. "I like all the stunts and that. The more you can take away the acting and just have real life reactions, the more realistic it is, and the better it is for everyone."

The fight means the crew of the Red Dwarf are no longer welcome on backwards Earth, and so they leave in Starbug. It was the end of a memorable show for many, but not a favourite among the cast, as Chris Barrie said: "*Backwards* wasn't an amazing show in my humble opinion." Even if it did have that wonderful moment for the Cat at the end when he decides to go behing the bushes — and realises, too late, what happens when you do that in a backwards universe.

Episode Two: Marooned

GUEST CAST
None

Story
With Red Dwarf heading for five black holes, Holly tells the crew to abandon ship while she steers a safe path through them. Lister and Rimmer plan to be away for only twelve hours, but Starbug crashes on a snowy moon and there's nothing for them to do but await rescue. As the days go by, how will Lister and Rimmer survive the freezing conditions without supplies? And, more importantly, how will they survive each other?

Funniest Moment (arguably)
Rimmer gains new respect for Lister after he sacrifices his guitar to put on the fire… or so he thinks until Lister takes his guitar from the cupboard where he'd hidden it right under Rimmer's nose.

Behind The Scenes
The confrontation between Lister and Rimmer was central to *Red Dwarf* in the early years. The bunkroom bickering had often been a highlight in those episodes, with some sparkling writing and some great performances. In *Marooned*, all of that came together with everyone at the top of their game. The actors produced some funny and poignant performances to match the quality of the script.

Craig Charles had to admit that his acting ability was much better than when he first took on the role of Lister. "I'd be a pretty sad smeg if it wasn't, you know what I mean? I think I've improved an awful lot. I'm not very proud of my first acting performances, but things have only looked up, things have got better. You've got to remember I didn't go to drama school, I didn't do any of that, so all my mistakes were made in public, made on television with millions of people watching. I'm surprised I've survived, really, but I enjoy it."

Chris Barrie agreed (when interviewed in 1993) it was a great episode and ranked it as his second favourite, behind the Ace Rimmer vehicle, *Dimension Jump*. "Things like *Marooned* and all that sort of stuff — fantastic dialogue. You look at *Marooned* now and there was nothing like it in the sixth series, it was just all visual effects. Which I'm not saying is a bad thing, but is the way the show has developed. I'd love to do lots of scenes where it's just talking."

There is something else noticeable in watching *Marooned*, a new sense of confidence in the way Chris and Craig play their characters. Perhaps it was the experience they were able to bring to the roles by that point, perhaps it was the makeover of the sets and costumes which made them more comfortable, or perhaps it was the reception they were getting from the audience.

Other members of the cast are hardly in the episode, with Cat and Kryten coming to the rescue in the final minutes. There are, however, some great lines for Holly, who's totally loopy as usual, having mistaken five specs of grit on the scanner scope for five black holes. The scripts had originally been written for Norman Lovett's Holly and the character remained basically the same despite being played by a woman. "There were lots of things of me still being called 'senile old git,'" said Hattie Hayridge. "I kept saying 'do you mind if we change this?' I don't mind being insulted as long as it's accurate!"

The idea of locking Rimmer and Lister in a room together wasn't the original inspiration for the episode. This came from deciding to set a story on a frozen moon and followed a meeting between the producers, director and visual effects supervisor Peter Wragg. "*Marooned* was an example of sitting down with the effects guys and saying, 'What can we exploit here?'" said director Ed Bye. "'Snow was easy,' they said. It was probably the most foolish thing he [Peter Wragg] ever said. He regretted those words so bitterly he could have bitten his tongue off! We shot a sequence for *Marooned* in a studio in Liverpool and in order to be like a blizzard we had to fill the studio with polystyrene little balls which are like snow, and soap flakes so it would stick to their faces. We had to pour all this in front of a fan which was fuelled by a VW Beetle's engine, so this fan is really strong. Then all the stuff would come out and Craig would have to stagger around with bits of soap flakes going into his eyes, up his nose, down his mouth, in his ears — everywhere! Having committed ourselves to this snow idea we had to crack on with it. It worked in the end, but it was hard."

Just to prove Ed's point, there's an outtake of Lister stepping out of Starbug into the snow and immediately falling out of shot. This was because the fan was so strong and the soap flakes were so slippery that Craig Charles simply fell over. The effect was so good, the outtake made it into the show.

The model work by Peter Wragg and his team also saw *Red Dwarf* reach new heights in terms of special effects. The shot of a fireball striking Starbug was so good it made it into the credit sequence, while the crashing of Starbug onto the snow-bound moon remains one of the most memorable of the series.

All these elements only helped to enhance what is effectively a two-hander for Rimmer and Lister in an episode originally titled *Men of Honour*. Director Ed Bye was still impressed with it years later when he re-watched the episode to make the re-mastered version for a DVD release. "I always liked *Marooned* because of that where they're stuck and they can't do anything... [I was] looking at the re-mastered and thinking, 'God, that was good'. The stuff they do, these two people sitting there who are completely different, but sort of trying to find the common ground somewhere, but failing... You're always disappointed when it's finished, you go 'I want more of that, give me some more of that stuff!'"

Episode Three: Polymorph

GUEST CAST
Genny… Frances Barber
Young Rimmer… Simon Gaffney
Mrs Rimmer… Kalli Greenwood

Story

A creature with the ability to change itself into any object stows away on Red Dwarf. It feeds on negative emotions and, one by one, steals Lister's fear, the Cat's vanity, Kryten's guilt and Rimmer's anger. The crew need to get the creature off the ship, but will a kamikaze Lister, slobby Cat, uncaring Kryten and pacifist Rimmer be up to the task?

Funniest Moment (no argument)

Kryten removing Lister's shrinking boxer shorts.

Behind The Scenes

This episode was notorious for what became known as 'the ten minute Polymorph scene'. As far as the studio audience was concerned, this was the funniest moment of the show — possibly ever! They laughed so much, none of the cast or crew could hear anything and they were unable to carry on with the rest of the show because the audience was in such hysteria.

In the story, the Polymorph has turned itself into a pair of boxer shorts, which Lister doesn't realise at the time when he puts them on. He's about the leave the bunkroom when the shorts start shrinking. He collapses to the ground in pain and Kryten rushes over to help Lister pull his shorts off. He's kneeling over Lister, tugging hard while the vacuum hose plugged into his groinal attachment flails around. It's all perfectly innocent, but to the audience it looks like… well, it looks like a robot in a vacuum attachment trying to take off a man's shrinking shorts — what else would it look like?

The audience reaction caught the production team by surprise. They knew the scene was funny, but that didn't know it was going to be *that* funny. It had been rehearsed during the week and in the dress rehearsal on the afternoon before the recording and it got laughs from the crew, but no one had fully taken into account the true comedy value of Kryten's groinal attachment. The vacuum hose was originally supposed to come out of his chest, but costume designer Howard Burden couldn't find anywhere to attach it on that part of Kryten's outfit and so, by a fluke, it ended up being put lower down. The audience certainly knew what Kryten's groinal hose could represent and literally screamed with laughter. On the finished episode the actors can be heard shouting their dialogue at each other because the squealing is so loud. It left Chris Barrie waiting in the wings for some considerable time before he was able to come in with Rimmer's punch line: 'you'll bonk anything, won't you Lister?'

The final scene is reputed to have lasted ten minutes and had to be cut down to fit in the rest of the episode. In the final version, it lasts about a minute and a half.

When the polymorph itself is revealed in its true form, it turns into a creature which Hattie Hayridge described as "the one with the big teeth, worked by levers". It was the first creature to be built by the special effects team for *Red Dwarf* and looked great. But it wasn't on its best behaviour on set and kept falling over, while its mechanics didn't always work. Hattie remembered the creature's final shot involved Rimmer running down the corridor to face it. "Just as he ran round the corner, the whole monster just collapsed," she said. "They had to rebuild the whole thing just for that one little bit, because they'd filmed everything else. It just collapsed ten seconds before it should have done, and all the levers fell off and everything. There was spot-welding going on."

The episode contains yet more complex exposition from Kryten which actor Robert Llewellyn always found difficult. But it was a speech where he insults Rimmer's mother by comparing her to a whole list of fish-related attributes which he couldn't seem to learn. To help him, bits of his speech were written on cue cards around the set. In order not to blow the jokes in front of the audience, they were turned round so no one could see them. Unfortunately, someone forgot to turn them back again before Robert delivered his speech and production manager Mike Agnew only realised this at the last minute. The only way to get to them without walking through the middle of the scene was to crawl between Robert's legs while the actor performed above him. He didn't manage to get to the cards before Robert got to the speech, but somehow he delivered the lines flawlessly without needing to read them.

Great moments for the cast come when the Polymorph steals Kryten's guilt, Cat's vanity, Lister's fear and Rimmer's anger. The non-angry Rimmer was originally written as a hippy, but it wasn't quite working in rehearsal and Chris Barrie improvised a whole load of alternative material. The writers noted it all down and re-worked it into the new, improved Rimmer speech, delivered by a bearded, be-spectacled man with a pipe and a 'Give Quiche a Chance' T-shirt.

More humour comes from the Polymorph's ability to change into almost anything. There's a sequence at the beginning where it morphs into 35 different objects including a teddy bear, a sock and a real live rabbit. "It took hours to get that rabbit just to stand in the studio," said Hattie Hayridge. "The rabbit kept running off under the cameras. It was the second shot and it took two hours to get this rabbit to stand there."

These transitions from one object to another were achieved by jump cuts. The camera was fixed in one place, the objects were placed before it one after another and the resulting footage was simply edited together. It works as a technique, but isn't very sophisticated, so when it came to re-mastering the episode, director Ed Bye decided to try using the extra budget and improved technology to do something different. "We were looking at *Polymorph* and I thought all those things that the Polymorph changes into, we'll morph all those so the Polymorph globs into one thing to another. We tried one — because that's all we could afford — and I thought 'Christ, that's not funny anymore', so it would have been useless anyway."

It goes to show that the success of an episode isn't always down to budget. "There's a balance," said Ed. "Yeah, sure, four times the budget please, that would be great, we could really make it out-standing! But one thing that doesn't really affect the budget — well, everything is affected by the budget — but to a certain degree, the comedy that you do on the night, it's going to happen then or it's not going to happen then."

It's probably fair to say, judging from the audience's reaction at the time, the comedy in *Polymorph* happened beyond expectations.

Episode Four: Bodyswap

<u>GUEST CAST</u>
Voice of Executive Officer Brown... Lia Williams (uncredited)
Voice of Auto-Destruct System... Mike Agnew (uncredited)

Story

One of the scutters goes mental and re-wires the ship, including the auto-destruct device. When Lister accidentally sets it off, Kryten uses the hologram discs to replace Lister's mind with that of a senior member of the crew who has the authority to shut it down. This gives Rimmer the idea of putting his mind into Lister's body. Lister agrees to the swap so Rimmer can put his body through a fitness and health regime. But will the temptation of bodily desires be too much for the former hologram?

Funniest Moment (arguably)

Lister sets off the auto-destruct by ordering from the vending machine. It looks like they're all going to die until it fails to go off — and the machine dispenses a milkshake and a crispy bar.

Behind The Scenes

Lister and Rimmer may have swapped bodies, but they kept their own voices. In order to make Lister's voice come out of Rimmer and vice versa, the action and dialogue was recorded as normal, with the voices dubbed on afterwards.

This led to on-set antics as both of them did impersonations of each other. Especially Chris Barrie, who used to make a living out of that sort of thing. "It was a laugh, sort of imitating Craig," he said. "I think I was getting on his nerves, though, because he kept walking around going 'do I really sound like that, man? Do I sound as whining and stupid as that?' and people would go 'well, actually Craig...'"

Hattie Hayridge, while playing Holly, got to watch the whole thing being played out in rehearsal and during filming. "It was quite hysterical watching them do that. Because Chris is an impressionist anyway, it was just like they had to keep stopping because they were giggling over him doing Craig. And then Craig, even though he's not an impressionist, was really good at doing Rimmer. It was quite funny really to see them do each other."

There was also a practical element to all this tomfoolery. The mimicry helped the mouth movements fit more accurately during the dubbing and convince the audience that a body swap had happened. Another technical trick was used to record all the background noises (such as footsteps) by recording the action twice, the second time with the actors miming the dialogue to create a clean sound effects track.

The technical nature of the episode meant it was impossible to film in front of a live studio audience. So the episode was recorded and edited, then shown to an audience to create a laugh track. Peter Risdale-Scott, who was still commissioning editor for *Red Dwarf* at BBC Manchester, remembered this did not go smoothly. "The evening was a disaster," he said. "We took over a small BBC theatre in Regent Street called *The Paris*. *The Paris* seats about three hundred to four hundred people and it became a small cinema and we projected the episode onto the screen. The audience loved it to death because we got all the fans in and there was their favourite series blown up on the big screen. The disaster was they laughed so much that when they laughed at one joke, three or four others would come before they'd stopped laughing. So when we got it back to the cutting room, it was totally impossible to use the track of the audience's laughter. It was just over everything. In the end it was shown to a different studio audience."

Bodyswap was the first working day on *Red Dwarf* for Robert Llewellyn in his new role as Kryten. As is normal for sitcoms, some of the location filming was shot in a block before rehearsal started and the first location for Robert was a hotel sauna. For a man who gets incredibly hot in the costume with his head covered in a rubber mask, to sit in a real sauna in a real spa was extra-punishing. He sweated copious amounts that day which caused unforeseen problems for the special effects department. The script required Kryten to light candles for Lister's dinner with a flame which ignited at the end of his finger. A device built into Kryten's glove was essentially a cigarette lighter attached to some wires, which the special effects team operated from behind the camera. It worked fine in testing, but in the hot confines of the sauna, Robert Llewellyn's sweat caused the equipment to short-circuit. So whenever the flame was due to appear, it failed to work and Robert was jolted with an electric shock. After that day, it's a testament to the actor that he came back for the rest of the series.

This scene was eventually completed, but didn't make it into the final cut for the episode and the tape was subsequently lost somewhere within the BBC archives.

The episode features some of the most spectacular spaceship sequences yet for *Red Dwarf*, with Starbug chasing Blue Midget across a rocky planet and crashing into the surface in a cloud of dust. Unlike the live action sequences (which were shot on videotape), these were shot on high speed film which, when slowed down, adds weight to the sequences.

For continuity buffs, a dialogue section just before the spacecraft chase refers to 'White Midget' which was the original name for what became Starbug. In the confusion of the hectic schedule, this accidentally got left in.

Episode Five: Timeslides

GUEST CAST
Gilbert... Robert Addie
Bodyguards... Rupert Bates, Richard Hainsworth
Young Lister... Emile Charles
Young Rimmer... Simon Gaffney
Thicky Holden... Stephen McKintosh
Ski Woman... Louisa Ruthven
Ski Man... Mark Steel
Lady Sabrina Mulholland-Jjones... Koo Stark
American Presenter (Blaize Falconburger)... Ruby Wax
Adolf Hitler... Himself

Story

Kryten develops some photographs in mutated developing fluid which brings the photos to life. When they are projected onto a screen, Lister discovers he can walk into the photos and interact with the people in them. It provides a gateway into the past, which Lister uses to get his younger self to invent the Tension Sheet. It changes Lister's life so that he never joined Red Dwarf and, instead, became rich and famous. Rimmer decides to pull the same trick and visits *his* young self at boarding school. But, as he explains everything, Thicky Holden is listening in the next bed. So, when Rimmer comes back, the time lines revert to the way they were: Thicky Holden is recognised as the inventor of the Tension Sheet, and Lister and Rimmer are once again stuck on Red Dwarf.

Funniest Moment (arguably)

Rimmer tries to persuade his younger self to invent the Tension Sheet, while Thicky Holden keeps interrupting the conversion, making a mental note of every detail.

Behind The Scenes

Timeslides again sees *Red Dwarf* utilise a great science fiction idea for comic effect. The idea of going back in time and changing the past had been a staple almost since the beginning of science fiction, but in the hands of writers Rob Grant and Doug Naylor, the idea comes across as new and fresh.

The story begins with Lister lamenting his life stuck on board Red Dwarf. He's sick of everything, of constantly finding more ingenious ways of wasting time, and doesn't want to join Cat in playing table golf. He wants a job, to meet people and girls, which is a bit difficult when you're the last human being alive.

To the rescue comes a mutated batch of developing fluid which Kryten discovers can bring photographic prints to life. These include a picture of a couple on a skiing holiday which Lister got back from the developers by mistake. The couple, in turn, got some gross photos of Lister's birthday party including a snap of him being sick. The episode originally included some dialogue of the ski couple talking about this, but during filming Craig Charles pointed out that, at the time the photo was taken, the couple wouldn't have yet received Lister's pictures, so the lines were cut. Also in the outtakes are several attempts to hit Lister in the eye with a snowball, later to show up on the *Smeg Ups* compilation.

It's not only photographs that can provide a gateway to the past: film footage can too, thus allowing Adolf Hitler to guest star on *Red Dwarf* 'as himself'. Lister's encounter with Hitler ends with him stealing the Führer's briefcase. It turns out to be the infamous briefcase containing a bomb, which Colonel von Stauffenberg hoped to use to assassinate Hitler. Realising what he has done, Lister kicks the bomb back into the film footage and it explodes, leaving Hitler unscathed. Lister's involvement in the whole affair thus makes it into history, as seen in the newspaper he is reading in the following scene.

(In actual fact, von Stauffenberg put a bomb in his own briefcase, not Hitler's briefcase, but why let historical accuracy get in the way of a good gag?)

Other parts were portrayed through the usual method of using actors as opposed to real historical figures. Of the most significance was Emile Charles, Craig Charles' brother, who used family resemblance as an advantage to play the young Lister. Alongside him in the band Smeg and the Heads were Bill Steer and Jeffrey Walker, two members of real-life band Napalm Death. *Om*, the song they are playing, was written by Craig and Craig's band also provided the incidental music for the scene where Kryten is dancing while developing his photographs, and for the scenes of Lister arriving at his mansion (the tracks being *Bad News* and *Cash* respectively).

It seems the timeslides not only allow people to walk into the past, they also enable them to change the past. Lister is the first to take advantage of this and persuades his younger self to invent the Tension Sheet, essentially a square of bubblewrap painted red with little pockets of air which are fun to pop. So, instead of the legitimate inventor — Fred 'Thicky' Holden — making millions, it is Lister who becomes a millionaire, meaning he doesn't join Red Dwarf, bring a cat on board or rescue Kryten.

Rimmer decides to go visit the rich Earth-bound Lister at his luxurious home, the scenes for which were filmed at Lyme Hall in Cheshire, a National Trust property which charged a budget-gobbling fee. A scene inside the dining room features Koo Stark as Sabrina Mulholland-Jjones, an actress made famous by her relationship with Prince Andrew before he married Sarah Ferguson.

The rich version of Lister, of course, doesn't remember Rimmer, so Rimmer decides to try the tension sheet trick on some timeslides of his own. Except when he goes into the past to talk to his younger self, the conversation is overheard by Thicky Holden who patents the tension sheet and puts time back to the way it was before.

It is, perhaps, a complicated plot with changing time lines and stepping into photographs, but under the assured writing of Rob Grant and Doug Naylor, it worked superbly. It remains one of the best examples of *Red Dwarf* with a cracking storyline and lots of funny bits.

Episode Six: The Last Day

<u>GUEST CAST</u>
Girl Android… Julie Higginson
Hudzen… Gordon Kennedy

Story

Lister receives notice that his Kryten mechanoid is reaching the end of its life and its in-built shut-down chip will automatically activate in twenty-four hours. With apparently no way to prevent Kryten obeying this command, Lister throws him a goodbye party. Kryten enjoys himself so much he decides he wants to live. There's just one problem: persuading his homicidal replacement Hudzen.

Funniest Moment (arguably)

Kryten's comment, after getting drunk at the party, "I feel a Jackson Pollock coming on!" — referring to Lister's story of being drunk in Paris, with a pavement artist selling his vomit as a work by the famous abstract painter.

Behind The Scenes

In what was to become a bit of a *Red Dwarf* tradition, the script for *The Last Day* came in rather late. While the episode *Backwards* was being filmed in Manchester, Rob Grant and Doug Naylor were busy in London trying to come up with a sixth episode. Which explains why the character of Hudzen was conceived at the last minute, giving little time for costume designer Howard Burden to do what costume designers are supposed to do. Instead, he pulled together a load of disparate elements from whatever was around, including a studded leather collar and motorcycle helmet to give the replacement mechanoid a hard-guy look.

Gordon Kennedy was hired to play Hudzen without having to

audition. The actor is usually a cheery fellow with a soft Scottish accent, but decided to toughen up his delivery at the read-through to produce a vocal-chord-grating deep tone for Hudzen's voice. Gordon Kennedy had previously been known for his role in the Channel 4 sketch show, *Absolutely*, and went on to have a successful career which has included playing Little John in the BBC's modernisation of the *Robin Hood* legend.

There's something very '*Terminator*' about Hudzen, the robot programmed to kill. As in *The Terminator* movie, the viewer gets to see scenes from Hudzen's point of view with the robot's digital analysis displayed as text across the screen. This being *Red Dwarf*, it reveals Hudzen's analysis of everyone he meets as being a viable target, apart from Lister who is human — but, the screen says 'what the hell!' and he becomes a target too. Similarly, there is something very *Blade Runner*-esque about the way Hudzen reacts when confronted with the fact that silicon heaven doesn't exist: he slows down and stops, very much like the Rutger Hauer replicant in the influential 1982 movie.

Religious commentary is woven into the episode alongside its humour, most notably with Kryten's explanation of silicon heaven which is where mechanoids and calculators go when they die. 'Humans don't go to heaven,' he tells Lister, 'someone just made that up to prevent you all from going nuts'. This prompts the viewer to ask if the mechanoid's idea of an afterlife is any more ridiculous than the human one.

Rimmer's speech about his parents' religion mocks the idea of taking everything written in a holy text a bit too literally. Their devotion as Seventh Day Advent Hoppists is a way of life based on a misprint. It echoes *Waiting for God* in the first series, where the Cat people had based their beliefs on Lister's slobby lifestyle and dream of living on Fiji.

Religion can be a controversial topic on television when it's challenged, but writers Rob Grant and Doug Naylor felt that including it in a space comedy stopped anyone from being too offended. "Funnily enough, I think if you do a lot of stuff in science fiction, people just don't get it and so they don't object to it," said Doug. "When we were in Universal [Studios in America trying to make an American version of *Red Dwarf*], they wanted us to Americanise one of the scripts. One of the scripts which we did was *The Last Day* and we thought this is really interesting. Of all the shows that we're doing, this is such an obviously religious show, and they didn't get it."

"There were times when somebody was saying to the [American] executive, 'are you going to do the religious satire stuff that *Red Dwarf* does?'" said Rob, "and he says 'oh, we'll address that when we come to it' — and he's got the script on his desk!"

Another theme to return to the show in this episode is Kryten's attempt to break out of his programming. He is programmed to shut himself down — effectively, to die — when triggered to do so, with only the promise of silicon heaven to look forward to. It is only at the end when Kryten 'lies' to Hudzen that there is no silicon heaven that he is able to break out of his programming and defeat Divadroid International who ordered his destruction.

One of the things which motivates Kryten's desire to keep living is a wild party which Lister and the crew throw for him in the officers' club. They each give him a present to celebrate the occasion, although originally Holly wasn't scripted to give him anything at all. A bit of persuasion from actress Hattie Hayridge got the script changed so Holly gave Kryten a gift after all. The party also allowed her to dress up a bit, which she rarely got to do on the show. "The wardrobe man, Howard, used to say 'I don't do anything with you, do I?'" said Hattie. "So he used to try and chip in a pair of glasses or a hat or something like that now and again. He did have a budget for me even though nothing was spent on it."

The party reveals, for the first time, Lister's background as having been abandoned in a cardboard box underneath a pool table as a baby; a story which would be re-visited in *Ouroboros* four series down the road.

The episode is cheaper than most in the third series, with no location shooting, grand model shots of smashing spaceships or legions of guest stars. It therefore allows *Red Dwarf* to concentrate on some of the other things which made it so successful, like dialogue, character development and being funny. There is even the opportunity for Robert Llewellyn to appear without his rubber head, as he plays Jim Reaper, Head of Sales at the Space Division of Divadroid International.

A good end to a good — and very successful — series.

Red Dwarf IV

Written & Produced by... Rob Grant & Doug Naylor
Directed & Produced by... Ed Bye

Rimmer... Chris Barrie
Lister... Craig Charles
Cat... Danny John-Jules
Kryten... Robert Llewellyn
Holly... Hattie Hayridge

Recorded: November-December 1990
First broadcast: February-March 1991

Red Dwarf IV was commissioned hot on the heels of the success of *Red Dwarf III*; an obvious move considering the show was gaining in popularity and reputation. But, for actor Robert Llewellyn, getting the call to come back and film another series was a total surprise. "When I did series three, 1989, we had a party at the end of that series and I thought that was the end of it," said Robert. "I had a really good time and I thought I was really lucky to get in on the end of this amazing series. It was like, that's how long series last, they do three and that's it. So we had this party and we were all saying goodbye and it was only two months later that they said 'do you want to do another one?'... Series four has always been the biggest surprise to me, 'oh we're doing it again? Oh, what again? Another *Red Dwarf*? Oh weird!' I really couldn't get my head around that."

For the new series, a new make-up designer was brought in, Andrea Pennell (later to become Andrea Finch) and she developed a new way of doing the Kryten make-up so Robert didn't have to spend so many hours in the make-up chair.

Also new were the studios. The move to Shepperton Studios was forced on the production because the ones at BBC Manchester were being refurbished, but it is generally considered to have been a blessing. It meant the end of shuttling back and forth between London, where the cast would rehearse during the week, and Manchester where the episodes were filmed in front of a live studio audience. This saved time and also saved the headache of making sure everyone actually got there (the original arrangement of flying the cast up to Manchester had been replaced by a specially chartered coach after certain cast members gained a reputation for missing the flight).

Hattie Hayridge remembered this changed the feeling of doing the show. "It was actually fun when we used to go up to Manchester because it used to be rehearsals in London and filmed in Manchester. Then they closed the studios up there for refurbishment. They got used to doing it in Shepperton and realised, I suppose, it must have been cheaper than giving us all a five-star hotel room in Manchester. It was fun to go down there, we used to get our own hostess coach, one executive Rapide coach with a woman on it, like a hostess, serving you tea and sandwiches. We used to watch videos on the way up on the telly. We stayed two nights. We'd go up on the Sunday, stay there Sunday night and then pre-record Monday, do the show Tuesday, then drive back Tuesday night. The Sunday we got there, we'd all go out for a meal and stuff, so it felt you were bonded together more than the other where you felt you were commuting to work and going home again."

The advantage of being in Shepperton Studios was there was no need to rehearse at the BBC Rehearsal Rooms in Acton. The cast were able to rehearse on the actual sets they would be performing in and did not have to work with pieces of tape on the floor to represent doorways.

For production designer Mel Bibby, keeping the sets up all the time meant it was easier to avoid the issue of wobbly sets which had plagued some BBC science fiction programmes in the past. "It's much easier at Shepperton," said Mel. "The first three series were done in Manchester and that was a bit of a nightmare. We used to do a pre-record day on Thursday with some of the sets in and then take out those sets and put other sets in for the following day and then put the audience in. So it was an overnight change around. That's when you get wobbly sets because there's such a rush. But in Shepperton the set stays standing during the series and it can be braced-off with scaffolding to avoid that. Basically the set's made up of pallets and they're very rigid, so it's not much of a problem. But we still get a few wobbles!"

Not as if any of these behind the scenes changes could be seen by the audience. Apart from a slight change to Kryten's make-up, it simply looked like it was going to be another brilliant series of *Red Dwarf.*

Episode One: Camille

GUEST CAST
Mechanoid Camille... Judy Pascoe
Hologram Camille... Francesca Folan
Kochanski Camille... Suzanne Rhatigan
Hector Blob... Rupert Bates

Story

Kryten discovers a female mechanoid called Camille when he investigates a distress call. The two of them seem made for each other until Camille meets the rest of the crew and appears to Rimmer as a Hologram, to Lister as a leather-jacketed human and to the Cat as himself! She is a pleasure GELF, made to reflect the desires of whoever looks at her. In reality, she is a green blob. Undeterred, Kryten continues their relationship, unaware that her long-lost boyfriend is still out there.

Funniest Moment (arguably)

Lister tries to get Kryten to learn the art of insults by calling Rimmer a 'smeghead'. But, still ruled by his programming, the best Kryten can do is call him a 'smeee heeee'.

Behind The Scenes

As a pleasure GELF, Camille cannot help but transform into everyone's perfect companion. For Kryten, when he looks at Camille, he sees a mechanoid just like himself, but in female form. So the search was on for someone who could play Kryten's love interest. Who better than Judy Pascoe, the real-life partner of actor Robert Llewellyn?

"I'd seen the results of Robert being Kryten for the last however many years it was," said Judy. "I was at home when he came back every night after wearing the rubber mask. When I talk to Rob when he's got the mask on it's so freaky because it's this voice that you know, but you don't know the face. It's a very strange experience. I think it does affect you psychologically. I think he needs a therapist on call 24-hours a day while he's doing *Red Dwarf*!"

Initially, it wasn't certain how she would play a female mechanoid and it was suggested she perform the dialogue in a Swedish accent. That didn't work so, instead she tried a direct impersonation. "I did it in Robert's voice, exactly the same as Kryten, and they just cracked up!"

She also tried mimicking Kryten's jerky robotic walk. "I was doing all that and they decided it just wasn't right. The other people who were playing the mirrors, or the ideal women for Chris and Craig, weren't doing exactly the same. It didn't seem right to mimic the accent or the walk exactly the same. So I did everything toned down a bit."

For the recording days Judy had to wear the Camille mask glued to her face for many hours. She had some idea what it would feel like because she had worn prosthetics on a different television show. The only person who wasn't prepared for it was her boyfriend, Robert Llewellyn. "He was just weird," she said. "He couldn't look at it, he just said, 'Oh God, it's too weird. Now I know what it's like.' So we sat in his dressing room like these outcasts the day that we did it. You go very inward when you have it on, I don't know why. But I don't think it's so much [of a problem] for him now, because they're all so used to seeing him. For two days a week he just becomes Kryten. He is Kryten for everyone else on the set because they're so used to it now. For other friends when they come to the recording and see him they go, 'Oh God! I just can't look, I just can't look.'

"I know the first time I saw him was in Manchester and I walked in and he had the Kryten mask on and he was wearing a T-shirt and smoking a cigarette — he still used to smoke then — and it was Robert, but it was like talking to the elephant man or something," said Judy.

"You just can't look at it because it's someone you know really well. So I knew he was going to experience the same thing."

Robert Llewellyn said the whole experience very odd. "I found it very disturbing when she walked on stage because it was like seeing your girlfriend with someone else's head on," he told *TV Zone Magazine.* "We did have a kiss when the cameras weren't on and it was so weird, it was like kissing when you've just come out of the dentist after a local anaesthetic and it's not possible — you can't feel a thing. We would have had very safe sex if we could have got through our plastic underpants!"

The mechanoid couple had several romantic scenes together, in a robotic sort of way. The fact that there was a real romantic connection under the masks made little difference. "He'd directed a play that I'd written, so we'd worked together before," said Judy. "We don't do it very often, but when we do it's completely fine because I don't even think of him as my boyfriend, I just think of it as Robert Llewellyn who I'm working with. It's weird how you can sort of switch off and leave the personal lives at home."

Judy spent one day pre-recording scenes in the studio as Camille, and the rest of the scenes live in front of a studio audience. "It's brilliant, it's just the best," she said of the live atmosphere. "It's a great way to film a sitcom. It's wonderful because it's like having the best of both worlds, it's like having the best of theatre and the best of television all at the same time. Normally when you do television or filming you miss having a live audience and the problem with a live audience is often you're in a play with only a hundred people [watching]. But to have an audience and to be doing it on television is to have the best of both things."

Judy got a break from being encased in a rubber head when Camille reveals her true form to the crew — and turns into a green blob. She continued to do the voice while the physical part of the blob was performed by Mike Tucker, a member of the special effects team, sitting inside it on an office chair with wheels. It produced a classic *Smeg Up* when the blob couldn't keep hold of her drink and kept dropping it, once losing the cocktail umbrella and cherry decoration in her soup.

This scene takes place in Parrots, a swanky cocktail bar so named in order to make the *Casablanca*-inspired joke near the end 'we'll always have Parrots'. A lot of the closing moments of the episode, including the 'this could be the start of a beautiful friendship' speech, are an homage to the Humphrey Bogart movie.

The set of Parrots, however, was not a favourite of production designer Mel Bibby. "That was a complete send-up — a disastrous one!" Mel recalled. "I didn't like it. We were just using bits of sets that we had previously acquired because we had run out of money — yet again! A lot of times when we get to the end of the series there are a lot of sets that have to be compromised on because of money."

Other guest stars were Francesca Folan, playing a female Hologram with a Rimmer-like fondness for telegraph poles and Hammond organ music, and Suzanne Rhatigan as a Lister-esque human. She wasn't the original choice, however, as the part was initially played by Tracy Brabin. The writers didn't feel she quite worked and so brought in Suzanne — Craig Charles' then girlfriend — for some re-shoots. This character was written to resemble Kochanski, but references to this in the dialogue were cut, so the end credits' reference to 'Kochanski Camille' seem a little odd.

The episode is also famous for its opening scene of Lister trying to get Kryten to lie when he asks him to name various pieces of fruit. Robert Llewellyn's performance in particular is hysterical, proving that *Red Dwarf* was still capable of producing superb self-contained dialogue scenes.

Episode Two: DNA

GUEST CAST
DNA Computer Voice... Richard Ridings

Story

The crew find a transmogrifying machine which can take a person's DNA and alter it into something else. When Kryten unwittingly gets trapped in it, the machine samples his organic brain and transforms him into a human being. Kryten soon realises he's not cut out to be a human and decides to turn himself back. But, while experimenting with the machine, the crew accidentally create the Mutton Vindaloo Beast from Lister's curry — and suddenly have a much bigger problem on their hands.

Funniest Moment (arguably)

Kryten asks Lister about the function of his human anatomy by showing him a picture of what lurks where his groinal socket used to be — an image which requires a double polaroid.

Behind The Scenes

Kryten's appearance as a human for most of the episode meant a respite from the hot confines of the rubber mask and costume for Robert Llewellyn. After almost two series of moaning about his lot (*DNA* was filmed at the end of the fourth series), it's easy to imagine what a relief it must have been for him. He may have been cooler, but he was a lot more nervous.

"I get very embarrassed in front of an audience when I haven't got it on," said Robert. "The one show, *DNA*, when Kryten got turned into a human being, I got really flushed and flustered when I first went on in front of the audience. It was like I had never done it before, it was very odd. Also I had nothing on and Craig kept showing them my bum. I was wearing a surgical gown, so naturally that had to be pulled apart for the audience's benefit."

This was the scene with the famous 'double polaroid' moment. The surprise on Lister's face when he sees the picture is reported to be genuine shock from Craig Charles because of what he was looking at. There have been so many jokes made by the cast about what the picture actually was, that the truth has been lost in *Red Dwarf* history, although it is believed to have been part of the human anatomy mocked up by the art department.

Kryten's new human look also allowed the wardrobe department to have a bit of fun. As commented by Lister in the episode, he may look human, but part of him is still mechanoid. Which explains his dress sense, which is totally without taste or co-ordination — hence one of the loudest shirts in the history of the universe with mismatched tie and jacket.

While dressed like this, he visits his old self in the guise of his three spare heads. It gives the character a moment to discuss what his new life is like with representatives of his old life. You could say that's quite a deep concept, philosophically. It's also very funny, especially with Spare Head Three being an grumpy old northern bloke.

The idea came out of a conversation with writers Rob Grant and Doug Naylor. "They asked me last year [1990] if there was anything I wanted to do," Robert Llewellyn told *Red Dwarf Smegazine*. "I said I'd love to do that sort of voice. I've done it for the studio audience — I've sometimes dropped into a grumpy old comic northern accent. In *DNA*, it suited the mask which kind of went all wrinkly. So I wanted to do something with that. I wanted to play Kryten's dad. You know [he puts on his northern accent]: 'I hate you, you bloody silly bastard!' So they did the thing with the spare heads, and that was very much Rob and Doug's idea."

It was also Rob and Doug's idea to change the continuity surrounding the Lister/Kochanski relationship. In the first two series,

Lister had lusted after her, but never plucked up the courage to ask her out. Here, Lister talks about breaking up with Kochanski after having a relationship with her. This wasn't a continuity 'error', but a deliberate decision by the writers.

"We felt that it was less mature," Rob Grant told the *Smegazine*. "It was kind of schoolyard mentality, that he wanted to go out with this woman and daren't ask her out."

Doug Naylor added in the same interview: "There's also this huge science fiction convention where you should be consistent from day one all the way through and people go absolutely wild if you're not. I find it very, very funny to be quite as inconsistent as we've been from the beginning."

"We do actually pay lip service to the continuity," said Rob. "If we make a change we sit down and weigh up whether it's better for the show, and if it makes the show better, we'll go for it."

Originally filmed last and scheduled for broadcast at the end of the series, *DNA* was designed to end on a bit of a cliffhanger, suggesting Kryten is stuck in human form. Although the crew return to the transmogrification equipment with the intention of reverting him to the mechanoid he once was, they don't get round to it in the course of the episode. They're too busy being chased by a Mutton Vindaloo Beast.

The creature, in true monster-of-the-week style, was a man in a suit. The man in question was Paul McGuinness from the special effects department, whose tall stature and skinny frame made him ideal for the job. He made the suit himself, with bits of curry-inspired latex hanging from it, and pulled an all-nighter to get it finished in time for the recording. So it's a very tired curry monster who's seen to chase the Dwarfers down the corridors. It is even said he dozed off on several occasions between takes.

To defeat the curry monster, Lister decides he needs to be transformed into the ultimate human fighting machine. The inspiration for his costume is clearly the science fiction movie *Robocop*. Holly's calculations are, however, a little off and turn Lister into a miniature version, which is far less frightening. But he still wins the day, even if destroying the monster causes it to explode all over him. This shot —where Lister gets a splat of curry in the chest — was done with such force that it really knocked him over backwards.

The monster is defeated because lager is 'the only thing that can kill a vindaloo' and has to be the first and last time a scary science fiction monster was defeated by something so mundane. How brilliant — and how very *Red Dwarf*.

Episode Three: Justice

GUEST CAST
The Simulant… Nicholas Ball
Justice Computer Voice… James Smillie

Story

Red Dwarf picks up an escape pod from a prison ship that may contain the first woman Cat has ever met in the shape of guard Barbara Bellini — or it could contain an escaped psychotic simulant. When Cat starts the revival process, the others decide to head for a disused penal colony to use its facilities in case the occupant isn't Babs. What they didn't account for was the screening process which probes their minds to check they have committed no crimes. Although the rest of them are cleared, Rimmer still harbours guilt for causing the accident which wiped out the crew — and is sentenced to 9,328 years imprisonment for the second degree murder of 1,167 people.

Funniest Moment (arguably)

The Dwarfers step into the escort boots and are made to walk around the complex.

Behind The Scenes

Justice features perhaps the best use of location on *Red Dwarf* so far with many scenes on Justice World filmed in Sunbury Pumphouse, a disused water pumping plant near Shepperton Studios. Its interior of metal gantries and rusting equipment were made more atmospheric by John Pomphrey's lighting and a bit of smoke.

However, the studio set for Justice World where Rimmer is put on trial was a let-down for production designer Mel Bibby. "That was a compromise," he said. "Ed Bye was directing that year and he'd just done a show where they had an infinity set where basically everything's done on perspective. But to do it properly you've got to ramp the floor so it looks as though it goes into infinity, but it's really only sixteen foot long. Well, we hadn't got room and we hadn't got the money to ramp, so we had to do it on the flat and it didn't work. It didn't look as though it was going into infinity, so a bright light was stuck at the end to confuse everybody."

The episode begins far away from Justice World, in the medical bay where Kryten is tending to a poorly Lister. It revisits the idea of space-age illness gone to the extreme first used in *Confidence and Paranoia*. This time, a space-age version of the mumps virus has enlarged Lister's head with a massive pus-filled bump on the top. Cunningly, the first shot is of Lister with his head under a towel, so when it is revealed, it gets a big reaction from the audience.

"That's when I really had sympathy for Robert Llewellyn," Craig Charles told a DVD documentary. "Because it took quite a while in make-up to get that space bumps head put on. And when it burst — oh God!"

The popping of Lister's head happens off-screen with only a sound effect to give a clue as to what happened. It gives rise to a classic Cat moment who, splattered with pus, walks into Starbug's cargo bay absolutely devastated, with the line: 'his head burst'.

The yellow and red pus effect was achieved with some KY Jelly courtesy of the make-up department. The special effects department, meanwhile, customised rat traps to make the superb escort boots which lock themselves onto the feet of the Dwarfers. They built the model of Justice World to resemble the Scales of Justice and were responsible for the objects that the simulant smashes over Lister's head at the end. These were made of wax so they would break easily, but not easily enough for Craig Charles who complained the scene gave him bruises.

The simulant is played by Nicolas Ball with an evil glare in his one natural eye, and a red glow emanating from the other eye socket set into a half-metallic face: another homage to *The Terminator*.

Some of the highlights of the episode are, again, the dialogue sequences. Robert Llewellyn does a superb job with Kryten's defence counsel speech outlining the depths of Rimmer's smeginess. Chris Barrie contributes with marvellous reactions from behind, getting increasingly offended as the insults build. He also looks genuinely scared during the scene earlier in the episode when he is found guilty of murder and given a jail sentence. A dramatic moment within a very funny episode.

The justice zone, if it were really possible to create such a thing, would actually work — as Lister demonstrates when he refuses to commit any more crimes (an attempt at arson causes his own clothes to catch fire). This is summed up in a lengthy speech at the end of the episode, in which Lister says that it is impossible to have perfect justice without giving up free will.

This speech was a last-minute addition to the episode, to fill a hole left by a deleted scene. Justice World was originally supposed to be on a planet, not a space station, and a scene was filmed with the crew walking round a park while Rimmer was incarcerated. In the deleted scene, Lister misses the rubbish bin with his lager can — at which point the Justice Zone Litter Birds retaliate by dropping a gooey bird dropping on his head. It was felt this scene didn't really work and was cut.

Episode Four: White Hole

GUEST CAST
Talkie Toaster... David Ross

Story

Kryten discovers a technique to boost the intelligence of a computer and tries it out on Holly. She becomes super-brainy with unparalleled knowledge of concepts such as string theory and quantum mechanics. The only problem is, the process has drastically reduced her life expectancy to mere minutes. The only recourse is to shut herself off, along with most of the ship's systems. When they encounter a white hole spewing time back into the universe, they decide to risk consulting Holly over what to do next. Her advice is to play pool with planets.

Funniest Moment (arguably)

Time occurs in random pockets as Kryten explains the concept of a white hole beginning with the Cat's question; 'what is it?'. As the conversation continues out of order, the Cat keeps repeating 'what is it?', just in case they weren't already confused enough.

Behind The Scenes

White Hole was the last episode of the series to be written and came after a period of head-scratching from writers Rob Grant and Doug Naylor. Running low on plot ideas, they raided their own *Red Dwarf* novel *Better Than Life* and thought about using a sequence where Lister visits a version of Earth which has become covered in rubbish.

They showed the idea to director Ed Bye, a man who normally took the difficulties of special effects under his wing. "I always see that as a bit of a challenge," he said. "There's been one or two times when I've had to say 'I'm sorry, I don't think that's possible'. Things like 'Lister mounts giant cockroach and flies to garbage world'. You think, 'Well with the best will in the world this is going to looking to look like a bad version of *The Muppets!*'"

So the garbage world idea was thrown out and another sequence in the novel, which involved a black hole, became the inspiration for *White Hole*.

The resulting episode was much easier for Ed Bye to direct. Or would have been, if he hadn't been ill. He'd had a bit of a week of it, if truth be told. At the beginning of the week, his wife had had a baby, and at the end of the week, he came into Shepperton Studios on the day of the audience recording only for it to be obvious to everyone he was too sick to work.

Cue an emergency call to former executive producer Paul Jackson, who had to brush up on his directing skills. "The fact is, I loved sitting in the chair directing," he told the *Red Dwarf Smegazine*. "But I wouldn't have been able to do it if that camera script hadn't been precise to the last detail. It was already forty minutes late when I got there, and we never would have finished the day if it hadn't worked perfectly."

At least he had an excuse for being late, which is more than can be said for Danny John-Jules who had the misfortune to choose that particular day to be a little tardy. He therefore had to suffer the big boss having a stern word with him in front of the cast and crew.

The whole set was, in Paul Jackson's words "a little busy" on that day. "That's the way it is when the boss comes in," he told the *Smegazine*. "I'm a cantankerous old bastard when I'm directing. Ed's much more easy going than I am. I'm the only guy who signs the cheques, so it was a little busy."

The scenes shot in front of the audience on that night included Lister pedalling away on a static bicycle to try to generate enough electricity to work the Cat's hairdryer and fry a couple of eggs. Danny

John-Jules unwittingly chose this moment to fluff his lines several times over, meaning extra sessions of pedalling for poor Craig Charles, already hot under studio lights and wearing Lister's fur cap. Viewers can therefore be assured it is real sweat on his face.

Also taking part was the well-loved Talkie Toaster: rescued from the garbage hold, fixed by Kryten and still driving everyone bonkers by repeatedly asking if they want any toast. The original appearance of Talkie Toaster was voiced by comedian John Lenahan, but the new incarnation was voiced by David Ross, the actor who played the original Kryten in series two. "That was wonderful that toaster because I didn't even have to learn the lines," he told the *Smegazine*. "I just went in and read it. It was wonderful, it was like doing radio. Of course, all actors like radio because it's the easiest job in the world, you just have to stand in front of the microphone and read it. The trouble is, the money's crap!

"With the toaster, it was also nice to feel part of the team again — it was nice to see Doug and Rob and Robert and all the other cast — especially in such a zany, one-off role. It's great to be able to say that you've played a toaster at one point in your career!"

White Hole was an opportunity for Holly to spend a little bit of time in the spotlight, which was unusual since the arrival of Kryten who had taken on a lot of the work explaining the plot. When she became a genius, she had a new look with slicked back hair. "That pleased the make-up department because they could mess around with me," said Hattie Hayridge. "At one point, one original idea was for me to be in a bald cap, but strangely enough they put it on and they thought it looked too good. They thought I'd be like a sort of egg-head. But lucky for later life, perhaps, being bald apparently suits me! So then they just said 'well it's not worth doing that then if it's going to suit her'. So they did my hair back with just one little curl thing at the front."

She also came out of the screen, appearing as a disembodied

head floating in the room. "That was really good when it came out of the computer. I thought perhaps they could have done that for series five — that possibly could have been a change, that she became super-intelligent and came out of the machine. It would have been a way to allow her to move about."

The episode is once again full of wonderful moments, from Kryten's observation that they can't hear anything because there are 'no sounds to hear', to the memorable scene where time occurs in random pockets. This scene, in which Kryten tries to explain the concept of a white hole with the Cat repeatedly asking 'what is it?', was *Red Dwarf* once again playing with time. It was filmed with a mixture of the cast repeating their lines and actions, and using jump-cut editing to show the conversation skipping to the end, to the middle and back to the beginning again. A classic moment.

Episode Five: Dimension Jump

<u>GUEST CAST</u>
Mrs Rimmer... Kalli Greenwood
Young Rimmer... Simon Gaffney
Cockpit Computer... Hetty Baynes

Story

In another dimension exists another Rimmer whose heroic antics are legendary within the Space Corps. It is his job to test a new craft which can break the dimensional barrier, so he leaves his old life and goes crashing into Starbug where he meets Lister, Cat, Holly and a very different version of himself. He saves the day, repairs Starbug, fixes Cat's crushed leg — but is there truly room for two Rimmers on board one spaceship?

Funniest Moment (arguably)

What a guy!

Behind The Scenes

Not surprisingly, Chris Barrie puts *Dimension Jump* at the top of his list when it comes to episodes of *Red Dwarf*. "[That's] probably my favourite of the whole thing because it was a joy to wear that wig and to play such a winner," he said, interviewed in 1993.

He'd been playing the anally-retentive smeghead Rimmer for several years, at the same time as having success as Gordon Brittas, the irritating leisure centre manager, in the BBC sitcom *The Brittas Empire*. He really needed a break from that sort of character and the writers decided to give him the opportunity to play a hero.

"I just thought I'd make him sort of a city boy," said Chris Barrie. "A yuppie kind of character with a slight internationally American kind of feel to it. But very obviously an English boy who's done well and joined the Space Corps and not public school, but sort of good grammar school and good at everything. Mr Popular, but with a conscience. A little bit of Sean Connery thrown in there, and the whole character generally was a bit of a James Bond figure anyway."

To make him look the part, the costume department provided Ace Rimmer with a gold lamé suit, complete with gold space helmet and flared trousers. Make-up provided a wig with a fringe which he could flick back and a tan-like glow for his skin. A small rolled cigar completed the image.

"I'm one of these people who puts on a costume, [and] it does help you for some weird reason," said Chris. "Like doing Rimmer, putting on that uniform you feel more like Rimmer, like a wanker, like a prattish, pernickety, fussy… I don't know why. Ace, when you put on the wig and you've got the whole flick going and you've got that funny silver outfit. The outfit — it was just so wild it was good! It wasn't actually what I'd thought of; I'd thought of a more traditional American jet-fighter pilot sort of thing and make that spacey. But Howard [Burden, the costume designer] did a very imaginative job and I don't know what I feel when I put that uniform on, but it was more the wig and the glasses and the Californian tan."

It not only transformed him when while he was playing Ace Rimmer, it also had an effect off-set. "It was quite extraordinary," said Chris. "Women who'd reacted to me as a bit of a tosser before, you could visibly see them looking at me — it was the kind of look you'd expect to get from a girl. Now I know what it must have been like for Robert Redford or Paul Newman in their heyday. [Women would say] 'Chris, you look better like that'. Someone like Andrea [Pennell — the make-up designer] would say something like, 'Chris, you're quite shaggable in that wig!'"

There was a chance for other members of the crew to play different versions of their characters, too, in Ace Rimmer's dimension. Craig Charles got to play Spanners, a successful engineer in the Space

Corps, while Robert Llewellyn got a break from the Kryten make-up again, as Rimmer's boss Bongo. Danny John-Jules was originally scripted to play a cleaner, but asked for a better role model and so the part got changed to a padre.

Hattie Hayridge got to appear outside of Holly's monitor for the one and only time as Melly, Bongo's assistant: a seductress with the hots for Ace Rimmer. "It was meant to be a Betty Grable type of thing," said Hattie. "The only thing with that costume is… it was one of these tunics that went down to between your thighs and your knees and it had a very strong zip all the way up, which is great for standing up, but if you sat down it looked like you were wearing an anorak and it all bunched up and looked horrible. I think it would have been better if it wasn't quite like that.

"At the end when we did it, I said 'what a guy' like everybody else did, but I must have said it wrong because it wasn't in the actual recording. So it didn't follow because everyone else says 'what a guy, what a guy' and then I don't. I'm sure I said 'what a guy', I didn't say 'what a tub of lard' or anything."

Later in the episode, she met him again as Holly, a moment not originally in the script. "I'd chip in with little bits of 'why don't I do this?'" said Hattie. "The swoon in Ace *Dimension Jump*, that was mine. They hadn't written me in as meeting Ace at all, and I said 'why don't I meet him?' And they said 'you know, the time to get the effects in and stuff like that, it doesn't add anything to the script that I meet him'. And I said, logically I should at least meet him at some point or other, so I said 'why I don't I just meet him and faint, at least it explains why I'm not in the rest of it.'" That was the only time Hattie has ever stood up while playing Holly. When she fainted and disappeared out of the bottom of the screen, she really was falling over!

One of the more trying scenes in *Dimension Jump* was an effects shot set up by Peter Wragg and his team, where Ace and Lister have to fix Starbug in a raging storm that included a heck of a lot of water.

"That wasn't very pleasant," says Chris. "I couldn't bloody breathe at one point, I was drowning. I had to have a bit of a rest. Bloody wind machine! It was fun. Old Wraggy, he kept up the old effects."

At the end of the episode, sadly Ace Rimmer has to bid his farewells. He just can't stay in the same place as smeghead Rimmer. Chris Barrie commented: "Really in many ways he's not as funny as Rimmer-Rimmer because he's straight and decent, there's no special reason for him to say funny or interesting things, so I think you always need smeghead Rimmer to keep the friction going, to feel the comedy."

Which is exactly how the episode ends. Ace leaves, but not without Rimmer plotting his revenge. With the help of a scutter, he rigs up a net of kippers above a door which he plans to drop on his other dimensional self. But it doesn't work and Ace Rimmer walks through without being kippered. In the original script, Rimmer then goes to check what went wrong and is deluged with the kippers instead. This part was filmed with the intention of ending on a freeze frame before they hit him. However, the sequence was deemed not to work and was cut, to be replaced by text scrolling up the screen explaining how Ace Rimmer went on to travel to many other dimensions and meet many other Arnold Rimmers, but never one as deeply sad and worthless as the one he met on Red Dwarf.

Just to prove it, the end credits roll with Rimmer telling the scutters to 'take it away' and play the closing theme on the Hammond organ, courtesy of *Red Dwarf*'s resident composer Howard Goodall.

Episode Six: Meltdown

GUEST CAST
Elvis... Clayton Mark
Hitler... Kenneth Hadley
Einstein... Martin Friend
Pythagoras... Stephen Tiller
Abraham Lincoln... Jack Klaff
Caligula... Tony Hawks
Pope Gregory... Michael Burrell
Stan Laurel... Forbes Masson
Noel Coward... Roger Blake
Marilyn Monroe... Pauline Bailey

Story

When Kryten discovers a device which can transport the crew to the nearest planet with an atmosphere, they find themselves on a world populated with wax droids. Over millions of years they have broken their programming and formed into two camps which are at war — the heroes and villains of history. The heroes are hopelessly outnumbered and without a military strategy... until Arnold J. Rimmer arrives to command them.

Funniest Moment (arguably)

Caligula repeatedly slaps Lister around the face every time Cat offends him.

Behind The Scenes

Yet another instance of a movie inspiring *Red Dwarf* and this time a whole episode. In *Westworld*, Yul Brynner played a gunslinger in a Wild West theme park populated with animatronic waxworks. In the movie, the Brynner character broke his programming and started killing tourists. In *Meltdown*, it's more like Madame Tussauds come to life with everyone from Adolf Hitler to Mother Theresa making an appearance. It led to the biggest guest cast yet for a *Red Dwarf* episode — with all of them required to look like famous people.

The location sequences with famous people training and fighting out in a cold and grim field were recorded in a real-life cold and grim field just round the corner from Shepperton Studios. Hattie Hayridge, who played Holly, wasn't required for the location shoot, but went along anyway to watch.

"Marilyn Monroe was brilliant," she remembered. "Also she wasn't mad, like some of the others. Some of them you felt really believed that they were that person… Queen Victoria was quite convinced, I think, that she was Queen Victoria… I mean Queen Victoria wouldn't speak to the make-up lady, she'd speak to Prince Albert and he'd speak to the make-up lady."

Meanwhile, the man booked to play Gandhi — Alex Tetteh-Lartey — was causing concern among the film crew. "Gandhi had to do these press ups in a freezing cold field in November and the first Gandhi that they brought couldn't actually get out of the car," said Hattie. "They were going 'oh my God, he's having trouble getting out of the car!' He was like in his eighties. They were saying 'oh no, he's got to do press-ups, he's going to die!' I think they sort of said, 'thanks very much for coming, but I think it'll be too physical for you'. So he was whisked off and they had to get another Gandhi who was only marginally younger, as you probably remember. And everyone was going 'oh my God' — exactly the same thing with him. But he reckoned he could do it, he'd be all right."

So it was Charles Reynolds who appeared on-screen as the legendary pacifist and was able to 'get down' and give Rimmer fifty.

Gandhi, Mother Theresa, Marilyn Monroe and all the others subsequently run across a minefield and get blown up. Hattie Hayridge was, again, watching. "That was the funniest one. It was just tears streaming down your face laughing, especially running down that field with all the explosions going off, because some of them seemed really close. They'd be running past and there was all these explosion-things coming out of the ground and they were getting covered in mud. It was really funny."

But the star of the guest stars, as it were, was Elvis Presley. Elvis impersonator Clayton Mark not only brought his own costume, he also brought his singing talent, hip-shaking moves and over-blown Elvis mimicry. During rehearsal, he would add in a few extra moments which ended up in the script. His immortal line, 'you've been wonderful prisoners, you really have' was one of his. "I just turned up and I ended up with more dialogue than when I started," said Clayton Mark. "I threw in a lot of it and they let me keep it."

Like most of the wax droids, he didn't have to audition. "They just called a lookalike agency I'm with and I turned out to be the only one she had that could sing. Plus I'm the only American one. There's another guy, but he can't really hold a note! It had to be an American because there was a load of dialogue."

After nearly getting blown up in a field, Clayton returned to sing the end title sequence as the King of Rock and Roll. "I had the flu when I did that so I don't remember doing it. I think we did it in about one take, two takes. I was only there about half an hour and then I left."

When it came to casting the former Roman emperor — and notorious madman — Caligula, writer/producers Rob Grant and Doug Naylor turned to an old friend: Tony Hawks, who had been playing bit parts in *Red Dwarf* since the beginning. "I think it was a bit of a laugh, really," Tony recalled. "Rob and Doug were looking through pictures of the various people that they wanted lookalikes for and they dug out various pictures of Caligula and apparently they reckoned I looked a bit like Caligula! So they gave me a call and said 'would I like to play Caligula?'

"On one side that's nice," said Tony, "but bearing a resemblance to this man who carried out all these atrocities and orgies and things and had very familiar relationships with horses, I wasn't too sure about!"

Tony was spared a visit to the freezing-cold field, as his scene was filmed in a cosy studio. He got to slap Lister round the face several times in punishment for anything the Cat said. "It was a nice little scene," said Tony. "We did that one in the evening in front of the audience so you spend the whole evening pacing around as Caligula backstage waiting to come out and do your five minute scene. It's one of those ridiculous things when you've known the words since early in the week, Tuesday, then half an hour before you go on you think you've forgotten them suddenly. But it was all right, it was fine. I think it was quite a good episode."

Other studio shenanigans made it into the *Smeg Ups* and remain some of the best outtakes of the series. They show Chris Barrie in full General's outfit entertaining the audience with his impressions of Kenneth Williams, David Coleman and mumbling jockey Lester Piggott. And, in the scene where Lister and Cat are teleported inside the chimney breast in Hitler's war room, Lister knocks on the wall and comments that it's made of 'stone'. Of course, it's a set and it sounds like what it is actually made of — chipboard. The audience thinks this is very funny, stopping the scene and causing Craig Charles to tell them: "we were going to sort that out in the dub". Which was never done because, in the finished version, Lister refrains from knocking on the wall at all.

Hitler's house looks to be an impressive location, but was easily acquired, as it is part of Shepperton Studios. 'Old House', as it is known, has been used by many film and TV productions. Shots of the bird-like monsters which chase Kryten and Rimmer through Pre-Historic World don't quite have the *Red Dwarf* touch and look a little out of place. This is because they are clips from a different film entirely — the 1967 Japanese movie *Daikyoju Gappa* — and edited into the episode.

Meltdown was originally due to be the first broadcast episode of the series, but was delayed because of sensitivities surrounding the 1991 Gulf War. *Dimension Jump* (originally due to be the second broadcast episode) was similarly delayed, which meant the two episodes ended up concluding the series.

Red Dwarf V

Written & Executive Produced by... Rob Grant & Doug Naylor
Directed by... Juliet May / Grant Naylor
Produced by... Hilary Bevan Jones

Rimmer... Chris Barrie
Lister... Craig Charles
Cat... Danny John-Jules
Kryten... Robert Llewellyn
Holly... Hattie Hayridge

Recorded: November-December 1991
First broadcast: February-March 1992

Red Dwarf V became more ambitious in its stories, concepts and visuals than ever before. There were complex storylines with *The Inquisitor* about a droid who travelled through time erasing people whose lives were not worthy; striking locations such as the flaming lake which the Dwarfers traverse in *Terrorform*; and ideas such as an hallucination which causes them to believe they are in a different reality in *Back to Reality*. "Every series is different," writer and producer Rob Grant explained. "We always try to move on, I don't see any point in just repeating yourself. And visually — I mean not counting the shows we directed ourselves — visually I think it's very spectacular, the stories are more sophisticated more complicated. We take advantage of the science fiction much more in this series, and it's a bit weirder."

Producing such an ambitious series on a sitcom budget with sitcom resources was always going to be a challenge, but it was one not to be undertaken by resident director, Ed Bye. He found himself booked to do another show instead and, as the show starred his wife Ruby Wax, he couldn't change his plans. "I had committed myself to another show almost the day before they got confirmation of another series and I couldn't really get out of it," he said. "And I thought I needed a break from it, to be honest, because it's a very tiring and difficult show to do. It's sort of like every rule is bent to try and get everything done in time to the quality that we wanted so we'd be working till three in the morning and non-stop stuff all the time."

Red Dwarf needed a new director and former executive producer Paul Jackson suggested Juliet May. She was an up-and-coming director who already had a BBC1 series under her belt, the Tony Hawks sitcom *Morris Minor's Marvellous Motors*, and had directed a sitcom pilot, *Heil Honey I'm Home*, for producer Paul Jackson. There seemed no need to look any further and she was hired.

This is where the problems started for *Red Dwarf V*. Juliet was only really starting out on her career in television and she didn't have the experience to cope with the challenges of an ambitious show like *Red Dwarf*. She had no experience of special effects, for example, and didn't instinctively know how to shoot things like split screen. She also had limited knowledge of science fiction, which was problematic when explaining complicated plots to the cast and crew. "The worst thing that compounded it was that she wouldn't ask for help," writer and producer Doug Naylor told the *Smegazine*. "She wanted to take it on her own shoulders really, and I think that's what... well, we basically didn't see eye to eye."

The *Red Dwarf* cast had also grown up together on the show and Ed Bye had been very much part of the team in the first four series. There have been some suggestions that they were resistant to change and, as time went on, they lost confidence in the new director.

Hattie Hayridge, who played Holly, remembered some of the difficulties on set. "I hardly got directed in a sense, not the same as the others," she said. "The main difference with the others was that with Ed, he would make like squares in front of their faces [with his fingers, like a miniature TV screen], so they knew when they would be on camera. Whereas Juliet didn't do that and assumed people would act whether they're on camera or whether they're not, which is true really. I guess that's what you're meant to do. They did want to know from the point of raising an eyebrow or something, there's no point in doing it if you're not going to be shown on camera, especially at a pre-record where there's no audience. You could be standing there making all the faces in the world and it won't really make a lot of difference. I think they found that difficult because they were used to Ed doing this brilliant thing of doing a square."

It became clear that Juliet was not going to work out and she parted company with *Red Dwarf* after the fourth episode. Chris Barrie remembered: "We thought the fifth series was, 'well, it's getting a bit difficult this year isn't it?' We thought that was maybe because Ed wasn't around; a new director — and then no director for a few of them!"

In actual fact, Rob Grant and Doug Naylor stepped in to jointly sit in the director's chair (crediting themselves as Grant Naylor), even though they hadn't directed before. Fortunately, they had an expert crew to quietly guide them, particularly in the shape of camera supervisor Rocket. But there were still problems with some of the footage that had already been shot and the cast were called back the day after the wrap party to do some hastily-arranged re-shoots. A lot of *Angels and Demons*, especially, was re-shot during this hectic day.

Juliet May went on to have a successful career after leaving *Red Dwarf*, with her name appearing on many hit shows, including *Dalziel and Pascoe*, *New Tricks* and *Miranda*. Some of her work in *Red Dwarf* V also looks stunning, such as the scene of Kryten in the crashed wreckage of Starbug and the Dwarfers canoeing through a lake with streaks of flame coming out of the water in *Terrorform*.

Doug Naylor told the *Smegazine*. "She was around for the first four [shows], and then we had to do some re-shooting, and spent a lot of time in the edit. In the end, though, her name is on four shows, and it looks like the best series, so I think she came out of it very well. It's one of the most difficult shows to direct. Unless you realise how difficult it is, you're going to be in big trouble. Ed had a hell of a time if you look at some of the early shows he directed, so this is no slight to anyone. It's just one of the most difficult shows with our budget, which isn't big, to direct on British television."

Episode One: Holoship

Directed by: Juliet May

GUEST CAST

Nirvanah Crane… Jane Horrocks
Captain Platini… Don Warrington
Commander Binks… Martin Friend
Harrison… Lucy Briers
Number Two… Simon Day
Number One… Jane Montgomery

Story

Rimmer is taken aboard a holoship, a spacecraft created entirely out of hologramatic light where he can touch and operate exactly like a living person — including having lots of sex. Rimmer wants to transfer to the holoship so he can become an officer and interact with the rest of the crew — including having lots of sex. Especially with Nirvanah Crane. The problem is, the only way Rimmer can join the ship is through a challenge which will see the losing member of the crew get wiped. Rimmer begs Kryten to help him, but what he doesn't realise is that his opponent is Nirvanah Crane, and to win the challenge is to lose the girl.

Funniest Moment (arguably)

Lister mimics the holoship captain who reports from Starbug using a handheld communicator by taking out a packet of cigarettes, pulling out one to use as an aerial and making insolent comments about the captain's chin and genitalia.

Behind The Scenes

Chris Barrie described *Holoship* as "one in the eye for old

Rimmsy." After years stuck on board a spaceship with no women, and the added disadvantage of being dead, Rimmer finally gets the girl. Chris Barrie gets to take all his clothes off, apart from a modesty towel, and turns out to have been hiding a toned body under Rimmer's smeghead uniform — who'd have thought?

Up-and-coming actress Jane Horrocks, who went on to acclaim in films such as *Little Voice* and to star in the BBC series *The Amazing Mrs Pritchard*, was cast to play Rimmer's love interest, Nirvanah Crane. Her busy schedule meant that the episode couldn't be filmed first, as had been hoped, because she wasn't available until three weeks into the shooting schedule. It would have been an easier episode to use as an introduction to new director Juliet May, as it was technically a lot simpler than the others.

Chris Barrie was a bit disappointed with how the episode turned out. "*Holoship*, I think, felt better at the time than it was. There were some great performers in that one. Matthew Marsh as the Captain was great; it's good to see an actor coming in and doing a big performance and really going for it. And Jane Horrocks — great actress. A lot of people would say she's not right for that part, but she was super."

People's memories of the filming of *Holoship* are understandably different from the finished product as the episode ran more than ten minutes over length and had to be cut down to size in the edit. Most significant of the cuts involved Rimmer and Nirvanah and the building of their relationship, including an entire scene of her trying to persuade him to have sex while he gets nervous and expresses an interest in playing table tennis instead. Part of the scene of both of them in bed together was another casualty. The plot also suffered with two significant trims being made to scenes which explained more about the mind patch and Rimmer's plan to use it to succeed in the challenge to join the Holoship.

A Holly scene also bit the cutting-room floor. This was a disappointment to Hattie Hayridge, who had already seen her role on *Red*

Dwarf dwindle as the stories got bigger and were increasingly taking place outside the ship. "That was the one where Rimmer comes running in from the Holoship and we have this whole thing of going 'Where's Lister?' [Holly replies:] 'Hello Holly, how are you?; Hello Arnie, how are you?' and he's just going 'Where's Lister?', just screaming 'Where's Lister?' and [Holly's] going 'what a rude pig he is and why can't he be nice?'. He was in this hurry and I was being really annoying to him. It was quite funny, but it wasn't an important part of the plot at all. It's an obvious scene to go because it's just a character thing of Rimmer being a git, and because everyone knows he is, they didn't need an extra character thing in there."

The design of the holoship itself was one of the most stunning of the series. The model was built by Paul McGuinness of the special effects team using perspex, which gave it that ethereal, translucent look. The interior, with its clean lines, white walls and lit panels was created by production designer Mel Bibby. *Holoship* required several sets to be built, from the command area to Nirvanah's bedroom, the lift and the corridors. As he sat down to design them, he had *Red Dwarf*'s tight budget in mind. "Fortunately we had the scripts for *Holoship* and *Back to Reality*, so when I designed *Holoship* I was also thinking about *Back to Reality* because it's the same set," he said. "You've got *Holoship* which is all crisp and clean and white, but if you look when we do *Back to Reality* where all the chairs are, the backing is *Holoship* which has all been sprayed down and a lot of moulding's been put in, a lot of engine work's been put in. So it's like getting two sets for the price of one."

The series therefore begins by introducing a bit of a new, sparkling look to *Red Dwarf*, as opposed to its usual grungy feel. It's such a shame that so much of the episode had to be lost in the edit. "I was really quite disappointed with *Holoship*," writer Doug Naylor told the *Smegazine* afterwards. "It didn't really have the emotional arc I had hope it would have. I wasn't moved by it at all, and it should have worked but it didn't."

It does, however, contain one of Chris Barrie's favourite bits. "One of my favourite lines in the whole fifth series was, 'I've come to know you as… people I've met.' I think I wrote that, I think I came up with that line, which I'm very proud of. I don't come up with many lines, but I think I did. I'll get all the letters from Rob Grant and Doug Naylor saying, 'well actually, Chris, we wrote that'. That was quite fun all that. Every episode of *Red Dwarf* has had something about it, some fun aspect about it."

Episode Two: The Inquisitor

Directed by: Juliet May / Grant Naylor

<u>GUEST CAST</u>
Inquisitor... John Docherty
Second Lister... Jake Abraham
Thomas Allman... James Cormack

Story

When a droid from the future arrives to judge the lives of the Red Dwarf crew, they know they're in trouble. They have to justify themselves as having led a worthwhile life, or be erased from history, to be replaced by a life that never had a chance. It's bad news for Lister and Kryten who embark on a time-travelling scheme to steal the Inquisitor's gauntlet and save themselves.

Funniest Moment (arguably)

The Dwarfers triumph at the end and Kryten asks Lister to 'give me five'. But Lister can do better than that, because he still has the other Lister's severed hand in his jacket: 'I can give you fifteen,' he says.

Behind The Scenes

The Inquisitor was one of those episodes which left everyone scratching their head in rehearsal. It was one of the scripts that was ready to go at the start of the series and was a candidate to film first, but the director wanted to start with a story which was a little less complex, so *The Inquisitor* dropped to second.

A lot of plot is packed into the half-hour. It begins simply with the idea of a droid going through time erasing the existence of people who've had worthless lives. But, before they die, the person gets a chance to plead their case. This was the idea at the heart of the episode, as writer Rob Grant told the *Smegazine*: "Having to justify your life was an interesting idea we thought, and that was the drive behind it, each one of them having to justify themselves. We just couldn't make that as interesting as we had hoped."

Like *Holoship*, a number of moments were cut from the final episode. These include some extra dialogue in Starbug's cockpit, the most missed being Kryten and Rimmer debating the relative stupidity of human and mechanoid-kind. A classic Cat one-liner was also excised.

The end sequence, where Lister confronts the Inquisitor after saving his life, originally saw the Inquisitor lift his mask to reveal actor Jack Doherty's face, but these moments were re-shot so he kept his mask on throughout. The most unfortunate loss was a scene where the Cat hits Lister and Kryten over the head with a spade. It wasn't necessarily sophisticated, but it was pretty funny and can be seen as an extra on one of the DVD releases, complete with the original audio recorded on set which makes it obvious that the spade is made of rubber.

The story begins, not on Red Dwarf, but with the Inquisitor, as he replaces the life of one hapless man with that of another who did not have the chance of life. This sequence was designed to go ahead of the opening credits, but the idea was subsequently dropped in favour of keeping the format the same as the rest of the series.

Naturally, the Inquisitor moves onto examining the lives of the Red Dwarf crew and, as Rimmer comments, 'we're in big trouble'. So they have to justify the worth of their lives, the twist being that it is a replica of themselves who interrogates them under the Inquisitor mask. It's perhaps a shame that this part of the episode is so short, and doesn't quite become the tour-de-force that the trial scene in the previous year's *Justice* had been. Kryten's reaction to being asked to justify himself is probably the strongest as, rather than submit himself to questioning, he turns the tables on the Inquisitor and asks him what right he has to judge humanity.

A lot of the action is carried by Kryten in this episode, leading to long and complicated speeches for Robert Llewellyn to learn. As a man who doesn't find learning lines that easy, it was a challenging shoot. It also gave rise to a little in-joke where, at the point of going back in time to save themselves, Kryten asks Lister to remind him of what he said the first time. As Lister recites the words, Kryten interrupts him with 'that's it, yep, that's it, don't tell me, I've got it, I've got it!' which is reminiscent of Robert Llewellyn trying to get his lines right, and one of many examples in *Red Dwarf* where the cast's personal traits have made it into the scripts.

Kryten goes back in time to take the Inquisitor's gauntlet, knowing he is going to get killed (having already seen it happen), leaving Lister to defeat the Inquisitor. Lister's plan is to use a time paradox double-bluff where he risks the Inquisitor's life in order to save him, knowing it will mean the Inquisitor can't kill Lister without killing himself.

If you've just had to re-read that last sentence because it made no sense, then you can understand how other people had a difficult time trying to keep up. "I have to admit now, after all these years," said Chris Barrie in a DVD commentary, "that there were some moments in *The Inquisitor* where I didn't know what was going on."

There are a lot of concepts in *The Inquisitor*, from the question of what it means to have a led a worthwhile life, to the consequences of travelling back in time. It reflects the fifth series' shift to bigger stories with more emphasis on science fiction ideas. Writer Doug Naylor told the *Smegazine*: "I think we made a conscious decision to lose some of the comedy and sacrifice some of it for the sake of the stories. You do that and then you get into the edit and go--" he buries his head in his hands and groans. "Ultimately, it's come out on the other side and I liked *The Inquisitor* and the kind of direction it was starting to take."

Episode Three: Terrorform

Directed by: Juliet May

GUEST CAST
Handmaidens… Sara Stockbridge, Francine Walker-Lee

Story

When Rimmer and Kryten land on a psi-moon, the land re-shapes itself into Rimmer's psyche. It creates monsters out of aspects of Rimmer's personality and he seems destined to suffer at the hands of the Unspeakable One. Kryten, Cat and Lister arrive to rescue him, but their bazookoids are useless. The monster only withdraws when Kryten describes Rimmer as part of the crew. But the moon won't give up Rimmer so easily and drags Starbug down into quicksand. Only by boosting Rimmer's self-esteem can they be saved. But, can Kryten, Cat and Lister really swallow their pride and say, with a straight face, that they love Rimmer?

Funniest Moment (arguably)

Lister and Cat are so dumbfounded by fear after Kryten's hand walks into Lister's boxer shorts, that they communicate their horror by typing it up on the computer screen.

Behind The Scenes

Once again Chris Barrie, as Rimmer, gets his kit off and gets to have intimate moments with good-looking women. In *Terrorform*, the scene with the handmaidens smearing a semi-naked Rimmer with oil is highly memorable and resulted in one of the most-used publicity photos of the series.

Chris Barrie, interviewed during a break on the set of *Red Dwarf V*, was clearly having a good time. "In this series I've had a bed scene,

I've had my little body smothered in lovely baby oil. This series for me has in many ways been the best."

"And I've been very angry about it," said Craig Charles, who was listening in. "The dead guy's getting all the girls, and that's not right, is it? The dead guy gets the chicks — is that right, or is that wrong?"

Robert Llewellyn couldn't help but agree. "Chris has had quite an astonishing amount of sex in this series."

One of the two women who played the handmaidens was Sara Stockbridge, a leading model for Vivienne Westwood, whose arrival created a little frisson on set. It was a very sensual scene, but Chris Barrie couldn't afford to be too distracted because he had to deliver a lot of dialogue. "They got Johnson's baby oil and rubbed it onto my body," he said. "But you may remember it was in that set where there's lots of wood shavings on the floor, so as the takes went by and the dust got kicked up, they were rubbing wood shavings as well as Johnson's baby oil into my skin. It wasn't quite as romantic as it might have seemed on paper. I didn't think about it before or after because of that long speech I had. I knew I would eventually start corpsing when I reached a certain point in the speech because she was going quite low, she was doing the business!"

The episode begins in a far less sexy way with Kryten severely damaged among the wreckage of Starbug. He's lost his short-term memory and that, along with the loss of his short-term memory, means he's not quite sure what has happened. The scene is visually stunning. Filmed in a studio made to look like a night-time exterior and pre-recorded before the live studio audience was brought in, it meant the lighting and camera work didn't have to be compromised. Actor Robert Llewellyn was buried in earth, so his real legs were out of sight and Kryten's damaged legs appeared to come out of his body. There were also two fake Kryten hands built for the scene where he removes a hand, places an eyeball on the end of one fingertip and sends it to go find help. The first was a simple prop which he could manipulate and the second was a puppeteered hand which was able to respond to Kryten with a wink of its eye as he gave it instructions. A third animatronic hand was built for the scenes of it crawling along the corridors of Red Dwarf with genuine flexing fingers. Although the actual crawling was achieved by pulling it along on a wire.

For some reason only known to Kryten's hand (and, probably, the writers), the hand decides to get Lister's attention by crawling into his boxer shorts. Lister is so stunned that, rather than tell the Cat what's going on, he types it up on a screen. Cat, similarly shocked, types back his replies. This was another scene which was pre-recorded and caused a certain amount of dismay when the original version was played back during the dress rehearsal. Writer/producer Doug Naylor decided it needed a drastic re-edit and spent most of the rest of the day in the editing suite fixing it. The result was one of the best comedy moments of the episode.

There were a lot of pre-recorded scenes on *Terrorform*. The scenes with the crew walking around the psi-moon at night look truly atmospheric. One sequence of them rowing across a lake was especially ambitious, even for *Red Dwarf*. Propane gas forks were installed in the lake which, when lit, appeared as streaks of flame rising from the water. During the shoot, Craig Charles decided it would be a good idea to light a cigarette on one of the flames and moved the boat closer to the fire, while the film crew on the bank envisaged the cast going up in flames and the boat capsizing. In the outtakes, a member of the crew can clearly be heard shouting 'Craig, don't bugger about!'. Fortunately, no one caught fire and the boat remained upright, which meant the waiting frogmen who were in the lake for safety reasons didn't have to do any rescuing.

Lighting director John Pomphrey was less fortunate. He mis-judged the point where the land ended and the lake began, and fell in, taking two engineers and some equipment with him into the water.

Back in the studio, more pre-recording was necessary for the

'Unspeakable One', the self-loathing beast, which confronts Rimmer after he has been oiled. This was one of the biggest disappointments for the special effects team, who built a fully working, six foot tall puppeteered and partly animatronic creature. In the end, only bits of it were seen on screen, and the only full-length shot was of its shadow.

The episode examines the idea that Rimmer is his own worst enemy, as the psi-moon takes all his negativity and turns it on himself. As each aspect of his self-esteem is destroyed, it is represented by a range of gravestones. They include generosity, self-confidence and honour. There is also a very small one for Rimmer's charm, suggesting he didn't have much of that in the first place.

The only way for Rimmer to be saved, and for the psi-moon to release Starbug, is to reverse that negativity. This climaxes in the rest of crew having to bolster Rimmer's confidence and pretend that they love him. Much of this scene, however, ended up on the cutting-room floor because it didn't work as well as it might.

"I really liked *Terrorform* an awful lot," Rob Grant told the *Smegazine*. "I thought the start of it came off very well and I really liked the look of the stuff when they were in Rimmer's mind and the weird stuff with the gravestone. It doesn't end terrifically because they never really got that scene right, the part where they pretended to like Rimmer… and yet, in the script, it looked like it was going to work."

Episode Four: Quarantine

Directed by: Grant Naylor

GUEST CAST
Dr Hildegarde Lanstrom… Maggie Steed

Story

The Dwarfers discover a laboratory where a hologram doctor has been working on synthesising positive viruses, such as luck and sexual attraction. The problem is, she has contracted a virus herself and gone completely mad. Meanwhile, Kryten has furnished Rimmer with a copy of the Space Corps Directives and Rimmer has decided to enact Directive #595 which allows him to shut the rest of the crew in quarantine for three months. The prospect of being trapped with each other's company is bad enough, but they then discover the person who is in charge of their incarceration — Rimmer — has gone completely mad. He has contracted the holo-virus and has started taking advice from a penguin glove puppet called Mr Flibble. What's even worse — Mr Flibble is very cross.

Funniest Moment (arguably)

Lister is injected with the luck virus and tries to hit a bull's-eye by throwing a dart over his left shoulder with his back to the dartboard. But it seems his luck has run out as the dart goes totally in the wrong direction and imbeds itself in the back of Kryten's head.

Behind The Scenes

Quarantine wasn't written when *Red Dwarf V* started filming, and writers Rob Grant and Doug Naylor had to work on the script while the other shows were being shot. Their original idea was that the crew would get psi-powers (telepathy, telekinesis, etc.) and these appeared in the first draft of the script, called *Psi-Man*. But, as the episode evolved, this idea became a minor part of the plot, with Rimmer briefly getting the power to move objects with his mind after contracting the holo-virus.

Uppermost in the writers' minds while developing the script was the need to keep it simple. They needed a relatively cheap show, especially following the expensive night shoots on *Terrorform*, and they wanted to make things a little easier for new director Juliet May. As it turned out, she left the programme before *Quarantine* was made and directing chores were taken up by Rob Grant and Doug Naylor (crediting themselves as 'Grant Naylor').

Location scenes were, once again, filmed at Sunbury Pumphouse, but problems really beset the production when they got into the studio. The scene in quarantine where Kryten, Lister and Cat discuss how they are going to cope shut in a room together was a nightmare to shoot. For some reason, all three of them had trouble with their lines. Like yawning in the doctor's waiting room, as soon as one of them started forgetting their lines, the others seemed to catch the condition. The relatively simple three minute dialogue scene took fifty-seven minutes to get through on the night and subsequently took between one and four days to edit (depending on which account you believe).

The set for the quarantine area of Red Dwarf is rather obviously the same set as Red Dwarf bunkroom inhabited by Lister and Rimmer. Production designer Mel Bibby remembered this was one of the many occasions where a lack of cash was the mother of invention. "A lot of times when we get to the end of the series there are a lot of sets that have to be compromised on because of money. I think *Quarantine* was one of them where we actually repainted the sleeping quarters on Red Dwarf. The argument was it was all modular systems, so they would be similar. We had to make it look similar, but different, and it didn't quite work out."

The audience, however, were probably not so much looking at the set as looking at the extraordinary costume Rimmer was wearing. The red and white gingham dress with matching hat and plaits sticking out on wires made him look suitably bonkers. But it was the addition of Mr Flibble that really finished him off.

The furry penguin glove puppet was never meant to be a guest star on the episode. The script required some sort of puppet and the penguin was brought in during rehearsal as a practice prop. The puppet was supposed to be replaced with something else when it came to the recording, but no suitable replacement was ever found and it was decided the penguin should go in front of the cameras.

"That was quite an interesting episode," said Chris Barrie of *Quarantine*. "Again it would have been nice to have a bit longer to do that one really well, to make Rimmer really evil. But it was funny, the whole chemistry of being mad and evil and having Mr Flibble and all that business was quite a laugh."

Writer Rob Grant agreed that time was an issue when making the episode, which merged the two ideas of positive viruses and shutting the crew in quarantine. "Out of all of them, I think that's the most intriguing science fiction idea out of season five, the idea that you can have positive viruses. It was a very interesting concept, but we were under such time pressures. I think if we had the time, we could have done a much better show set entirely in quarantine."

Episode Five: Demons & Angels

Directed by: Juliet May / Grant Naylor

<u>GUEST CAST</u>
None

Story
Kryten thinks he has a solution to Red Dwarf's supply problem — a triplicator which takes one object and makes two more. He
tries with a strawberry and creates one succulent fruit of divine
flavour, and another filled with maggots. Something is not quite
right, so he reverses the process — and creates two copies of Red
Dwarf: one full of divine copies of the crew, the other with their evil
counterparts. To get the real Red Dwarf back again, they have to get
pieces of the triplicator from both copies, but the ships are unstable
and they're running out of time.

Funniest Moment (arguably)
"I've been to a parallel universe, I've seen time running backwards,
I've played pool with planets and I've given birth to twins. I never
thought, in my entire life, I'd taste an edible Pot Noodle." — Lister

Behind The Scenes
Demons and Angels — originally titled *High and Low* — was
the first episode of the series to be filmed. New director Juliet May
decided to do it ahead of *The Inquisitor*, which she really didn't understand and *Holoship*, which couldn't be filmed until the third week. It
was one of the toughest episodes a new director could be asked to
shoot because there were three versions of every character. To have
two versions of the same character on the screen at the same time,
they are filmed one at a time and joined together down an invisible

line using the split screen technique. Juliet hadn't done split screen before and later admitted that she joined *Red Dwarf* without knowing what a split screen was.

Even in terms of *Red Dwarf*, it was an ambitious show to shoot and it's those production problems that colour the memory of the episode for the writers. "It was the show that we were always in trouble with," Doug Naylor told the *Smegazine*. "We re-shot maybe half of it, we edited it, and there were still three or four scenes that we really wanted to get rid of, but in context, they were surrounded by scenes that worked, so the whole thing was lifted. You had the music and everything else, so actually by the end of it, we were saying very cautiously to one another 'it's okay, it's not the biggest turkey of all time.'"

"It was a nightmare of a show to shoot," Rob Grant remembered in the same interview. "Because you had all the splits, the costume changes all over the place and we fell behind on the initial filming and never really caught up with it. In the end, the dark halves were a lot funnier in rehearsal and Robert was doing all this jerking which never made it onto the screen."

Demons and Angels was a rare opportunity for Holly to have a larger role. Unlike a lot of episodes in the fifth series which took place on psi-moons and holoships, this episode was contained within versions of Red Dwarf. Actress Hattie Hayridge got to wear an angelic headdress in one incarnation and a black wig on the evil ship. Sadly, she didn't feature as much as she could have.

"I think Juliet never quite understood the technical thing of how they filmed me," said Hattie. "I wasn't filmed on my own ever in that episode, which is a shame because that's the only episode where I ever looked any different. She just filmed the set and I was in the background. There wasn't the separate reel that was just me. So that was what affected me most in that respect. Especially when you've spent three hours having this wig put on and you're like a postage stamp in the back of the screen."

Costumes for the rest of the cast were even more extreme. Robes and sandals were de rigueur on the angelic ship (a little cooler for the ever-suffering Robert Llewellyn as Kryten), whereas the evil ship was peopled with some scary dudes: Lister as a malevolent cowboy with blacked out teeth, a grungy version of Kryten, Cat with a set of teeth so large he had difficulty keeping them in, and Rimmer in an extraordinary pair of stockings.

"People would say, 'oh, so that's what you look like in suspenders!'" said Chris Barrie. "I quite enjoyed that because I did like the characters who did that all the time--" placing his hands together and bowing "—'Brother Cat' — I quite enjoyed all that."

Meanwhile, there were mishaps on the set as a couple of the cast received minor pyrotechnic burns. A sparking 'grenade' got slightly too close to angelic Cat's foot, hurting Danny John-Jules, and a squib came loose from the breast plate under Kryten's costume, resulting in a jolt between Robert's thighs when the pyrotechnic went off. As always with this sort of thing, the actors dramatized their anecdotes of the incidents, while the special effects team insist it was all perfectly safe and can't imagine what they were complaining about.

More minor injuries occurred in a scene where evil Kryten bashes through a wall and strangles Lister before pushing him to the ground. This was choreographed beforehand, so Robert Llewellyn would strike two marks on his side of the wall in order to reach through to Craig Charles. But, on the first take, Craig was a bit too far over to one side, so when Robert punched through the wall, he hit him in the back of the head. When Craig fell forward, he hit a metal barrel, and he can clearly be seen shouting in pain in the finished episode.

But even after all that struggle, the episode wasn't finished. There were bits considered not to work and parts of the story with holes in which meant a lot of it had to be re-shot. There was no time to do any of it during the official recording days of *Red Dwarf V* and so, the day after the end of series wrap party, the cast were called back for some last-minute filming. They only had one day to do it because the studio was due to be handed over to another production after that.

"That was the plan," Doug Naylor told the *Smegazine*. "But we had no time to rehearse. We wanted to make adjustments and it was a matter of 'okay, we'll start with the first scene, and go along and try to pick up all the worst scenes and do as much as we possibly can… There was this very funny scene where Rob was actually in the director's chair and I was right behind him writing and passing the stuff to him. He would read it, and we would dash down to the floor and say 'there isn't enough time to get this photocopied; here it is, here's your lines, we'll block it now and we'll shoot it one scene at a time. Right, ok, let's do it' and we would dash back up to the box. Everybody had a hangover and did not want to be there."

"It was really difficult, it was not fun, we didn't have a lot of laughs that day," Robert Llewellyn told a DVD documentary.

Despite the stress going on behind the scenes on *Demons and Angels*, the finished product is one of the better episodes of *Red Dwarf V*. The concept of the good and evil Dwarfers is a simple one and works well, you can't see the join between the original footage and the re-shoots and it includes a lot of humour with some outrageous costumes. It was all building up nicely to an impressive series finale.

Episode Six: Back to Reality

SS Esperanto Director: Juliet May
Directed by: Grant Naylor

GUEST CAST
Andy... Timothy Spall
Cop... Lenny Von Dohlen
New Kochanski... Anastasia Hille
Nurse... Marie McCarthy
New Lister... John Sharian

Story

The crew arrive at an underwater world where every life form has committed suicide. It seems they were all victims of the despair squid, which starts to infect Kryten, Lister and Cat with its depressive power. They try to escape in Starbug, but the squid comes after them and they crash...

...The words 'Game Over' appear. They had been playing a total immersion video game and the last four years were all make-believe. In reality, they are Sebastian Doyle, his half-brother William Doyle, Cybernautic Detective Jake Bullet, and Duane Dibbley... or are they...?

Funniest Moment (arguably)

Duane Dibbley.

Behind The Scenes

Back to Reality had a real impact when it was first broadcast, not least because many people really thought it was going to be a change of format for the show as the characters stepped out of a computer game into a different world. They weren't the only ones to be fooled.

"We actually handed that script into the production team first and [former *Red Dwarf* producer] Paul Jackson read it," said writer Rob Grant. "It was set as show one and he simply thought we had changed the entire set-up and the whole situation. He thought we were going to write a whole series about Colonel Sebastian Doyle and Duane Dibbley!"

"Without telling anyone," added writing partner Doug Naylor. "Not set designers or anything!"

"For a long time we thought it would go out as the first show, but it was clearly better at the end," Rob continued. But he dismissed the idea that the series could have ended without returning the old gang to Red Dwarf. "It was a possible ending, but it's a bit too close to Bobby Ewing stepping out of the shower! I don't think we could have lived with it."*

The moment where the crew wake up as different people in the virtual reality suite is a real shock moment that nobody could see coming. The costumes and the cast's reactions help to sell the concept, along with the set, which production designer Mel Bibby was proud of. "I like the reality seats and the room. That particular set I was really pleased with because it just looked as if it was right. My idea with that was they'd been locked in this game for six years and nobody ever comes to see them, they probably change their bags and that's it. It's not going to be crisp and clean, it's just left to mildew on the walls, we really aged that one down."

Also brilliant was guest star Timothy Spall, as 'Andy' the game technician. The consummate actor was well known for Geordie drama *Auf Wiedersehen, Pet* and subsequently went onto even greater fame and achievement. *Red Dwarf*, however, was his first sitcom in front

---

* This is a reference to 1980s American soap opera *Dallas* where actor Patrick Duffy left the show and his character Bobby Ewing was killed off, only to return a year later by stepping out of the shower and revealing that the whole thing had been a dream.

of a live studio audience and he was incredibly nervous. So much so that, in the first take, he gabbled his words at an impossibly fast pace. If he made a mistake he would simply keep going which risked blowing the jokes in front of the audience and dampening their reaction for the final take. A lot was riding on that scene, his dialogue contained a lot of exposition and some great gags, so the production team were getting very worried. But then he came on and did it again and produced a brilliant performance — with unsurpassed use of the word 'twonk'. A lot of people were relieved.

Another fabulous character was Duane Dibbley. Danny John-Jules always plays the Cat brilliantly, but the role is usually about two things — his vanity and his one-liners. Suddenly Danny is called on to be someone totally different and he rises to the occasion — helped by some impressive teeth and a pudding basin wig. The latter came from the Ray Marston Wig Studio in London. "We went to Ray Marston's for the wig and he said we haven't got one of them, it'll cost X amount of money," said Danny. "Then he took out a load of these wigs and the make-up lady went, 'where did you find them?' and he said, 'in the basement under a load of boxes and stuff'. So it was just some piece of thing in the basement of Ray Marston's. We put it on and everyone went, 'that's it, that's Duane Dibbley!'"

Costumes for the others consisted of a snazzy half-rubber / half-metal head and a cool detective suit and tie for Kryten as Jake Bullet, a wig and a smart suit for Lister as Sebastian Doyle and a tramp look for Rimmer as William Doyle. "Getting to play someone who's not such a slob's quite good," Craig Charles said during the filming of the episode. "This is a bit more like what we're like in real life."

"It is, actually," said Chris Barrie. "[I've been on] a night out with Craig and he's spruced up to the nines. Whereas I'm a bit of a scruff- ball, holes in my jeans."

They were joined for one of these scenes by American actor Lenny Von Dohlen who appeared impressively oppressive as the cop in the other reality. He had recently been in the David Lynch TV series *Twin Peaks* and is said to have been encouraged to take the part by Frances Barber who appeared in *Red Dwarf* two years earlier in the episode *Polymorph*.

Lister, Rimmer, Kryten and Cat (or is it Sebastian, William, Jake and Duane?) make a quick getaway from the cop by jumping in Sebastian's limo and driving off, while being chased by the other cops. At this point, the action cuts back to Starbug with Holly trying to tell them that they are hallucinating. It's at this point that the audience starts to understand what is really going on.

Not only was it a pivotal moment in the episode, it was also a lot cheaper than filming an actual car chase.

While the Dwarfers hallucinate, the action is played out in Starbug with them all sitting on crates, leaping up in the air when they go over bumps and leaning over with the sharp bends. This all took a bit of co-ordinating as they had to do it together. In the end, Hattie Hayridge drew a map of the car chase and held it in front of them so they knew when to go over the speed bumps and round the chicane.

This sequence also provided a classic moment for the *Smeg Ups* tapes as, in the heat of the car chase, Chris Barrie's crate tips over backwards and sends him crashing to the floor. He emerges moments later, red-faced, and with his fellow cast members laughing around him.

The episode was filmed in three blocks, the first of which took place at the beginning of the schedule when Juliet May was still directing and involves the location scenes on board the Esperanto (where they discover the people who committed suicide). The other two blocks were directed by Grant Naylor after she had left and involve location work in the other reality (the carpark and the alleyway), and the studio recording in front of the audience.

For some reason, when these segments were first edited together,

the episode didn't work at all — at least, not according to the producers. One of the things which didn't help was the lack of laughs from
the studio audience at the moment where the Dwarfers hallucinate
they are Duane Dibbley, Sebastian Doyle and co. It's thought that
the audience were so shocked at the thought that the whole series
had been part of a virtual reality computer game that they couldn't
bring themselves to laugh.

Rob Grant was so depressed about the whole thing that he went
home for three days. Doug Naylor was similarly disheartened. "You
can have a show that looks good, is terrible before the sound dub,
then goes through the dub and is okay," he told the *Smegazine*. "I
wanted to kill myself after *Back to Reality* before they dubbed it — I
just thought 'this is so hopeless.'"

But he persevered and stayed in the editing room trying to sort
it out. When it was finished, he called Rob and persuaded him to
come back to take a look because, he told him, 'it's quite good now'.
It's surprising to think that the creators didn't realise what they had
achieved at the time. *Back to Reality* was, and remains, a fan favourite
and ensured *Red Dwarf V* went out on a high.

Location Report: Back To Reality

Author's note: *In 1991, I visited* Red Dwarf *on location for an article for* Starburst Magazine. *It was only my second magazine article and my first one about* Red Dwarf. *Reading back, it gives a little bit of an insight into what it's like to film* Red Dwarf *— with the need to re-film sequences several times, the waiting around between takes and the playfulness of the cast — so I thought it was worthwhile including as a bonus chapter.*

One thing I remember about that day, but didn't put in the article, was that Craig Charles was furious that he had to come into work on a Sunday when he had tickets to see a Liverpool football game. It seems that this would normally have been a day off for everyone, but they were called in for an extra day, possibly because of the change in director. It's interesting that Rob Grant — having suddenly found himself directing the episode — seemed perfectly at home. He was also excited about the prospect of an American version of the Red Dwarf, *which would later fail to take off (see the chapter on* Red Dwarf USA *later in this book). Another project which failed to happen is the science fiction comedy series* The Oo-wee-oo Dimension, *which Rob Grant also talks about in this article. It's interesting that, at this point, it seems like it was virtually commissioned and it's a shame that it never happened.*

In a multi-storey carpark at Shepperton Studios, draped in black velvet sheets to keep out the outside world, the cast and crew of *Red Dwarf V* are creating an alternate reality. The cars are covered in dust sheets and shrouded in mist from several smoke machines. Beside one of the cars is a robot, a cat, a dead man, and a three-million-year-old Liverpudlian: Kryten, Cat, Rimmer and Lister.

Lister approaches one of the cars and lifts off the dust sheet — a man concealed out of camera shot ensures it falls smoothly off the car.

Directing the action is Rob Grant, one of the writers, who is making his director's debut in the last two shows of the series. "I don't actually know what it feels like at the moment, because I did my first show last Friday," Rob explained. "It's exciting, I will say that.

"When you write the script, it's all perfect in your head, the performances are all perfect, and the locations are the best, and magnificent. And it always degrades gradually through the process as it goes through the actors not to say gets worse, but it changes. When you actually have the chance to position the cameras where you actually imagined it, it certainly solves communication problems between you and the director… The product is more in line with what we, sort of, visualized at the beginning."

Rob Grant writes all *Red Dwarf* with Doug Naylor, who is also at hand on set. "We sort of do it between us, really," said Rob. "We go through the camera script together, we write it together, and he sits behind me in the scanner and taps me on the shoulder when he thinks it's going wrong, and that kind of thing. It's actually freed us, so that Doug looks after the producer's side of things, and I don't have to do quite as much of that 'cos I'm doing the directing. It's working out very well at the moment."

While the crew are setting up for yet another shot of Lister getting into the car, Craig Charles (Lister) has spotted my unfamiliar face in the crowd. "Who are you?" he asked. I explain. He slaps me on the shoulder and drags me in front of the camera — "You must meet the rest of the cast," he said. I said hello to Chris Barrie (Rimmer), Danny John-Jules (Cat) and Robert Llewellyn (Kryten). Craig explained *Starburst* is a big fan of the show and the cast have to be nice to me, before allowing me to retreat behind the camera again.

For all Craig's clowning around, he is very professional when filming. In one shot he is careful to check the position of his hands from a previous take to avoid a break in continuity.

It's true what they say about the time spent waiting around on a film set. It is an especially long wait for the actors between each take.

Danny John-Jules starts singing and dancing to relieve the boredom and Robert Llewellyn joins in by kicking his legs in the air — it is rather peculiar to see a mechanoid dancing!

While this is going on, Chris Barrie is teaching one of the make-up girls to waltz and their feet are all over the place! It's a far cry from Rimmer's lonely image. "He's deeply sad," said Chris about Rimmer. "If you read through the lines, he's actually the saddest. And in many ways one can really feel, if you really think about it, more sympathy for him because he's got so much shit around him. Where it comes across that he's the git, it's because he does not know how to improve the situation, and when he does he gets very nasty, because he's stupid. So he has nothing going for him. But the good thing about Rimmer is, in many ways, he's the linchpin for many of the plots… he's the fall guy, so he has, in many ways, got to be there and it gives me the opportunity to do lots of things."

While close-ups are being filmed of some of the other characters, Kryten leaves the set in search of a straw. He's thirsty and it's the only way he can drink something without disturbing his make-up. It now takes only two hours to apply the make-up every day, whereas it used to take four. For Robert Llewellyn, it gets very hot under the studio lights: "It's just as hot as you could possibly imagine you ever being. It's like going into the hottest room of a Turkish bath with a plastic bag over your head." But Robert enjoys the series: "It's been hard but fun… A lot of difficult speeches, sawing my hand off and getting cut in half by Craig, and generally being blown up."

It's also been an eventful series for Lister. "I got exploded through a load of boxes," said Craig.

"I punched you in the back of the head," Robert added, "that was fun!"

"I've been battered," Craig continued. "I think every muscle in my body has been bruised at one stage during this run. I've had cuts, grazes, bruises. It has been fun getting blown-up a bit… I think

Lister's come of age in this, really, kind of grown up a bit, much more the voice of reason."

The characters and situations have certainly grown from the early episodes which were more like a sitcom, as Rob Grant explained. "When we first started the series, that's what we meant, it was meant to be a sitcom. The first three shows we wrote didn't really have any Science Fiction. I mean the pilot, of course, has science fiction, but we did a couple of very *Likely Lads*-in-space, *Porridge*-in-space kind of episodes, with *Balance of Power*, and actually we wrote a show that never got transmitted. And then we wrote *Future Echoes* and suddenly thought, 'Oh, actually, it will be a lot more fun this, to do science fiction, to do stuff that hasn't been done before'. That's what we tried to do thereafter."

The show has been phenomenally successful, selling widely abroad and now the fifth series is nearly in the can, the BBC have booked a sixth series and the cast have been optioned for it. "We might have dreamed it, but not imagined it," said Rob. "We thought we'd be lucky to get to the sixth show, never mind the sixth series! We've only got five people in our universe, we can't have the comedy milkman coming in for a co-starring role, so we didn't think thirty shows would sustain that necessarily, but the more we get into it, [the more we feel] we could go for sixty, or ninety, I think."

Back on the set, Robert Llewellyn is drinking happily from his straw and is getting ready to film a quite complicated shot with Lenny Von Dohlen, the Cop. The camera is tight on Lenny as he trains his gun on an urchin girl. Lenny has to jolt to the sound of six shots, and fall down, then the camera pans over to see Kryten's smoking gun. Not only does the camera work have to be precise, but there are the added complications that none of the guns really fire. Kryten's gun doesn't actually smoke and Lenny can't actually fall over because the camera is right behind him.

Visual effects man, Andy Bowman, fills the tip of Kryten's gun with some kind of liquid which smokes as it hits the air. But when it reaches the vital part of the scene where the camera focuses on Kryten's gun, the gun has finished smoking. The scene is re-set.

But this time, after the gunshots, Lenny hits the camera as he slumps.

Rob Grant decides the scene needs some more pace for the next take. Julian Scott, the associate producer, is instructed to shout 'Bang, Bang…' to simulate the gun shots. But on this take, the camera picks up Kryten's face too early.

It is set up for the final time, and everything goes smoothly. The video tape is rewound and Julian hears himself on the play back. He rises to receive his accolade for shouting 'Bang' six times, which will later on be dubbed over with sound effects.

After that, it's about time to break for lunch.

As everybody rushes for their fish and chips, Rob Grant takes some time to talk more about *Red Dwarf* between mouthfuls.

"We kind of run out of ideas just as we finish the last show every series," said Rob, "and we think, 'Oh God, that's probably it, isn't it?' and then we get a new burst of energy and enthusiasm when we're about to do a new lot."

Not only are they heavily involved in making *Red Dwarf V*, they've also been talking about a new American version which is going to be made into a pilot. "We'll be involved, in fact," said Rob. "They're going to use our story lines, but they've got to cram them in to twenty-two minutes, and of course there's a new religious broad-casting law just been passed in the States, so a lot of our episodes wouldn't make it through that. We have high hopes for it — and if it doesn't work, it doesn't work."

Red Dwarf's writers have also been working on something a little closer to home. "We've in fact got a new series, which we're supposed to be making next year for Carlton," said Rob. "It's for a mainstream channel, [it's] science fiction, a comedy version of *The Twilight Zone*, called *The Oo-wee-oo Dimension*, you know like 'oo-wee-oo'" — Rob sung a couple of notes of the theme tune to The Twilight Zone — "So that should be quite exciting, actually getting some viewing figures for some science fiction. Because they are so stupid with science fiction, it constitutes so many of the best-selling films of all time. I mean, in the top twenty [films] I think there are something like twelve — stupidly over-balanced. And yet on television, they think you can only show it at 6pm for kids."

"I think there are a whole bunch of people, probably about fifty million in this country, who will never watch something because it's science fiction, specifically because of that," Rob continued. "They think it's silly and for kids. But we play to science fiction fans. [In *Red Dwarf V*] we've got a couple of episodes that aren't very hard science fiction, but we're letting rip a bit more with the bizarreness of the ideas."

Rob's little boy, Joe, who has been sitting on his mum's lap at the table throughout the conversation has spotted Kryten coming into the canteen.

"Who's that? He's a funny man, isn't he?" observed Rob.

Robert Llewellyn, in full Kryten make-up, stops by the table and squats down to face Joe.

"Who's this, Joe?" said Rob, as his son stares wide-eyed at the mechanoid. "It's Kryten! What's happened to his head?"

Rob asked if Joe wants to touch Kryten's rubber head, but Joe is reluctant. "You don't have to, don't worry," Robert assured him. "It's all a bit too much, isn't it, having a funny man looking at you like that." Robert leaves to eat his lunch; leaving, no doubt, a bemused little boy.

Back on the set, Doug Naylor can be seen with his camcorder taking a private video just before the crew are ready to resume filming proper. The call comes for quiet on the set, but little Joe has other ideas and after a couple of minutes, his mum has to take him out to watch the filming from the outside broadcast van.

A few more scenes in the can, and the crew breaks to film in an alleyway just around the corner. These outside scenes are filmed in advance and then played on video screens when the rest of the show is taped in front of a live studio audience. The actors are then able to see which bits the audience finds funny. "It always surprises me when people laugh at Rimmer," said Craig Charles. "Sometimes it would be nice to do it without an audience, because they do tend to laugh in the wrong places. They laugh in the build-up and miss the big woofer! Whereas if they'd been quiet for a little bit longer, they could have got the big woofer, you know? Sometimes they can laugh over — especially on the PVT [pre-recorded scenes] — they can laugh over the big joke, whereas live we can just hang on and deliver the line."

In a show as technical as *Red Dwarf*, the actors have got used to imagining effects which are to be added at a later stage; but Craig said this is more difficult for the audience: "Sometimes when things get played in for them, they can't see the actual special effects happening at the time, so it's difficult for the audience imagining what's going on… Sometimes on the special effects we don't get as many laughs as we should because it's not quite finished."

Craig Charles came to *Red Dwarf* from the entertainment world rather than from an acting background. In fact, all the main cast are from a non-acting background, but Craig doesn't think that's a problem. "Acting's easy," he said. "It's easy to do; very difficult to be very good at. Over the years, me and Chris — because we go back to series one — our performance has improved about five thousand per cent in the actual acting stakes."

With a programme as successful as *Red Dwarf*, the cast attract quite a lot of attention from the fans, which has grown as the programme has gone on. "We get a lot of adulation, I suppose," said Craig. "People collect the cigarette butts that I smoke when I'm filming. I've had conversations with taxi drivers going, 'I had a girl in who'd been watching the show last night and she had the straw that you drank out of; treasuring it, she was' — you know, things like that. We're not really in it for the adulation, we're in it because we like doing the work, we like each other, it's funny, [and it's] seven weeks a year. I have very little in common with a lot of the people who like the show. I like different things. I'm in it because I like the comedy. A lot of people, the fans especially, like the science fiction angle of it more than the comedy angle.

"I always think that staying away from the fans is a good idea anyway," he continued. "Because when they see you as Lister and they see you in space, in costume and all this kind of stuff, then [for them to see you in real life] you're shattering all their illusions."

The crew set up at an alleyway round the side of the studios where the next scene is to be filmed. With only a couple of props, the alleyway has been transformed into a future England with a heavy American influence. While the crew prepare, Chris Barrie resumes waltzing with the make-up girl — "One, two, cha cha cha!" She seems to have got the hang of it now.

It's getting colder, and the crew are warming their hands on the huge film lights. Danny John-Jules is walking around in somebody else's coat trying to keep warm. He has to develop a different voice for Cat in this alternative reality. He tries a wimpish voice which the cast finds very funny, but Doug Naylor says it's "too weird". Danny tones it down a bit for the take.

Rob Grant calls 'it's a wrap' and the crew leap into action. It's late and everyone wants to get home. Make-up artists grab their make-up bags, the camera crew grab their gear and everyone literally runs out of the alley with their equipment. Within minutes, the scene is transformed to look, once again, like a walkway between two studio buildings.

Red Dwarf VI

Written & Executive Produced by... Rob Grant & Doug Naylor
Directed by... Andy DeEmmony
Produced by... Justin Judd

Rimmer... Chris Barrie
Lister... Craig Charles
Cat... Danny John-Jules
Kryten... Robert Llewellyn

Recorded: February-March 1993
First broadcast: October-November 1993

The BBC were so keen for another series of *Red Dwarf*, they put in their bid even before *Red Dwarf V* had finished filming. There was just one problem: they wanted to show it in the spring of 1993 and the writers knew that didn't give them enough time to get the scripts together. Rob Grant and Doug Naylor asked for a broadcast date later in the year, but the BBC were unsympathetic. Either there was a new series ready to go out in the spring, or there would be no series at all. Rather than see the show die, the producers decided to pull out all the stops in order to get it done.

It meant filming started in 1993 with only half the scripts available. "We've got three scripts, but not the other three," said Chris Barrie on his first day filming as Rimmer. "It's been a bit seat-of-the-pants getting it all sorted."

But Doug Naylor assured everyone it was *Red Dwarf*'s usual hectic schedule — if it was, maybe, a bit more hairy than previous years. "We've still got a lot of work to do on the first three [scripts]," he said at the start of production. "We're re-writing them as we go along and there's no difference really between the last three and the first three, except the second three haven't officially been handed in."

In fact, in order to get all the scripts done, Rob and Doug hired a house near Shepperton Studios and moved in together to maximise writing time. Even so, as the production went along, the scripts got later and later and there were constant last minute changes. The script was so late on the last episode, *Out of Time*, that there was no chance for the cast to learn their lines and the whole thing had to be put on autocue.

By the end of production, the writers were feeling the strain of working themselves so hard. "Umm, just a bit!" said Doug. "Rob's been home — what is it? — three times this year?"

"It's been awful for us," said Rob. "We're going to spend six months in a nursing home!"

After all that hard work, the BBC ironically changed their minds. They decided not to show *Red Dwarf VI* in the spring after all, opting for a slot in the autumn instead.

It was a tough shoot for everyone, no one more so than the cast. "It was difficult," Craig Charles told the *Smegazine*. "It's not supposed to be easy."

But it was Chris Barrie who spoke out about it more than anyone. And he didn't pull any punches. "It is getting more and more difficult, it seems, to do it in front of an audience," he said. "Because of the time factor, we haven't enough rehearsal. And, because there's visual effects, everyone gets in a vaudevillian situation, when you've got two-and-a-half hours recording time and you're doing a show, people get a bit tetchy and adrenaline pumps and you can almost have accidents. So I think it would be good for everyone if there was more time."

Once again, the series was without its original director Ed Bye and new personalities were on the scene to oversee day-to-day activities. Chris lamented the loss of Ed and, with the writers ('the boys' as he called them) in ultimate control of production, he was critical of the way things were handled. "If you did have an Ed Bye figure, he would get the scripts in early so we'd have enough time to do it properly. When you've got the boys in complete control, there's no one to hurry them along with the scripts, apart from their agent. Then you will always get their style of production, which is by committee and slowly inching forward and sometimes keeping people in the dark. I've said it to them several times over the last two months, to their faces. I've decided if you've got an opinion, I just say it these days because at least people will know where you stand."

It is fair to say that, since then, Chris Barrie has mellowed somewhat over *Red Dwarf VI*. He took a bit of a sabbatical during the following series and subsequently was able to return to the series with new enthusiasm. "The thing about *Red Dwarf*, it is an exciting show on paper," he said. "The scripts, the stories, in many ways make the struggles worthwhile."

The new director for *Red Dwarf VI* was Andy DeEmmony, whose previous job had been on *Spitting Image* which he had directed for many years. He relished the chance to do something new. "For me, it's a perfect combination for what I do, which is effects and comedy," he said. "Something like this has got a lot more visual going on. I enjoy the characters and the character side of it. I hope to use the effects in a subliminal way to work with that, rather than trying to work against the character comedy."

Andy, a genial man with a firm control over the filming process and a calm exterior — despite the pressure he was under — got on well with the cast. "Working with Andy DeEmmony was quite good," Craig Charles told the *Smegazine*. "We started calling him a South African because he's got the name DeEmmony and he's Dutch… And Chris Barrie does a brilliant impression of Justin Judd, who produced it. We had a good laugh taking the piss out of everyone we were working with."

As was the case with the new floor manager, Simon Wallace. One of his jobs was to make everyone shut up when the cameras were about to roll and he would do this by calling out: 'quiet please'. The way he said it was as if it were out of the corner of his mouth, with a trailing hiss at the end, so it was more 'quiet pleasssss'. This left him open to ridicule by the mischievous cast who would mimic him whenever he said it. So, instead of the words 'quiet please' causing a hush to fall over the studio, it lead to a chorus of 'quiet pleassss', 'quiet pleassss', 'quiet pleassss' from members of the cast. He took it in good humour, but the poor man, who had been using this phrase in the industry for something like twenty years, couldn't quite figure out why it was suddenly happening to him.

One of the personalities sadly not to appear on *Red Dwarf VI* was Hattie Hayridge. Her character, Holly, was written out when it was decided to move away from the Red Dwarf ship and have the crew stranded on Starbug instead. In previous years, it had been more and more difficult for the writers to give her something to do in the episodes. The stories had increasingly been set off-ship and Kryten's role had somewhat overtaken hers when it came to exposition.

The decision to drop the character was made by Rob Grant and Doug Naylor who called Hattie Hayridge to their offices in 1992 for a meeting. "October the 16th," said Hattie. "Not that it's imprinted on my brain or anything!"

The news came as a total surprise. In fact, she originally thought the meeting was going to be about giving her a bigger role. "I went in in a very good mood, 'oh hi, how are you?'" she remembered. "And they were like, 'oh fine'. They were very sort of like — if I say 'sober' it sounds like sober as opposed to drunk — sober as opposed to light-hearted, let's say. They said 'we've got, um, something, um, not very nice thing to say' and I said 'oh, are you going to give me the sack?' in my jokey way! — I just thought they were going to talk about 'oh, we've decided you're going to do this, you're going to do that' — and they said 'oh yes, kind of, I suppose it is'. I was clutching a coffee cup that I almost tipped down my frock! I went 'oh right, oh yeah, okay'. I said 'why?' I went through this list of possible reasons that I thought it could possibly be, like 'you hate me?' 'No.' 'You're saving money?' 'No.' 'You think I'm shit?' 'No.' I think they'd had more months to think about it than I had. I think they were quite surprised that I was quite shocked.

"When I got home that night from the meeting I was the tiniest bit pissed off," she said. "I phoned up a friend and I said 'oh, I'm not in it anymore' and he said 'well, you don't want to be a computer all your life do you?' And that was the best thing he could have said really, because other people said 'oh no, what a shame, what are you going to do?' which gives you a real panic feeling, you think 'oh, God!' whereas when this friend said that, it was 'yeah, that's the way to look at it.'"

The change was part of the new direction for *Red Dwarf VI*, with the Red Dwarf ship stolen and the regular characters stuck on Starbug with limited supplies. "We just didn't want to do another series that was exactly the same as the others," said Doug Naylor. "I think Rob and I — when we do the writing — we've got to get excited about it all over again and it's much easier if we've got a new impetus and a new freshness about it. It's kind of like recession-hit *Red Dwarf*.

There is no Red Dwarf, it's all set on Starbug, it's all set two hundred years after the previous series. Red Dwarf has been nicked by people unknown and they spend the entire series chasing it."

"[It's] much more streamlined in that the whole series has a direction, a quest going through it," said director Andy DeEmmony. "It ties in better than just random episodes. All the crew have a direction, they have an aim in common, which is much better than just aimlessly wandering. I think it's good, it's potentially better than the previous series because of that."

It meant a whole new set and a whole new look. Once again, production designer Mel Bibby was there to see it through. "When we went to the first planning meeting for that, we thrashed it out and said, 'where does it come from, where is the logic on this?' Everybody just said that Kryten's been alive for three million years, so Kryten's been upgrading the ship for three million years. That was our internal excuse for bringing an airlock door in and a kitchen and sleeping quarters."

Also new was the use of computer graphics to create some of the special effects in the series. This was 1993 and technology had improved considerably since *Red Dwarf* started in the 1980s. A company — SVC — was brought in to provide the video effects which appear at various moments in the episodes, one example being Kryten contracting a virus in *Gunmen of the Apocalypse*. It was effectively two guys working hard at their computers for many-a-long hour simply because they loved the show and wanted to do the best possible job. It's fair to say the production got their money's worth out of them, as the company had put in a competitive bid for the chance to work on *Red Dwarf* in the hope it would be a showcase for potential future clients.

After all that hard work, the production got its reward with *Red Dwarf*'s first ever Emmy Award, for the episode *Gunmen of the Apocalypse*.

"It gets harder every year," said Danny John-Jules, who played Cat.

"It's been hard for me because I'm too old," added Robert Llewellyn, who played Kryten. "These kids that I work with, these young children! I've got a year older doing this show now, I don't want to say how old, but I'm the oldest person in the gig, aren't I? By hundreds of years."

Even Chris Barrie had to acknowledge the results were there for all to see. "It's been funnier than most of the sitcoms you see on the television," he said. "It's more interestingly shot than most of the drama you see on television. When things like *Have I Got News For You* is winning best television comedy programme in certain award ceremonies, you always think, 'television?' That's a radio programme put on television, made visual. Whereas the visual creative impact that *Red Dwarf* can produce — that's real television."

And, speaking before all the episodes were edited, Rob Grant could relax a little and be pleased at what they had achieved. "We made a conscious effort to make it as funny a series as we could and it certainly has been getting bigger laughs in the studios," he said. "It's very hard to tell when you're so close up to it. There's many a slip betwixt recording and broadcast because they change so much in the edit and in the dub, but I really don't think there's a bum show in it. I usually think, 'oh that one's going to be a bummer', but I don't really think that's happened this time."

Then Rob stopped and thought about what he had said for a moment. "I may revise my decision."

Episode One: Psirens

GUEST CAST

Professor Mamet... Jenny Agutter
Pete Tranter's Sister... Samantha Robson
Captain Tau... Anita Dobson
Crazed Astro... Richard Ridings
Kochanski... C.P. Grogan
Temptresses... Zoe Hilson, Elizabeth Anson
Featuring the hands of... Phil Manzanera

Story

Lister, Rimmer, Kryten and Cat are on Starbug in pursuit of Red Dwarf which has been stolen by an unknown person, persons or life forms. Their course takes them through an asteroid field littered with the remains of other spacecraft. It seems all the craft have been lead to their doom by psirens who can appear as anything to lure in unwary space travellers and suck out their brains. As the illusions get harder to resist — appearing as Kochanski in trouble and as a duplicate Lister — the crew agree to go into stasis while leaving Kryten in charge. As a mechanoid, he believes he is immune to the psirens' call, but that was before one appeared as his creator, whom he is programmed to obey.

Funniest Moment (arguably)

Kryten emerging from the waste compactor as a squashed cube.

Behind The Scenes

The episode begins with Lister waking up from deep sleep after more than two hundred years. He's a bit disorientated after so long, and Kryten has to remind him of who he is and where they are. It works as an introduction to *Red Dwarf* for viewers new to the series and for people who needed reminding eighteen months after *Red Dwarf V* had been shown.

It's revealed that they are stuck on Starbug, chasing Red Dwarf, and low on supplies. The re-invented setup gives the series a whole new motivation. They need to investigate any other ships or worlds they encounter in order to get supplies, while negotiating potentially hazardous areas of space in order to catch up with Red Dwarf.

"In many ways it was scary," said Doug Naylor on the set of *Psirens*. "Because when we told people there was no Red Dwarf, we had no guarantee — we still haven't — that it's going to work. But, in the end, it does give it a different feel. Whether it'll be better or worse, it's impossible to say, but it will feel slightly different."

With supplies running low on Starbug, Kryten is having to be inventive with what he serves for dinner. All their grain has been eaten by space weevils, so Kryten uses a bit of lateral thinking and grills a dead space weevil for Lister to eat. In reality, the weevil was glazed bread and made by Alan 'Rocky' Marshall of the special effects department: "He ate it, it tasted vile, but he ate it," said Rocky.

It was not the only gross thing Craig Charles had to do in the episode, as he also had to kiss a slimy psiren creature. Lister is lured into the kiss by an hallucination of a skimpy-clad woman he remembers from his childhood, Pete Tranter's sister. The woman playing her was Samantha Robson, who had to endure freezing temperatures in a quarry off the M25 on a night in February while wearing a revealing outfit. The hallucination then disappears and the psiren's true appearance is revealed to be an insectoid beast with gooey snout and a straw that will suck out Lister's brain. The creature was played by tall and skinny special effects man, Paul McGuinness, in a costume which had a latex snout covered in KY jelly for extra sliminess.

The scene was partly an in-joke from the writers who had heard Craig Charles complain during *Red Dwarf V* that he didn't get any girls on the series. So they gave him what he wanted — in a twisted kind of way. "Here I am one minute snogging a babe and the next I'm snogging a fluid-dripping... yuck!" Craig told the *Smegazine*, "It was dripping spermicidal fluid into my mouth! But I thought the scene with me and Samantha worked quite well, I thought it was sexy and quite realistic."

The episode was littered with impressive guest stars. One of the most eagerly awaited from the fans' point of view was Clare (C.P.) Grogan who was back after a three series break. She was surprised that people still remembered her as Kochanski from the early days. "It was a really lovely part, it was brilliant fun doing it, but it was such a long time ago," she said during a break during location filming for *Psirens*. "I'm absolutely thrilled to be back. It's *déjà vu*, it really is. I was pretty surprised to get the phone call."

Joining her was Anita Dobson as the psiren hallucination, Captain Tau. The actress had become a household name as Angie Watts in the BBC soap *EastEnders* in the mid-eighties and was offered the role because the producers hoped her husband, Brian May of rock band Queen, would agree to be Lister's hands in the scene where he plays the guitar like a pro. The idea was that they could do the show together, but in the end Brian May was on tour, so Anita came in on her own. "They just rang up and said would I like to come and guest on the show," she said. "It's such a huge cult favourite and especially for kids, so my street credibility has gone up in huge waves since I've agreed to do it. I'm having a great time."

Some people have suggested Anita was enticed into appearing on *Red Dwarf* because she was a fan of the show, but that wasn't the case. "I don't really watch much television, so I only know about it from what other people tell me," she said, on the day she was at Bankside power station for some location filming. "I've only seen tiny snatches of it, but I think I could possibly become a huge fan because everybody loves it so much, it's really caught people's imagination. It's a wonderful feeling around here. Just putting the costume on today and getting ready I've been as high as a kite. It's terrific fun. Everyone looks great, they're really into the programme and you just feel like you're part of the family."

The role of Lister's guitar-playing hands were eventually taken on by another famous guitarist, Phil Manzanera of Roxy Music. He simply crouched behind Craig Charles and put his arms around him and played an impressive riff.

Rounding off the star guest list for *Psirens* was Jenny Agutter, an actress famous for roles in films such as *The Railway Children*, *Logan's Run* and *An American Werewolf in London*. She had just the one scene, playing Kryten's creator Professor Mamet, and did so with great authority while looking stunning in a short tunic and knee-high boots.

Episode Two: Legion

GUEST CAST
Legion... Nigel Williams

Story

The crew hope to find some decent salvage on a space station once inhabited by research scientists. Kryten's scans show no life on board, but when they arrive, they are greeted by a being who calls himself Legion. At first, they are eager to accept his hospitality, until Legion refuses to let them leave. When they try to escape, his reason becomes clear as Lister pulls off Legion's mask to reveal his true face — an amalgamation of all four of them. Without their presence on the space station, Legion would not exist. The only way to defeat him is for Kryten to knock everyone unconscious.

Funniest Moment (arguably)

Kryten attempts to knock Rimmer out by bashing him over the head with an iron bar while Rimmer smashes his head against the wall.

Behind The Scenes

Nigel Williams' smooth and assured voice gives Legion a sense of calm and control. But, although he sounded good, his costume did not serve him well. Time and budget constraints meant costume designer Howard Burden hadn't been able to do what he wanted to do and had to compromise. So the idea of having coloured liquid circulating in tubes around his body was jettisoned in favour of a cheaper and less-effective all-in-one body suit with a moulded mask and breastplate.

The suit was made to zip up at the back, but when the actor arrived on location for his first day of shooting, the costume was too small, the zip broke and he had to be sewn into it. "We only had one fitting," said Nigel Williams. "We never really had a final fitting after it was made. I think it was always intended that it would be fitted on the day, as it were. Which, in fact, happened. It's pretty much a one piece swim suit. It looks very warm, but I don't know if you've ever stood in an unheated building at half past eleven at night in February in a swim suit. That's what we were doing on the OB recording, and it was very cold."

The cold location was, in fact, the Marco Polo House in London which doubled for the interior of the space station with its glass architecture and lift made of glass. The rest of the scenes were shot in studio sets. These included the banquet which was eaten with anti-matter chopsticks. The idea of the chopsticks was to remotely lift the food from the plate and propel it through the air into the mouth of the diner. The props the cast were given for this scene were powered by batteries which, when turned on, caused the ends of the chopsticks to twirl around. The idea was good, but in practice the ends kept falling off as soon as the cameras rolled.

The flying food sequence was one of a number of scenes which had to be pre-recorded because effects meant they couldn't be per-formed live in front of an audience. "It was a long day," Nigel Williams remembered. "It was nine fifteen in the morning, till nearly eleven o'clock at night. A long day, but it was very complicated stuff. It's very ambitious to try and do that on videotape in such a short time span, the twirling sticks and all that stuff. And the stuff going in your mouth has to be run backwards because it's rather difficult to get the stuff to zoom into your mouth, but it's much easier to pull it out of your mouth. So it was recorded backwards, and they play it backwards."

As for the food itself, this was also made by the special effects department. "I had to stick it in my mouth, which was bad enough, but I didn't have to eat it," said Nigel. "Chris was the only one who had to actually consume any of it. I think he said it was quite nice. I didn't challenge him on it, in case he gave me a bit!"

More difficulties were bestowed upon the actor playing Legion because he had to spend virtually the whole time acting behind a mask. Not only did it hide any facial expression that he might have used to convey the character, he also couldn't see very well. "Not at all," said Nigel. "You could see sort of straight ahead of you, but there's no peripheral vision. That was the biggest bind because there were things here [at the side of my face] that you'd walk into because you literally couldn't see them. It's all a bit throwing not being able to see. And the chemicals that make-up the glues inhabiting the inside of the mask were pretty overpowering… It was like talking through a blanket. You couldn't see anything, it was very hot and clammy inside, and very cold on the body — but, apart from that, it was a joy!"

The mask was necessary because it hid Legion's true face, a face that is made up of all the people he is drawing his energy from. Lister reveals the truth when he rips off the mask and sees a grotesque mix of all of their four faces. There were considerable complexities in filming this — especially with the technology available in 1993. The images of the four characters were amalgamated in post-production by Karl Mooney and his computer, using several of elements filmed for the purpose on set. In order for the shot to work, it had to be static, and that meant all of the cast members had to be filmed with their head in a brace so they couldn't move. The images were, therefore, interchangeable and allowed Karl Mooney to manipulate them into the final result.

The removal of the mask makes Kryten realise that Legion is a gestalt entity. There is a clue in the character's name for anyone who knows the Bible, as it comes from the quote: 'my name is legion, for we are many' (Mark, 5:9) and refers to the story a man possessed by many demons who is healed by Jesus. In order for Legion in *Red Dwarf* to be defeated, Kryten has to knock out all the others so he can't draw on their consciousnesses. This involves a superb slapstick routine as Kryten whacks Lister over the head with a chair, punches

Cat on the chin, hits Rimmer with a succession of vases and then tries using an iron bar at the same time as Rimmer is banging his own head against the wall.

This was filmed the same day as the scene of eating food with anti-matter chopsticks and the effects shots that had each character with their head in a brace. By the time Kryten got around to smashing vases over the head of Chris Barrie, it was getting really late. "It would have been so lovely to be able to spend a long time over it," said Chris. "A scene that is tailor-made for timing and comedy and performance. We'd all had a long day, and to try and shoot it, something of such importance [in such a short time, was] difficult and wrong."

Such a scene was made possible because of Rimmer's new hard-light drive. When he first encounters Legion, Legion is dismissive of the primitive technology of his lightbee and upgrades it into 'hard-light' which means that Rimmer can now touch things. The idea was only supposed to last for the one episode, but once the writers had put it in the script, they decided to keep it. "We felt that it helped the cowardly side of his nature if the danger he was in was more physical," Rob Grant told the *Smegazine*. "It's always been a bit of a bone of contention that he was a coward even though he was basically undamageable."

For Chris Barrie, who had been playing a hologram for many years, it was a welcome change. "It was a relief to be able to actually behave normally and touch things," he said. "It's one of those things where you can imagine Rob and Doug saying 'well, how are we going to make Rimmsy touch things? I know, get a hard-light drive.' That's the great thing with science fiction, you can do anything."

Episode Three: Gunmen of the Apocalypse

GUEST CAST
Loretta... Jennifer Calvert
Simulant Captain / Death... Denis Lill
Simulant Lieutenant... Liz Hickling
Lola... Imogen Bain
Jimmy... Steve Devereaux
War... Robert Inch
Pestilence... Jeremy Peters
Famine... Dinny Powell
Bear Strangler McGee... Stephen Marcus

Story

Rogue simulants hunt down Starbug and infect it with a deadly virus. Kryten comes up with a plan to defeat the virus by contracting it himself and tells the others to 'watch my dreams'.

Kryten is dreaming he is a sheriff in an old western, but he is losing the battle and has become a drunkard. The others join him in an artificial reality programme where they become cowboys. They sober Kryten up to face the bad guys in a duel in the centre of town. It is then that Kryten realises his guns, with their dove motif on the handles, are a dove programme which he can use to defeat the bad guy virus.

Funniest Moment (arguably)

Sheriff Kryten tries to leave town, but the sharp-shooting of the Cat, as The Riviera Kid, is too good for him. He fires a shot which ricochets off a series of metal objects before striking the rope holding the town sign which swings down and knocks Kryten on the head.

Behind The Scenes

While producing the scripts for *Red Dwarf VI*, the writers came up with a brilliant — but ridiculous — idea. How about a *Red Dwarf* cowboy episode?

They knew they wouldn't be able to afford to build a Wild West town from scratch, so decided to test the water and told the rest of the production team that the script was written and they needed to find a location. The team came back to say they had found an actual Wild West town in Kent, called Laredo, where enthusiasts would spend their weekends living as cowboys in the most authentic way possible. With a town at their disposal, they had a location which meant they could do what they wanted to do. Rob Grant and Doug Naylor went off to write the script which became *Gunmen of the Apocalypse*.

"That's the most fun I've ever had on *Red Dwarf*, and I wasn't even doing it," said Rob. "Everybody, especially the men, when they got on the set, you just feel like you're twelve years old!"

The owners of Laredo pulled out all the stops for the production crew and provided the extras for the episode — which was handy, as they all had their own costumes. Nevertheless, the pressure was on because there was a hell of a lot of footage which needed to be filmed during that one day at Laredo, and in early March, it wasn't going to stay light too long into the evening. But director Andy DeEmmony was prepared and had storyboarded the whole shoot so he knew exactly what he needed. He then filmed out of sequence, placing his camera in one position and shooting everything he needed from that point of view first, then moving the camera and doing it again. It cut down the time it took to reset and ensured everything was in the can by the end of the day.

"I remember everyone saying, 'oh, it's going to be a hell of a day,'" said Chris Barrie. "Everyone was panicking over what they were going to do... We wasted about forty-five minutes to start with, but after that everyone was so excited that the weather was so good and everything was how it should be, once we got it down, we got it moving pretty quickly and everyone was good. The horses were well-behaved. One of them fell over at one point, I don't know why... falling asleep on his feet or something, but he just fell over. Quite funny, quite odd. There was a bit of mucking about, but when you get a gun holster in your hand and there's bullets and there's horses and those buildings there, it was just fun."

The horses were an extravagance for a sitcom, as hiring them is quite an expensive business. The horses also had to share the limelight with a mischievous *Red Dwarf* cast, who consisted of two people who could ride, Danny and Robert; and two people who couldn't, Craig and Chris. For Chris Barrie, mounting astride such a beast was a daunting prospect. "Frightening," he said. "I'd never ridden a horse and the most frightening moment was that last [bit], the fly-past bit. Danny went 'yee-hah!'. The horses know what that means and off they bloody-well went!"

Robert Llewellyn's day did not get off to a very good start. He had to be at Laredo earlier than most because he had to get into the Kryten mask. He was in the make-up trailer, having his rubber head stuck on when "someone stepped in the caravan, the whole thing wobbled, and glue went in my eye," he said. "I had a wonderful day after that, but glue in my eye wasn't a good start."

A lot of the scenes that needed to be filmed that day featured Kryten as a Wild West sheriff, one of the most nail-biting of which was towards the end of the day. In the scene, Kryten tries to escape from the town, but is stopped by the town sign which swings down and hits him on the head. It wasn't difficult to do on paper, but involved a lot of coordination which could have all gone horribly wrong. The timing was crucial and Robert somehow managed to get to the sign at the right moment, it swung down and hit him on the first take. Someone was smiling down on the *Red Dwarf* crew that day.

The scenes inside the Wild West town were all shot on a saloon set built at the studios in Shepperton. These included a smattering of Laredo extras and some stuntmen to help with the fighting. The instances of bullets being shot out of the air and the whip which pulls Kryten's bourbon bottle out of his hands were achieved using computer-generated effects, so no bullets were actually fired or whips cracked next to the faces of actors.

The models shots for *Gunmen of the Apocalypse* were also spectacular, with a sequence of Starbug crashing into a lava planet in a fiery splashdown and later emerging again with lava dripping off its body. After so many planets made of rocks or covered in snow, the orange glow of the lava made the sequences look really different. Ironically, this was not the original plan. The writers, when putting together the episode, wanted to give Peter Wragg's special effects team an easy time of it and had Starbug crash onto an ocean planet. Water would be easy and look good, they thought, because it had been done before. But when Peter saw the script, he knew it would be difficult to achieve because water droplets don't scale and it would be obvious that Starbug was really a three-foot long model. He found Rob and Doug during rehearsal and suggested doing lava instead. They instantly agreed.

The icing on the cake was Howard Goodall's music which provides some atmospheric honky-tonk piano for the saloon scenes and a marvellous western-style theme used both in the episode and during the closing credits. With the music, location, script and comedy performances, all the elements came together to make *Gunmen of the Apocalypse* the most successful episode of *Red Dwarf VI*.

That was despite nay-sayers in some quarters voicing concern. There is a famous story of Janet Street-Porter (Executive for Youth and Entertainment at the BBC) being horrified when she saw the script. She insisted the whole thing was impossible on the budget they had and declared it couldn't be done, only to be told by Rob and Doug's agent, Charles Armitage, that the film crew had just come back from Laredo and they had already achieved the impossible.

The atmosphere on set was certainly buzzing after the cast came back from location filming. They instinctively knew that they had made something exceptional. Danny John-Jules wanted to go back. "I think it should be 'Return to Laredo,'" he said. "'Return to Laredo' would definitely be a good Christmas special."

"Fulfilling your dreams of being a cowboy was wonderful," said Chris Barrie. "Some good performances by the guests and a fun story. I think everyone rose to the occasion in that one and made the best of what we could do. We had a beautiful day down in Laredo, with Gerard the stuntman, a good egg, doing the biz."

Other people agreed with him because, after the episode was shown, it was given the prestigious International Emmy Award for an Outstanding Popular Arts Programme.

Episode Four: Emohawk: Polymorph II

GUEST CAST
Computer… Hugh Quarshie
GELF… Martin Sims
GELF Chief… Ainsley Harriott
GELF Bride… Steven Wickham

Story

The Space Filth charges the crew of Starbug with looting Space Corps derelicts. As they try to escape, the vessel fires on them, damaging the Oxy-Generation Unit beyond repair. The only way to get a new one is to trade with GELFs — with one slight hitch: the GELF Chief wants Lister to marry his daughter in return. So a plan is hatched to go through with the wedding and rescue Lister while the GELFs are asleep. But Lister gets wedding night jitters and legs it with the rest of them — angering the GELF Chief who sends an Emohawk after them. An Emohawk is a domesticated Polymorph and it's hungry for Rimmer and the Cat's emotions.

Funniest Moment (arguably)

Lister runs from his amorous new bride out of the GELF village with the cry: 'change of plan — *leg it!*'

Behind The Scenes

The GELF village featured in *Emohawk* was a set built outside on the back lot of Shepperton Studios for a medieval television drama called *Covington Cross*. Just like Laredo in *Gunmen*, it allowed *Red Dwarf* to utilise an impressive location at little cost. When writers Rob Grant and Doug Naylor found out about it existence, they wrote it into the episode — so the location came before the script. "Yes, absolutely," said Rob. "We wanted to use it in *Rimmerworld* and the logistics wouldn't allow us to get round to it. We'd had the idea for a long time of them having to trade in this settlement where Lister's forced to stay."

The GELFs — or Genetically Engineered Life Forms (because there are no aliens in the *Red Dwarf* universe) — were three men dressed in shaggy costumes, one of whom was TV chef Ainsley Harriott — not as if it was possible to tell under all that hair. "I'm the one that offers my daughter for marriage, the one that does the funny handshake that leans over with Kryten," he said.

It may seem an odd casting choice, but before Ainsley became famous for programmes like *Can't Cook, Won't Cook*, he was performing on stage at the Comedy Store, so was part of the tradition of *Red Dwarf* guests coming from a comedy background. More unusual, however, was the dialogue he had to learn. The GELF language may have been made up by the writers, but it was carefully scripted and the actors had to get it right. "It was all this woomba, woomba, woomba," said Ainsley. "It linked up with other conversations or things I was doing with Kryten, so it had to be right. So I was going home and going 'hhhrraagggh, wooobbbh' and it had to make sense because Kryten was waiting for his line to follow on."

Robert Llewellyn was heard to joke while filming the location scenes: 'I've never complained about a line before — but a foreign language?'

Described in the script as 'warty yetis', all three GELFs were played by men, including Lister's bride, who was played by actor Steven Wickham. "The prosthetic make-up takes about two hours to put on," he said. "It's a horrible warty face mask with a big shaggy wig and a big shaggy furry body with a big belly and a bosom and a huge bum and a rubberized costume, so it looks horrible. The costume itself is like a body suit, body stocking thing with all the bits stuck on. The stomach and the bottom are strapped on so they're okay, they're quite loose-fitting. But the face mask has to be glued on quite firmly, so if I lift an eyebrow, the mask moves with it."

At one stage during the filming, Craig Charles went over to one of the GELFs to discuss the up-coming wedding scene, only to discover he was talking to the wrong one. 'They're all the same, these yetis!', he said before going in search of his bride.

This was, of course, the bride whom he had to kiss after the wedding ceremony. It followed on from the slobbery snog in *Psirens* and was another way to make fun of Craig's request to do more kissing. "I was coughing up a fur ball for about an hour afterwards," he said. "It was funny though, the first time I've ever kissed a guy."

The wedding scene was filmed on location in the *Covington Cross* village of straw huts, lit with flame torches and pieces of set dressing to make it look more GELF-like and less medieval. It was shot at night-time in March and it was chilly, to say the least. "That was cold," said Steve Wickham. "It might have looked like we had big heavy costumes on, but the rubberized chest wasn't warm, it absorbed the cold. Then underneath, all we had was like a body-stocking, so it got progressively colder on Thursday night and the cold wind just cut through. It was freezing, it really was."

Even Robert Llewellyn was seen with an anorak draped over the top of his usually warm Kryten costume. Cast and crew were kept warm with hot drinks from a dispenser until production manager Kerry Waddell came by and asked people quietly: 'would you like a drink?'. They would reply something like: 'I've got a hot chocolate, thank you'. To which her response was: 'no, would you like a *drink?*' and she produced a bottle of rum from under her jacket. A shot of rum in a cup of hot chocolate did much to warm the cockles on that particular night.

It's therefore not surprising that Robert Llewellyn had to have a few of the words from the GELF language written up on boards so he could read them. "I'd just had a drink of tea with rum in it and I don't drink, so I was completely pissed," he said. "It's actually much easier being Kryten when I'm absolutely sozzled, I mean I can't do the walk or the lines or anything, I didn't know what was going on."

More respite for the crew came with the arrival of the catering. Rather than pay for a catering van to be on site, the production just rang up the local takeaway pizza company. They arrived during the filming of a scene, but it had to be completed before everyone was allowed to tuck in. Robert Llewellyn told the director not to shout 'cut!' but to shout 'pizza!'. He doesn't normally eat while wearing the Kryten mask, but even he tucked in that night, rolling bits of pizza up into little balls and trying to slot them into his mouth without touching his lips. He later claimed it's possible to see pizza juice on his chin on the footage filmed after supper (although, in reality, he seemed to have got away with it).

The scenes inside the mud hut were filmed on a set inside the studio. One of them included a real open fire which was incredibly hot under the studio lights and had to be put out during rehearsal so people didn't expire from the heat. Those fire extinguishers were also very much on standby during the recording, as the wardrobe department feared the GELF's flammable hair might get too close to the flames.

The episode ends with a twist as the Emohawk gets inside Starbug and, like the Polymorph before it, sucks emotions out of some of the crew. The first to succumb was the Cat, who was turned into Duane Dibbley.

"I adore him," writer Rob Grant told the *Smegazine*. "It was one of our intentions at the start of writing series six to have the Cat encounter some kind of space problem where he constantly becomes his alter-ego Duane Dibbley in times of stress and trouble; so they were all trying to keep him calm so that Duane wouldn't go around screwing things up — pulling the steering wheel off things. But we found it got in the way of stories. We were desperate to bring Duane back and we finally found a way."

It was certainly an audience pleaser, as Duane's appearance, then the return of Ace Rimmer (after the Emohawk had sucked emotion from Rimmer), made the fans in the studio go wild. It caused director Andy DeEmmony a headache during the edit. "American shows leave that in and they love it — big cheers, whoops, claps, everyone corpses on stage and they leave all that in. I would hate to leave that in, because it takes it out of reality. I find the laughter quite difficult to keep it real anyway, but if it's racing along and people are concentrating, the laughs sort of go with it, but if you stop all the action, it's out of reality. It doesn't happen in real life, nobody stands still for ten seconds and waits for clapping to die down."

Chris Barrie thought Danny John-Jules playing Duane Dibbley was "hilarious", but wasn't so convinced about the return of his own character, Ace Rimmer. "It was, in a weird kind of way, an anti-climax," said Chris. "I think I would have liked to have had the same uniform and everything, and it wasn't the same wig as last time. You'd be surprised at how much difference that can make. That was a pretty good wig we used, the other wig. But the wig we had in the fourth series was a super wig, it looked like normal hair. With someone like Ace, who's got to look right, if it looks too wiggy then it looks like Chris Barrie playing this sort of character, whereas the wig was so good in series four, *Dimension Jump*, that the whole thing really had a magic about it. But it was fun to do the character again."

As for what happened to the original Ace Rimmer wig, the answer remains a mystery. All that is known is that it went 'missing' sometime after *Dimension Jump* was recorded.

Episode Five: Rimmerworld

GUEST CAST
Rogue Simulant… Liz Hickling

Story

The Starbug crew return to the simulant ship to scavenge as many supplies as they can before the unstable infrastructure breaks apart. But they didn't count on the Rogue Simulant still being there. As she holds them at gunpoint, Rimmer sneaks off to save himself and climbs into an escape pod. The others also escape, but not before Rimmer's pod has fallen through a wormhole and landed on a desolate planet. All alone, Rimmer uses the supplies he finds on the pod to create a new environment called Rimmerworld, which he populates with clones of himself. It takes six centuries for Starbug to catch up with him, by which time the generations of clones have imprisoned him for being un-Rimmer-like.

Funniest Moment (arguably)

While locked in a cell with Rimmer, Lister comes up with an elaborate escape plan which involves jumping a guard and fighting their way back to Starbug. 'Or,' says Kryten, waiting until he has finished, 'we could use the teleporter'.

Behind The Scenes

Unusually for *Red Dwarf*, the plot of Rimmerworld begins by picking up on a loose end from a previous episode — the simulant spaceship still hanging around after the exploits of *Gunmen of the Apocalypse*. It was a chance to re-use the fantastic model created by the special effects crew, before blowing it up in a spectacular manner. It was also — in the environment of recession-hit *Red Dwarf* — a chance for the crew to scavenge some supplies from the wreck. They do this using their newly-discovered teleport device.

It is on the simulant ship that Rimmer's cowardly character is revealed, when they are confronted by the rogue simulant. Believing they are all going to die, he abandons them and escapes in one of the ship's pods. This aspect of Rimmer is later magnified when he is cloned over and over again on Rimmerworld.

Meanwhile, eagle-eyed viewers will have noticed something familiar about the interior of the escape pod. It's the same set as was used for the command centre of the simulants ship in *Gunmen*. "In retrospect we should have repainted it," said production designer Mel Bibby. "But we thought it was such a small clip [in *Gunmen*] and it was shot so tight that nobody would notice. But everybody did and people wrote in: 'why is it the same ship?' Being as he stole it off the alien ship, we argued that it's a modular system."

The alien planet where the escape pod lands is a desolate wasteland. In reality, it was a gravel pit just round the corner from Shepperton Studios. "It was freezing on that sand bank, that's what I remember of that," said Chris Barrie. "Bloody freezing! The wind-chill factor, I think, was the extraordinary thing. I had thermals on underneath, but it was just a wild, windy day."

Rimmer sets about creating a civilisation by accelerating evolution using supplies on board the pod, and populating it by cloning himself. The first clone to emerge from the pod stands naked in front of him, but it didn't require any naked acting from Chris Barrie, as the man in his birthday suit was a stand-in. "It wasn't me," said Chris. "He didn't look anything like me at all. He must have been freezing, he looked quite cold, but he was a bit of a commando, he was used to that kind of thing."

Being cold was a bit of a theme when it came to locations for *Red Dwarf VI*. That's the main memory of the rest of the cast when looking back at the scene where they arrive and first meet some Rimmer clones, dressed as Roman soldiers. In the script, it was referred to as an Eden-like world, but it was actually the woods at the back of Shepperton Studios which had been used for many-a-*Red Dwarf* episode. It was also early March, as *Rimmerworld* was the third episode to be filmed, and the woodlands were dormant. Not that this mattered too much to the audience, who hadn't read the script and didn't have to endure the weather conditions.

The cloning technology employed by Rimmer meant that around every corner there was a different Rimmer — including the women! They were played by real women, with a pair of twins playing the concubines that sit either side of the emperor. Veils over their faces concealed their true Rimmer faces, only revealed when the emperor removes one of their veils to kiss her. "I had to snog myself, which looked really grim," said Chris. "It was cut quite well, it looked quite creepy, but it didn't feel creepy because I was actually kissing the girl."

The main joke of the episode is that even in a world where everyone has the same values as him, Rimmer still ends up at the bottom of the heap. His characteristics, such as cheating and cowardice, are magnified down the generations of clones and he becomes imprisoned in a world of his own making. Chris Barrie enjoyed the episode, but wished there could have been more. "I don't think there was enough time put into the Rimmerworld Emperor and those kind of people. We could have done so many super things with the concubines and all that sort of business."

They manage to escape using the teleporter which, due to a miscalculation by Kryten, takes them a little bit into the future, where they meet themselves — minus Lister. The future Rimmer tells him that something 'hideous' has happened to him. Originally, this was to have turned out to be a practical joke, as Lister was missing only because he was in the toilet. This scene was filmed, but cut, as it was decided that it was better to leave the audience wondering about Lister's fate.

Episode Six: Out of Time

GUEST CAST
None

Story

Starbug makes its way through an unreality bubble minefield to find a derelict space ship capable of time travel. They strip out the time drive, install it in Starbug and temporarily enjoy deep space in the fifteenth century before returning to the present, where they encounter their future selves. Kryten allows their future selves on board so they can copy some components of the time drive to fix their own. In their future incarnations, Rimmer is fat, Cat is balding, Kryten is wearing a toupée and Lister is a brain in a jar. They tell tales of travelling through time to sample the best food and wine and meet some of the most notorious figures in history. The present crew of Starbug are horrified, refuse to help them and shoot at them. The future, more advanced, Starbug fires back, killing Lister and the Cat, and knocking out Kryten. It means the only person left to save them is Rimmer.

Funniest Moment (arguably)

Kryten's tearful reaction to finding out Lister will become a brain in a jar.

Behind The Scenes

Red Dwarf VI was originally to end with an episode where Starbug catches up with Red Dwarf, but the idea was dropped as the script for *Out of Time* was being written. The script itself — filmed under the title *Present from the Future* — was very late. Late to the point of sending the cast home in rehearsal because they had nothing to rehearse. Half the script did eventually arrive, followed by the other half later in the week. It was at this point that the strains were really showing. Because there was no time for the cast to learn their lines, they were written on autocue and screens were hidden all over the set for them to read.

"We had a bit of help with the boards and things which is very sensible, as we saw," said Chris Barrie. "Really you should learn them, it's the best way. Mastering the art of using a prompter or a board is very different to acting. It's nice to know the line and act it one hundred per cent but if you get the scripts that late, what can you do?"

Craig Charles was the only cast member able to learn his lines for the live recording in front of the audience. Somehow he managed to do it in the hour or so between the end of rehearsal in the afternoon and the performance in the evening.

At the beginning of the episode, the effects of passing through an unreality bubble make Kryten believe that Lister is an android, leading to some fun moments where Lister is made to serve the rest of the crew. "That's something we've talked about for ages and ages," said writer Rob Grant. "We liked the idea of how that would change Kryten's attitude to him. When you get these ideas you never know if it will be good for a show or it'll just be a scene or a few scenes."

When they later meet their future selves, the original plan was for future-Lister to have become an android, one which clearly looked as if it was a mechanical body with Lister's consciousness inside. Writers Rob Grant and Doug Naylor asked the special effects department if they could make a Lister android for the episode, but with no time and no budget, Peter Wragg gave them a flat 'no'. 'How about a brain in a jar?' he suggested, and they had no option but to agree.

It was the make-up department got to work making the rest of the cast look older. The wardrobe department gave the aged Rimmer a new yellow hologram costume and a fat suit to show how much he had been enjoying the hospitality of the past. People on set said it made him look like everyone from First World War Secretary of

State, Lord Kitchener, to sports presenter Des Lynam. "The padding is hot," said Chris Barrie. "The novelty of getting the laughs and walking around like a fat git wore off…. It was quite weird seeing the ideas of aging. I'll keep those little photographs and think when I get to fifty or fifty-five or whatever, and look upon it. I think if I look like I look there, facially, it'll be all right, but I hope I don't put that much weight on!"

Danny John-Jules, as the Cat, felt he had to do more to act being old than allow hair and make-up do it for him. "I think it's all in the eyes," he said. "It happens to people you know in real life. You think 'that's not him, is it?' Then you realise you went to school with this guy in the same class — he looks like your Dad!"

There was a lot of tension on the set in that last week, especially during the scene towards the end when the crew all die. This involved Rimmer running out of the cockpit, picking up a bazookoid, running out of the door and into the corridors of Starbug. This was pre-recorded late in the day with studio time rapidly running out. Floor manager Simon Wallace was literally counting down the seconds until the lights went off. It was this sequence that produced one of the best outtakes of the series, as Rimmer tries to run through a door carrying the bazookoid sideways and is stopped short as both ends of the gun bang against the doorway because it isn't wide enough.

Come the final day of shooting, tension had eased somewhat and, in rehearsal, there was a feeling that the end was in sight. There was no worry about remembering lines — because they were all written on autocue — so there was a lot more joking around. At one point, Chris Barrie and Robert Llewellyn tried on Craig and Danny's hats. At another point, Craig discovered the sink in the kitchen area was loose, so he took it out of its mounting and wore it on his head. Danny, meanwhile, pulled his jeans halfway down his bum and did an impression of producer Justin Judd by walking around saying 'there's no money left'.

The series wrapped that night, but the ending the audience saw was not the ending that was broadcast. Originally, Rimmer continued to run through Starbug with the bazookoid to the timedrive and shoot it to pieces. Because he destroyed the timedrive, they could never use it to become the future selves they had seen. It meant future-Starbug could not have destroyed them, because the time line didn't exist — and so the crew become alive again.

To celebrate their escape from death, they celebrate with some margaritas. In rehearsal, the cast all took a sip and Craig ad-libbed that it wasn't a margarita, 'this is urine re-cyc!'. The writers heard him, thought it was funny, put it in the show and within minutes were talking to the make-up department to see if they could give all the cast foam moustaches as part of the gag. This became the ending the studio audience saw, but it wasn't the ending in the finished episode.

The decision to change the ending was made during the edit and several ideas were bandied around. One idea was to have Starbug catch up with Red Dwarf after all, and have a model shot of the two ships in space as a cliffhanger. But a better cliffhanger, they decided, was to kill everybody off and so they dropped the margarita scene. The BBC had already indicated they wanted more *Red Dwarf*, so there was every chance the cliffhanger would be resolved and the characters wouldn't be dead forever.

The special effects department was asked how much it would cost to film a shot of Starbug being blown up. A budget was drawn up, but this was more than the production could afford, and the final shot of Starbug exploding was created electronically with an explosion being superimposed over an existing model shot.

The final frames of the episode include the legend: 'to be continued…', but it was more than three years before viewers would find out how that would happen.

Red Dwarf VI Special Effects
Journey Through An Asteroid Field

This article, compiled during a visit in 1993 to the now-closed BBC workshops in Acton, details the everyday trials of the special effects team as they work to film Starbug travelling through an asteroid field for the episode Psirens *and speaks to special effects cameraman, Peter Tyler.*

Entering the BBC Special Effects Workshop in West London is like going into another world. After passing through a maze of corridors, you enter a room housing giant gnomes, toadstools and other bizarre objects from long-forgotten BBC shows. The workshop itself smells of glue and paint and is a hive of model-making activity. Dotted around the room on desks covered in obscure-looking pieces of plastic are members of the *Red Dwarf* effects team, all engrossed in building spaceships.

Further into the building lies the model stage where all the sequences set in space and on alien worlds are filmed. Inside, Starbug is suspended on wires in front of a black backdrop. The black cloth is covered in tiny holes and, when lit from behind through a white sheet of paper, it turns into a starfield. The sprawling nebulae are actually white paint sprayed onto the cloth and lit from the front by coloured lights. When the coloured lights are switched off, the nebulae disappear.

In previous years, each element of a sequence would be filmed separately and then merged together using a process called 'matting'. This would usually involve the camera making all the movements to simulate travelling through space, as opposed to moving the ship. But that method has been scrapped for the effects shots in *Red Dwarf VI*, as cameraman Peter Tyler explained: "We're doing everything in one go, we're not matting anything at the moment. Whereas before we used to shoot a spaceship against black, make a travelling mat of it and then put the stars on separately. That takes much longer. What we're doing now, we're doing everything in front of this star backing, and hanging the models on wires."

The reason for changing the method of filming is down to *Red Dwarf*'s tight budget and schedule. There are more shots to film for the sixth series and a limited amount of time. "It's about twice as much this year and half the money," said Peter. "We spent thirty-four days shooting last year and this year so far we're fifteen days in, which is half the time. But we will go to about twenty-five days I reckon, which is ten days less. So it is less — less time, less money, more shots."

Although the sequences look dramatic on screen, they appear very different when they are being filmed because everything is done very slowly. For most of the shots, the camera is run at around four frames per second, as opposed to the normal running speed of twenty-four frames per second. The camera and the crane, which holds the model Starbug, are both controlled by a computer. A program determines how both of them will move during a sequence, to create the shot.

Using wires may save on filming time, but they cause an additional set of problems. The wires can sometimes shine under studio lights, which would spoil the illusion of being in space and ruin the shot. This is solved by Peter Tyler's little pot of magic paint. Any time he spots one of the wires shining, he approaches it armed with the paint pot and sprays mat-black powder paint onto the wires, which will hopefully disguise them.

The other problem is that wires wobble. If the spaceships are wobbling when they are filmed, especially when filming so slowly, it will look shaky when it is played back at the correct speed. Peter denied this alternative method of filming would affect the quality of the special effects shots. "No," he said definitely. "It's more difficult. We're still using motion-control, we're using a computer to run the axis which moves the model on its wires, but as you've seen, we've had a lot of problems with getting the wires to settle out, stop swing-ing about, so that's slowed us down a bit." Each time a shot is set up, they have to leave the model stage to let the wires settle down. This means they get more tea breaks, but it is a frustratingly slow process.

In the sequence where Starbug is flying through an asteroid field, even more wires have to be employed. The small rocks, made out of painted polystyrene, are threaded onto wires suspended between two poles, like a washing line, while some of the larger asteroids in the foreground are stuck onto poles.

It has taken Peter Tyler and his assistant Colin Watkinson, about a day to set up the asteroids before any filming can begin, which is indicative of how much work goes into creating an intricate shot like this: "It's all more complex this year," said Peter. "Like, this shot is just ridiculously complicated. When it ends up on screen they'll probably use about four seconds of it. It's taken us nearly a day to do it, but it's in the script so you've got to do it."

Even though the process of turning a few words of descrip-tion in a *Red Dwarf* script into something which will be shown on screen is time-consuming, it represents only a fraction of the time companies like George Lucas's Industrial Light and Magic (who have produced effects for everything from *Star Wars* to *Star Trek: The Next Generation*) would take to do a similar shot for a feature film. "We couldn't do it any other way," said Peter. "The traditional way, the ILM way of doing this, is to shoot most of those asteroids separately and matte them all together and spend a couple of weeks doing one shot, but we're not ILM, so we can't do that."

The sequence where Starbug travels through the asteroids is filmed several times to make sure they get the shot in the can, but the number of times they would normally film a sequence varies, as Peter explained. "It depends how much it wobbles!" he laughed. "If it doesn't wobble at all we just do one, if it looks like it's wobbling we do another one to try and make it better."

After they finish filming one sequence, the model stage has to be re-set for Starbug to be filmed flying through a different part of the asteroid field. Fortunately, this doesn't take too long as it just involves moving the asteroids around a bit and changing the camera angle.

The shot description in the script is: 'a tiny Starbug flies between a group of asteroids, all with wrecked spacecraft embedded in them'; however the budget doesn't stretch to building several spaceships specially for one tiny shot. Most of the ships are more famous for appearing in other programmes and have been borrowed from other places, notably Peter's private model collection. One of the model ships is from *Aliens* and was made from "a really nasty kit'. *Star Trek* fans may be able to spot a Klingon ship in the background. And other eagle-eyed viewers may recognise a ship from *Space 1999*. According to Peter, the large ship in the foreground has been knocking around for ages: "That's been used on all sorts of things," he said, "*Blake's 7* originally, and *Doctor Who*." A less-famous ship suspended from a wire at the back was designed by Peter himself for a film he made at college. And the ship embedded in the asteroid near the camera? "That's a bit of the Klingon ship," he said, "a bit that broke off."

As Peter is making the final adjustments to the asteroids and spaceships, he hits his head on one of the wires. All the polystyrene rocks and plastic spaceships start bouncing around like a collection of washing lines in a gale-force wind. It will take a long tea break before they settle down again!

For the beginning of this shot, Peter puts Starbug very close to the camera so it starts very large in the frame, before blasting off into the distance. He said he would have liked more freedom to film intricate and interesting shots, but that hasn't been possible this year. "I had intended to have more dramatic angles of Starbug going into the asteroids. Starbug would have been bigger in frame at the start and had more depth, but it's just so much time to rig, which is time we haven't got."

The Starbug being filmed among the asteroids is medium-sized, and one of a collection of five. As well as a second medium-sized ship, there are two bigger models for closer shots — one of which is used for crashing. There is one smaller one which is used for long shots where Starbug has to look really small, but Peter insisted you can't tell they are different once they are on film. "They're all identical," he said.

The medium-sized model is also more versatile. For an overhead shot, it is just suspended on its side from a couple of wires. The larger models are too heavy for that sort of thing, as the wires find it a strain even at a normal angle. Peter supervised most of the shots that involved the larger model by walking behind it just out of shot. This saved a lot of heartache during the early stages of filming when Starbug over-balanced, and he caught it just microseconds before it smashed to pieces on the ground.

About halfway through the effects filming schedule there have been a few near-disasters, but Peter seems reasonably pleased with the results. "One or two [shots] look a little bit shabby," he said. "Not too bad. Well, a bit simplistic, maybe, but there's no choice really. Like on this shot, it would have been nice to have the engines glowing, but that would be another run." The ship has to be filmed twice making the exact same movements; once with the engine lights switched on and once with them off. The two images are then merged to show the engines glowing. "We put the engines on separately to make them a lot brighter and have a filter in front of the lens to make them glow. It makes them a lot more interesting, [but it takes] twice the time to shoot it, and if it wobbled the second time we'd have to start again."

The major problem facing the effects crew is the number of difficult shots they have to do. "There's nothing been simple yet," said Peter. "Sometimes [in previous series] we just had a shot in a hangar or something, with landing something and that's quite easy to do. There's nothing like that this year, because the basic way the series has gone has changed a lot. There's no Red Dwarf, so there's no landing or taking off in the hangar, which used to be stock footage we shot a couple of years ago. There's none of that, so all the stock footage has to be re-generated, has to be different. I suppose that's why we've got a lot more shots."

A chart in the office by the model stage details the progress of the *Red Dwarf VI* model shots. Each shot is represented by a pencil sketch. Those that have a red tick beside them have already been filmed, but at the halfway stage, less than half had been ticked off. It's almost certainly down to the skill and dedication of the effects team that the model shots for *Red Dwarf VI* were, in fact, completed (almost!) on time.

Red Dwarf VI Special Effects
The Lava Planet

This article was written following a visit to the BBC Special Effects workshop in London when the Red Dwarf *team were filming the spectacular lava planet sequences which appear in the episode,* Gunmen of the Apocalypse *and includes an interview with the late* Red Dwarf *special effects designer, Peter Wragg.*

Starbug dives screaming from an orange sky into a mass of gooey lava. Then with a giant "yee-hah", it emerges from the red lava lake and blasts off into the sunset. And so ends *Gunmen of the Apocalypse*.

But that wasn't the original ending. Early drafts of the script had Starbug crashing into water. Water, thought the writers, would be easy to shoot because it's freely available and has appeared on *Red Dwarf* before. But using water in a model shot can be a dead giveaway because water droplets stay the same size no matter how big the model ship is. The script was changed after the protestations of special effects designer, Peter Wragg.

"Water gives us greater problems," said Peter. "Water's got its own scale and there's nothing you can do about that. And to get Starbug to disappear into water would be almost impossible because water is very dense and Starbug would have to be made out of cast iron for it not to break up the minute it hits water at that sort of speed."

Halfway through the day that Starbug's descent into lava is to be filmed, and the set still looks like a junior school model display. The planet's sky is a painted backdrop hired for the occasion and the planet's surface is made from a group of polystyrene rocks. One of the visual effects crew is hard at work painting the 'rocks', trying to make them look less like polystyrene and more like volcanic formations.

The lava lake isn't finished either, it's still a wooden tray with a perspex bottom. The lava is being made with industrial food thickener in another room, while the base of the wooden tray is covered with orange and yellow polythene. The lava is then poured in and lit from below, so it glows orange.

Finishing touches to the lava lake are achieved by building rocks around the edge of the tray using crinkled black aluminium foil. Special effects cameraman Peter Tyler urges the team to be sparing with the foil because it costs fifty pounds a roll — "from my camera budget!"

Peter Tyler's ironic motto for the day is "cameramen aren't supposed to get their hands dirty", which he repeats several times while he is up to his elbows in industrial food thickener, adding the final touches to the lake.

"It wouldn't be possible to get it done if there wasn't the commitment of the boys," said Peter Wragg, as preparation for the day's filming dragged into the evening. "Everyone's commitment is really terrific which helps to make it all happen and hopefully makes everything as good as it does."

The lava lake begins to take shape as rubber dust and pieces of brown cork are sprinkled on top of it like floating bits of volcanic rock.

When most of the scene is set up, they need to check the trajectory of Starbug to make sure it falls into the lake without crashing on the rocks. To do this, a flat polystyrene model of the ship is hoisted up to the ceiling on a wire and allowed to sail down onto the planet. From the camera's point of view, it appears to land in the lava lake, but in reality it disappears into a concealed hole in the 'floor' of the planet.

To make the planet look extra volcanic, they have decided to have flames shooting into the sky. The fire comes from several metal tubes — somewhat like Bunsen burners — which throw flames into the air when a blast of gas is blown through them.

"The flames are something we're doing ourselves just to try and make it look a bit more interesting," explained Peter. "I mean, at the end of the day, we're making a rod for our own back. Then that's what you're doing most of the time, making a rod for your own back by trying to add a bit more and do something a bit different."

When the flames are tested out they burst very high into the air, enough to singe the eyebrows of anyone standing too near to them. James, who has set them up, is told to turn the gas down a bit before setting something on fire! The flames look great, especially as they also shower sparks into the air. This wasn't by design, but happened by accident when some of the rubber dust on the lava lake was inadvertently sprinkled inside the tubes.

When the finishing touches to the set are completed, it is time to bring in the Starbug model. The ship's descent onto the planet is achieved by putting Starbug on a wire right at the top of the ceiling. Once they let go, it is supposed to sail down the wire and disappear into the lava lake. It is filmed at five times normal speed, so it looks more realistic when played back.

Mike Tucker, who helped build the Starbug models, warns that the ship is likely to break up on impact, so they'll have to be prepared to get it right the first time. However, as a precaution, he brings in a couple of pillows which he puts on the floor to cushion Starbug's landing.

"Ninety per cent of it is crossing your fingers," explained Peter Wragg. "You've worked out everything that you think might happen, then at the end of the day you cross your fingers and hope for the best. Shooting at 120 frames, you never know quite what you've got until you see rushes the following day."

Everyone gets set up for the big moment. One person is by the lava lake, sloshing it about gently to make it look as if it is flowing, Peter Tyler is behind the camera, Nick Kool is standing by with his finger on the flame-thrower button, Mike Tucker is standing on the gantry high up by the ceiling holding onto Starbug, and Peter Wragg is directing it all from behind the camera. When the camera starts rolling, Peter Wragg will call to Nick to fire off one of the flames, then to Mike to let go of Starbug, and again to Nick to fire off another flame.

The camera turns over. Peter Wragg shouts "Nick! Mike! Nick!" one after the other. Flames burst into the air and Starbug sails down the wire, bounces off one of the polystyrene mountains and lands well away from the carefully positioned pillows. It is all over in a fraction of a second.

One of the effects team retrieves Starbug from where it has crashed and broken into two pieces. It has to be glued back together before they can re-assess the ship's trajectory and try again.

"It's nice to be left to do all this," Peter Wragg said, looking at the impressive volcanic planet. "We are given a lot of trust, I suppose, in just getting it done because no one knows what we're shooting… Andy [DeEmmony, the director] keeps saying he would desperately like to get down here and see what we're doing because he hasn't seen anything, he hasn't seen what's happening. He's just seen the tapes that I deliver and say 'this is what we've done'… It's probably a new experience for Andy this year, having to go through the waiting and see whether the shots live up to what he's been expecting of them.

"It's all looking very good," Peter continued, "but ideally we would have another day, so we'd shoot this as a test, see rushes, see if we wanted to change anything, then do it again the following day. That's what we'd do ideally — shoot a test first — but we haven't got that luxury."

In the second attempt to film the sequence, Starbug successfully journeys onto the planet without hitting any of the mountains. It happens so fast that there is no way to tell if it's going to look all right. As it turned out, when they got the film back from the developers the following day, the flames looked totally out of scale and they had to re-film it. They replaced the flames with bubbling lava, which was achieved by blowing through tubes hidden at the bottom of the lava tray.

That first day of filming finished at around midnight with the crew well on their way to achieving one hundred model shots. "We'll get to one hundred slates and there will be a bottle of champagne at least," laughed Peter Wragg.

"It's a fairly standard thing on shoots that on slate one hundred, champagne comes out," he added. "It doesn't normally happen on model filming because you don't normally get to slate one hundred, but we're up to slate ninety-one now and I think everyone's determined to get to slate one hundred, come what may!"

Two days later, they had well exceeded their one hundred target — a first for a *Red Dwarf* series! That evening, they downed two bottles of champagne between them to celebrate the end of what had been a hard, but successful time making the special effects for *Red Dwarf VI*.

Red Dwarf VII

Executive Producer... Doug Naylor
Written by... Doug Naylor with Paul Alexander, Kim Fuller,
Robert Llewellyn, James Hendrie
Produced & Directed by... Ed Bye

Rimmer... Chris Barrie
Lister... Craig Charles
Cat... Danny John-Jules
Kryten... Robert Llewellyn
Kochanski... Chloë Annett

Recorded: May-August 1996
Audience viewing (laughter track): October 1996
First broadcast: January-March 1997

Fans had to wait for more than three years to get their next fix of
Red Dwarf, and they were lucky to get it at all. All sorts of problems
intervened after *Red Dwarf VI* ended and, for a while, it seemed that
no more episodes would ever be made. The writing partnership of

Rob Grant and Doug Naylor split up, Craig Charles had some highly publicised personal problems and Chris Barrie was making noises about not wanting to do it.

It is almost certainly down to the determination of writer and executive producer Doug Naylor that *Red Dwarf VII* got made, and got made in a very different manner to the way it had been made in the past. He set out with a clear idea, not only of how to get everyone back on board to work on the series, but also of what he wanted the new series to be like.

"I wanted it to survive and for it not to be awful," said Doug Naylor. "I wanted Kochanski to come in and affect the whole chemistry and re-define everyone's relationship. I wanted to get back to the early dialogue-based *Red Dwarf*s when it's not the monster-of-the week and we're coming across a derelict with something weird on it and we'd be swirly-thing alerts and lots of stuff in the cockpit. I wanted to find Red Dwarf, but not until the end of the series. I wanted to get Kryten away from being that kind of know-all exposition character where he just looks at the psi-scan and tells you everything — I always thought he was so funny and if he could just be funny, he could be funnier."

Doug Naylor had been left holding the baby after Rob Grant decided he didn't want to work on *Red Dwarf* anymore. The pair of them had been friends since childhood and spent their entire writing career as a team. But the last few years of working together had been incredibly intense and, it seemed, their partnership couldn't survive. The previous series had seen the pair of them work under immense pressure to deliver the scripts. It was followed almost immediately by writing and directing a mainstream sitcom pilot, *The 10%ers*. That pilot was successful enough to be commissioned for a whole series, but Rob Grant decided, at this point, to pull out of the writing partnership, leaving Doug in charge of the Grant Naylor production company.

Nobody seems to know the full reasons for the split, but former *Red Dwarf* producer, Paul Jackson, perhaps expressed it best on the television documentary, *Comedy Connections*. "I think it was very sad that two people who were so close and such good friends, just at the moment of their greatest success, suddenly, for some reason that — I don't know anybody who knows the reason — couldn't talk to each other."

Suddenly out on his own, Doug decided to go ahead with a new series of *Red Dwarf* and draft in new writers to help. "The plan was — and it's a perfectly good and sensible plan — if there's going to be more *Red Dwarf* series you don't want to write them all, so get a writing team who can write them. You put together the writing team and it can go on for years, and that's what the cast wants and wouldn't that be good?"

The plan, however, didn't turn out as well as he had hoped. "It was very difficult to find the team who wanted to do it and who were available and who could write the plots," said Doug. "Getting them to do plots has been very difficult. It was made more difficult because we've got a new character and the chemistry's slightly changed and they couldn't get their heads round something that they hadn't seen… I remember being in a restaurant in December talking about a script with a writer and then doing a massive re-write on it nine months later, thinking: 'what's happened in the first nine months? Why do we not have a script that's in a good stage to shoot now?'. That was one example of the script where it was almost a year in the writing."

The new character was, of course, Kochanski. But not the Kochanski who had appeared in previous episodes — played by Clare (C.P.) Grogan — but a new actress, Chloë Annett. Unlike the rest of the cast, she came from a traditional acting background and had a list of credits to her name, including a co-starring role in the BBC's time travel detective drama, *Crime Traveller*. Her job was a difficult one: to fit in with a very close-knit and established cast. "I was very excited about the job and I was looking forward to it," said Chloë. "It was slightly nerve-racking, obviously, because it had been going for years and they knew each other and they were all funny and I wasn't! But it's been great, the best fun I've had in a long time."

"I really felt sorry for her, it's a tough gig to have to do," said Robert Llewellyn, who had many scenes playing Kryten alongside her. "But she can hold her own and she's very funny and rude. And she's so good on the screen. If there was a scene that she was in and I wasn't and I could sit and watch, [I could see] she just burns off that screen. She's a natural. I think she has less experience of comic acting than the rest of us, and certainly of stand-up comedy like Craig and I have got. She was intimidated by the fact that she thought we knew everything about comedy, but she's such a natural. She's got something. The best thing is when people aren't aware of it, that always makes it better. So she'll do something and we'll all be cacking ourselves laughing and she says 'what?'. I always say 'don't think about it, just carry on, it doesn't matter, you're just doing it'. You don't need to know why or what it is, as long as you can do it again, that's all that matters."

One of the reasons for bringing in Kochanski as a regular cast member was to prepare for a potential *Red Dwarf* movie (likely to be financed by American backers who wanted a woman in the cast). The second was because Chris Barrie had decided not to do most of the series and the loss of Rimmer left a void. "She was never intended to replace Rimmer," said Doug Naylor, "because I always expected Chris to come back. It would, in many ways, be so much easier to go 'oh the hologram's face has changed' and re-cast someone else as Rimmer and we know that chemistry works and it will be fine. But I didn't want to do that because I expected Chris to be back."

Chris Barrie, having spoken out about the way *Red Dwarf VI* had been made, was reluctant to do any more. But, after discussions with Doug Naylor, agreed to come back for a limited time. Clever writing saw him stay as part of the Starbug crew for two whole episodes, while he made guest appearances in a further two.

"At the time, when the offer came and the contract came I didn't fancy doing another twelve weeks working in the way that we did before," said Chris. "It was something to do with series four, five and six when we moved to Shepperton. I thought at the time… we were trying to produce something more than a sitcom, but without the facilities that sitcoms had. I was doing *Brittas* at the time, which is a very straight forward situation comedy; you've got the TV studio with the TV gantry and it's all very straight forward to do. We had moved to a film studio in series four of this [*Red Dwarf*] and we were trying to do little films, but it had to be sitcom, because of the nature of the show. The whole thing didn't fit and I just found it a little bit uncomfortable, I just thought I didn't want to be involved at the time. But I never said; 'no I'm out of *Red Dwarf* forever and ever and ever.'"

One of the things which enticed Chris Barrie to come back for the series, albeit in a small way, was the decision not to film in front of an audience. It was a dangling carrot which Doug Naylor used to tempt many people back to *Red Dwarf* after the hiatus.

Returning director, Ed Bye, already knew it was possible, having directed another comedy series for the BBC without a studio audience. *The Detectives*, starring Jasper Carrott and Robert Powell was shot like a drama, using a single camera rather than multiple cameras in a sitcom-style studio setting.

But the decision to apply the technique to *Red Dwarf* was not one he took lightly. "I was slightly worried about it because a lot of the performances in sitcom are influenced by the audience," said Ed. "But, to be honest, these guys have been doing it for such a long time and are so professional that once they got that mind-set, it was fine. They knew there was an invisible audience out there so they worked to it. It didn't make it easier, but it made it easier to make it look the way it does without the audience. And it helped a lot with the performances as well. It took a lot of pressure [off. They weren't thinking] 'oh I've got to get it right by the third time or they're going to boo me.'"

It also helped with that other long-running concern on *Red Dwarf*: money. "There's a lot of invisible money that disappears when you've got an audience," said Ed. "One of the things about having an audience is it does mean that half the studio is not available to you because an audience is sitting there, so we've got half a studio that we could use to make the sets bigger. And the other thing is you make it glossier by lighting in a different way because you don't have to light for an audience. Normally, a set is flat across the studio wall and the audience is the other side, but with this we could make a set all twist around on itself. Also shooting without an audience means you can chop and change your shooting days around a bit so we could spend a little bit more time shooting outside the studio than we would normally have, which gave us the opportunity to go to some sexy locations."

The decision was a hit with the cast, but it was a different way of filming and it meant they couldn't be certain how much of it was funny until the finished episodes were shown. "It was very different and the first couple of weeks it took a lot of getting used to," said Robert Llewellyn. "When we were out on location then that's the same as it's always been, but when we were in the studio, I kept looking round the set to see where the audience were and there was nobody there. And also when you did lines that we knew, from experience on *Red Dwarf*, would be a big laugh and there was absolute silence, you have to leave a gap. After a couple of weeks I was really into it because you could concentrate so much more and the intimacy, particularly in scenes with me and Craig, were done very small and tight, one little camera on you, two people there and you're in a little room, you could really go small."

"Doing it in front of an audience is a bit like doing exams

sometimes," said Craig Charles, who was back playing Lister. "You've got two or three chances — at the most — to make it, then the audience wants you to move on, so the performances always suffer. It also means you can light it better, it looks better, the performances are more considered and if you get it wrong, you can go back and do it again."

The cast also enjoyed having Ed Bye back with them. His involvement in the first four series of *Red Dwarf* had helped shape the programme and, no matter how good other directors who came in might have been, he had been missed. "There's this enormous affection and respect for him from all the cast," said Doug Naylor. "He's so good at doing both sides of it, he's very good on the comedy, but he's also very good with them individually. He was the first person I went to when I knew there was going to be another series. It would have been a very difficult situation working with a director I hadn't worked with before, I couldn't have coped with that."

For Danny John-Jules, who was back playing the Cat, it helped having someone familiar in charge. "Ed was definitely a big inspiration, he always has been," said Danny. "It was like having the full crew back. Ed had to constantly convince us because we've never been down that road before, so he had to keep saying 'it's going to be great' and reminding us to keep our spirits up because obviously you do miss the audience. For the first couple of days, I was lost."

Things did go wrong during the making of the series, of course — it wouldn't have been *Red Dwarf* if they didn't — and money was just as tight as it had always been. The production had been able to get a larger commission out of the BBC, for eight episodes instead of the usual six, but early episodes like *Tikka to Ride* and *Stoke Me a Clipper* looked lavish compared to later and budget-challenged episodes like *Epideme* and *Nanarchy*. There were also huge problems with the special effects model shots which were filmed in the middle of production and, because scripts were changed in the meantime, no longer fitted the episodes. A last minute call to computer graphics artist Chris Veale was able to produce some hastily created visual effects, but with hardly any time and ninety-five per cent of the effects budget already spent, his efforts were not appreciated by many in the audience.

Doug Naylor, having worked hard on making the series, was conscious of the weight of expectation on his shoulders. He clearly felt he had put his reputation on the line by returning to do *Red Dwarf* without his long-term script partner Rob Grant. "I knew if it fails I'm in big, big trouble," he said. "I promised Craig when he was having his problems that we would do another series and so I was always honour-bound to do that. And I thought that I'm secure enough to know about my contribution in the first six series. Whatever anybody says or what anybody thinks, I know I wrote a couple of jokes in the first six series and if this is hopeless and a complete disaster, well so what? The fans will always say 'he's the complete talentless jerk', but there's nothing I can do about that."

The cast, however, were more optimistic. Danny John-Jules, for one, wasn't going to take any negative comments from fans. "What more do they want?" he said. "Chris is in it, Craig, Robert, myself, we're all there, and the original director's back. We've re-invented Kochanski — I don't see what more anyone could ask for. I think a lot of people thought that because Rob and Doug had parted ways that it would go down the Swanee. But I think the series has aged and progressed at the same time. You cannot do a show for ten years and things not change."

Craig Charles agreed. "I was concerned about it because Rob wasn't involved in it and Chris was only doing four," he said. "It was like people leaving a sinking ship or something. No offence to Rob Grant, but I was really concerned about him being missed. Then I read the scripts and I thought, 'these are as funny episodes as we've ever done!'… It's weird because when we got together it was like we had never been away. We were very conscious of the fact that people were waiting to write our obituaries — well, people have been writing mine for years! — so we just didn't want to give them the satisfaction. It had to be good, really."

Robert Llewellyn also remembered having nerves at the beginning, but these were swept away as he performed the material. "I think we were all slightly reticent at the beginning because we had no idea it was going to work," he said. "It had been such a long time, we've all got a bit older and done a lot of other things and it was sort of like, 'are we going to get on? Is it going to work? Is it going to fire off?' I think for the first couple of weeks, which was all OBs [outside broadcasts], all bitty things, it was 'Ooh God!'. I couldn't remember how to do the walk, I didn't know how to do the voice — I just couldn't remember it! I couldn't remember any of the lines, but then it just started to click back in. And when we did some scenes in the studio it was magic. I suddenly went 'oh I remember why I did this, this is fun.'"

"Now I only remember the good bits," Robert concluded. "I remember the enjoyment of doing really good scenes that raced along, and just forget the fact that I had a rubber head on and my temperature was one thousand and seven centigrade."

Episode One: Tikka to Ride

Written by... Doug Naylor

GUEST CAST
John F Kennedy... Michael J. Shannon
Lee Harvey Oswald... Tony Aspin
FBI Agent... Peter Gaitens
Cop... Robert Ashe

Story

Lister wants to go back in time to order a large supply of curries, but Kryten won't let him because of the risk of changing history. So Lister replaces Kryten's head with Spare Head Two, removes his inhibitions and persuades him to take them all back in time. But, due to a miscalculation, they end up in Dallas in 1963 and accidentally stop US President John F Kennedy from being assassinated. It re-writes the future, meaning there was never a Red Dwarf and they have no Starbug to return to. They try to make it possible for Oswald to carry out the fatal shot, but fail. The only way to solve the problem is to get John F Kennedy to assassinate himself.

Funniest Moment (arguably)

Lister beams into the Texas Book Depository, steps backwards and knocks Lee Harvey Oswald out of the window.

Behind The Scenes

The assassination of President Kennedy in 1963 is one of history's 'what if' moments. Many have speculated what would have happened if he had not been killed on that day in November 1963, and here that classic idea is used in typical *Red Dwarf* fashion.

Recreating an historical event which is so etched in people's minds was not an easy task. Archive footage of the president's motorcade travelling through the streets and the panic as the shots rang out is very well known, and recreating that was always going to be a challenge — especially on a *Red Dwarf* budget. But some clever staging by director Ed Bye managed to achieve it beyond expectations.

A car was hired, Michael J Shannon was booked to play President Kennedy and extras were strategically placed, matching the positions of the real people from the motorcade. The costume department dressed a small number of extras in clothes matching those worn by the crowd in the archive footage, and they were filmed up close to give the impression that there were more of them than there really were. Director Ed Bye was thrilled at how much they were able to make it look like the real thing. "It was tough because if it hadn't been sunny, we would have been really shagged!" he laughed. "We did a lot of research, Doug and I spent a lot of time pouring over archives and books and everything else and it was just getting all the little bits right. It was quite tough. And also, Dallas was full of hundreds of thousands of people. But a few things landed us on our feet. Kennedy was actually shot towards the end of the cavalcade so there weren't actually that many people there so we could recreate it pretty accurately.

"In actual fact, I originally put that in as a cut to black and white to make it look more realistic, but it actually looked as if I'd stolen a piece of footage and bunged it in! So I put it back to colour again."

The weather was kind to them and the Dallas scenes were shot in bright sunshine under blue skies, avoiding the cold and damp conditions that had been so obvious in previous episodes such as *Meltdown* and *Better than Life*. Most of these scenes were filmed at Farnborough Airport, which doubled extraordinarily well for Texas. The runway gave them a clear space to shoot the motorcade, while some old empty buildings looked suitably like 1960s America to film the street scene afterwards.

"It was hard but we were lucky," said Ed Bye afterwards. "We got good weather and the crew were great. The guy who played Kennedy was excellent too. The assassination scene at the end I'm particularly pleased with because that *had* to work. If that fell a bit flat the whole story would have been a bit flat because it's a dramatic moment: there's nothing funny about shooting the President."

Not that it was all plain sailing. Filming at airports has its own difficulties. "[That] was quite funny," said Robert Llewellyn, "because every time they said 'action' three fighter jets would come in to land right over our heads! Chris [Barrie] said he thought they were flying round above, waiting until we started, and then they'd say 'Delta Tango Charlie, they've just said 'action', come in to land!'"

The scene of John F Kennedy being transferred to a prison van at Idlewild Airport was shot at RAF Farnborough, while other inserts were filmed at the luxurious location of the carpark at Shepperton Studios. This included the scenes of the crew looking out of the window of the Texas School Book Depository, which was a set. "*Tikka to Ride* was probably about the biggest," said production designer Mel Bibby about his work on *Red Dwarf VII*. "Because we had to build the book depository, treat it in the studio and then move it outside. Peter Morgan, the lighting director, didn't want to try and create daylight so we moved it out into the outside lot and shot it in daylight."

Earlier sequences were filmed in an enormous wind tunnel outside Farnborough. Director Ed Bye was always on the lookout for good locations for *Red Dwarf* and, having found this one, decided he could use it for Starbug's cargo area.

"That was just staggering," said Robert Llewellyn. "It was a wind tunnel which is a sixty-foot diameter white steel tube with a fan at the end of it. I don't know how big the fan was — enormous. Just the quality of the picture and the image. What you see on the telly is like a tube with a fan in it and then suddenly this door opens and these four figures walk down and that's us coming down this ladder.

To be in this place was just staggering… They can make the wind in this thing go up to Mach Five, we were told, which is five thousand miles an hour. Luckily they didn't turn it on while we were there because we'd be mashed up."

It certainly looks impressive on screen. "It looks like something out of a big movie," said Danny John-Jules. "I was looking back at that picture raw without any treatment or anything and just going 'ahh, that looks like a movie.'"

Craig Charles thought it was a great place to play around. "I'm a bit of a nutter," he said. "I was seeing how high you could get, running and jumping to see how high you could get. It killed me! Not as if I was going to let anyone know. I spent the whole day filming in agony, but it was my own fault for acting silly beggars. You know sometimes your elbow pops out and you have a big lump on your arm? I had a big lump on my arm all day. So there, that'll teach me for not growing up."

Earlier on in the episode, things started with the usual introduction and daily life aboard Starbug. First, there was the little problem of the last series' cliffhanger and the fact that the crew had all appeared to die. The explanation given by Lister as to what happened was similar to the original ending filmed (but not shown) for *Out of Time*: that, by destroying Starbug, their future selves destroyed the time drive and changed the future, meaning they would not be able to go back in time and kill themselves.

There had, after all, been more than three years between *Red Dwarf VI* and *VII*, and everyone just wanted to get on with new stories. These included Kryten having his guilt chip removed: meaning he had no qualms about using his groinal attachment to stir the crew's tea. The sequence worked well, which was somewhat of a relief to Robert Llewellyn. "I think the groinal attachment seemed alright," he said. "When I first got that, I went: 'we can't get away with that, that is disgusting, I don't want my children to see this, truly obscene!'"

Something that went less well, however, was a plan for Kryten to appear 'naked'. The idea was that he had so few inhibitions, that he didn't think there was any problems with walking around Starbug in just a pair of Bermuda shorts. But the pink nude suit turned out to be the wrong shade of pink, as it had been matched to the colour of Kryten's gloves, which turned out to be different to his mask. For the actor underneath, there was also an issue of making it fit. "I cannot tell you how hot I was, ten times more than usual — and it didn't work! That's why you don't see it. It was no one's fault, it was just technically beyond the limit of what we can do at the moment. One day it will be possible and I will be even hotter and more uncomfortable than I can dream, but the amount of effort that went into that! That's what you don't see on the screen. There's me standing there with five men trying to zip the back up and sellotape it and put straps on it and then we go 'all right, forget it' and hours and hours of work is put to one side discreetly."

Other work which had to be put aside were some extra scenes which were filmed but lost in the edit because of the pressures of time. Among them were an extra dialogue scene in Starbug's cockpit with Lister talking about a dodgy curry that once stopped him getting off with a girl, and more discussion about the dead man found on the streets of Dallas. These moments were restored in a DVD release along with newly created (and much better) CGI effects, and an extra sequence at the end.

The extra sequence reunited Chris Barrie, Craig Charles and Robert Llewellyn for a new ending which showed Lister going back in time to stock up on curry by stealing Starbug's own supplies. There's also an explanation as to why they can't use the timedrive to go back to Earth to live in their own time period. This was the ending that had been in earlier versions of the script, but was cut because the script was too long.

The broadcast version of *Tikka to Ride* was, arguably, the best episode of *Red Dwarf VII*. It certainly impressed the cast the first time they saw it at a press screening to launch the series. "Looks great, doesn't it?" said Craig Charles. "I'm really pleased. I hope everyone's reaction is as honest as mine. I came with an open mind to see if I was impressed by it and I think it's the best thing we've done. Exceptional quality for the budget of a sitcom… I'm just so glad I'm still involved. I'm so glad I said 'yeah, I'll do it.'"

Episode Two: Stoke Me A Clipper

Written by... Paul Alexander and Doug Naylor

GUEST CAST
The King... Brian Cox
Captain Vorhese... Ken Morley
Queen... Sarah Alexander
Good Knight... John Thompson
Princess Bonjella... Alison Senior
Lieutenant... Mark Carlisle
Gestapo Officer... Mark Lingwood
Soldiers... Kai Maurer, Stephen Grothgar, Andy Gell

Story

Ace Rimmer returns! Fresh from escaping from Nazis, he's been hit by a bullet and is on the way out. He needs another Rimmer to take his place and looks to his parallel dimension self to take over the Ace mantle. But the cowardly Rimmer doesn't think he has what it takes to take over the heroic role — even after training. So Ace secretly recruits Lister to boost Rimmer's confidence and, after Ace dies, Lister takes Rimmer to see the coffins of all the other Rimmers who became Ace before him.

Funniest Moment (arguably)

As two German soldiers watch Ace Rimmer escape they are squashed by a falling crocodile.

Behind The Scenes

When it was known Chris Barrie wanted to leave *Red Dwarf* (at least for the seventh series), but would agree to a limited amount of filming, it was decided to send him off in style. Ace Rimmer had always been a favourite character for the actor, as it was for the fans and the writers, so it was the obvious choice.

The episode, filmed under the working title of *Natural Born Rimmers*, begins with some heroic action from Ace Rimmer. Director Ed Bye remembered the genesis of this idea came from his and the writers' love of James Bond. "It was such a long time ago that the Bond movie [*Golden Eye*] was quite recent then and the lovely idea of Bond movies is they always had insane stunt work at the beginning of the film. We wanted to do our own version of that, but tongue-in-cheek."

Like many of the scripts, *Stoke Me A Clipper* went through a series of changes. At one stage, the opening sequence was to be set on board a simulant ship with Ace escaping on the back of an alien. In the end, it was decided to go for something more Earth-bound and reminiscent of World War II action movies.

Chris Barrie, naturally, loved it. And it made him change his mind about leaving *Red Dwarf*. "I really wanted to come back after we started to make this because all the new ways of making the show were so good," he said. "That first sequence of *Stoke Me A Clipper* was one of the most exciting things ever to have been done. It really is good, it worked wonderfully. And working with people like [special effects designer] Peter Wragg who we'd worked with for years, and Ed and Doug it just felt so wonderful, as if *Red Dwarf* had come of age and has a whole future."

Just as *Tikka to Ride* had replicated 1960s Dallas, the opening of *Stoke Me a Clipper* doubled convincingly as Europe in the 1940s. The exterior scenes, where Princess Bonjella was rescued, were filmed at RAF Northolt on a cold and damp day, giving the scenes an authentic touch. Adding to the authenticity were two German actors, Kai Maurer and Stephen Grothgar, who were hired to play the Nazi soldiers with the most German dialogue, while Ken Morley (who played Vorhese, the Nazi in the plane) looked very much the part as he had played a German officer in Second World War sitcom *'Allo 'Allo*. He had also reminded the casting director of Goldfinger in the *James Bond* movies and did an excellent job of stroking his pet crocodile as if it were a fluffy white cat. "That was great fun," said director Ed Bye, "and that crocodile was real, you know. Actually the crocodile gets a credit at the end of the show. She's called Allison, a very fine actress!"

She does, indeed, get a credit at the end of the episode, with a "special thanks to London Zoo", even though the entire sequence of Allison in the plane, being wrestled by Ace and being used as a surfboard to reach Vorhese's freefalling body, were all clearly played by a stunt double.

This annoyed some of the production crew. There was never any chance that a real crocodile could take on the role, but the original idea was that it should at least *look* real. It was hoped that the special effects department could rustle up a realistic-looking animatronic creature, but due to one of the many cock-ups which plagued the special effects in the seventh series, the request for such a creature came too late, and so Allison was formed using an existing crocodile mould. There were two versions, one was just the front half of the creature with some animatronic controls to move its lips and eyelids; the other one was a full size foam rubber model which Ace had to wrestle with. In the end, that's precisely what they looked like — not that viewers seemed to mind, as Ace wrestling with a rubber crocodile seemed to match the over-the-top style of the opening sequence.

Then, straight after the opening titles, the episode went into another lavish sequence — this one in virtual reality with Lister in a medieval world trying to win the Queen in a jousting contest. The scenes look extravagant in bright sunshine with extras from The Medieval Combat Society and the Plantagenet Medieval Archery & Combat Society appearing in the background and jousting in the foreground. But it didn't look like that the first day the *Red Dwarf* team arrived on location at the ruined castle. "It poured with rain from the minute we got there," remembered Robert Llewellyn. "Only people with four-wheel drive cars got home, basically, we were really bogged in, it was like the Somme. [It rained] the whole day until about ten minutes after the last car eventually got off, and then it stopped raining — as it always does. We were covered in mud, we couldn't shoot anything. The whole lot had to be re-done."

Fortunately, the day they returned it was a beautiful sunny day. This caused unexpected consequences for Robert Llewellyn when dressed as Kryten. "You walk out into the sunlight and go, 'ooh no, that hurts so much, what on Earth is going on?' I had it explained to me by the make-up woman Andrea [Finch]: it's like if you put two cones of silver paper around your eyes and go out in the sun you'll find you get a headache very quickly and you'll go blind. This is effectively what's happening [in the Kryten mask]; you've got these reflective panels under your eyes that are bouncing the sun right in. Direct sunlight is absolute agony to be in. There were days when we were shooting in bright sunlight and then they point a huge five hundred kilowatt lamp right into your face and it's 'arrrgh!' That was bad. I complained a lot and got no sympathy from Craig — as usual!"

The problem was eventually fixed. "We tried lots of different things, but eventually an umbrella proved to be the best thing," said Robert. "Just to be under an umbrella out of the sun."

Sadly, Emmy Award-winning actor Brian Cox, who played the King, was unable to return to the location to enjoy the sunshine, and so his close-ups were re-shot in a carpark at Shepperton Studios. If you look carefully at the long shots involving the King in sunny conditions, you might just be able to tell it is actually costume designer Howard Burden dressed up to look regal.

Lister's fun in the medieval world is interrupted by the arrival of Ace Rimmer who has been hit by a fatal Nazi bullet and wants to hand over his heroic duties to the less-than-heroic version of Rimmer. This was the chance for Chris Barrie to go out on a high. Playing both versions of Rimmer, he got to play a death scene and to go through a period of introspection as he wonders if he's got what it takes to be Ace. Unlike previous series of *Red Dwarf*, none of it was done with a studio audience watching. "I probably enjoyed it better not doing stuff in front of the audience," he said. "I like concentrating on the character. I mean, if you've got the audience there you're half concentrating on them, in getting a laugh, or timing something properly, whereas when there's no audience there you can concentrate on the bit you're supposed to be doing."

There was some sadness that this was the last proper episode for Rimmer, but at least it sent him away in style. "There're highs and lows in every life," reflected Chris Barrie at the end of filming, "but, at the moment in terms of *Red Dwarf*, it's a major high."

Episode Three: Ouroboros

Written by… Doug Naylor

<u>GUEST CAST</u>
Frank… Gary Bleasdale
Barmaid… Juliet Griffiths
Flight Announcer… Adrienne Posta
Baby Lister… Alexander John-Jules

Story

A Starbug crew from another dimension get in contact through an opening in space-time. In their dimension, Kochanski is the one who survived on Red Dwarf and Lister is a hard-light hologram. She wants to have children, but before she can collect Lister's contribution to make this happen, she becomes stranded. As she tries to get back to her dimension, Lister begins to realise what it meant when he was abandoned by his parents in a cardboard box, with the word *Ouroboros* written on the side.

Funniest Moment (arguably)

Kryten is upset that the arrival of a woman will get in the way of his special relationship with Lister and asks if Lister would prefer folding sheets with Kryten, even if Kochanski is all naked and saying 'make love to me, you horny dude'.

Behind The Scenes

Ouroboros was Chloë Annett's first episode as Kochanski. She had the tough job of coming into an established cast who had known each other for years and onto a show which was already a success. "I was so excited," she said. "I love the programme anyway, and they're funny guys. They're stand-up comedians and I come from straight drama, so I was a bit nervous, but they made me feel so at ease and they were such fine actors. I know they call themselves 'performers' — they're not 'actors' — but I think they are really incredibly fine actors; really very good and very funny. And they've made me feel very at home. It's like a big family. And I wasn't sure at first, you don't know how they're going to accept you — *if* they are going to accept you — but they did, right from day one."

Chloë became an actor through the traditional route of going to theatre school and being brought up in a showbiz family (her father and brother are both directors). But the rest of the cast seemed to accept her. "She did really well," said Craig Charles. "She didn't have an easy job. Imagine coming into such an established show as a principal character, it must have been a nightmare for her. And with us all knowing each other so well and all the in-jokes, and all the history which she could not possibly relate to because she wasn't there. It must have been really hard for her. She fitted in like one of the lads in the end."

"A real tough gig that," admitted Ed Bye. "These guys have been doing it for a long time. And that was the other thing, they're guys and she's a girl. She had to fit in to a family and it was tough, very tough for her. But she fitted in really well and by the time we got to episodes where she was seated in, it worked really well."

As the director, Ed Bye was very much involved in the audition process for Kochanski. He knew from the outset the type of person he was looking for. "Principally somebody who could fit in, in terms of comedy, somebody who could understand comedy and make it work, perform it. Because the biggest killer is an actress that can't deliver a comedy line, however else good they are, that's important. Also she had to be completely believable. What we didn't want to have is somebody who was 'Mrs Terminator' or 'Mrs Damsel in Distress'. It had to be somebody who could stand up on their own two feet and be their own identity without being the girlie, while at the same time being female."

The episode establishes Chloë Annett's Kochanski in the history of *Red Dwarf* with a flashback to the days before the crew got wiped out. It reminds the audience who Kochanski is and is a chance to feature Rimmer in one of several cameos. The flashback scene was also an opportunity for the costume department to redesign the old uniforms which had been less than popular back in the early days of *Red Dwarf*. Howard Burden and his staff decided to go for a blue design with white piping, although this design was later discarded in *Red Dwarf VIII*. This scene was also Chloë's first day.

"The first day, the first scene, I was seriously hyperventilating," she said. "I did a little scene with Chris and I can remember it. We have one very short scene together when I'm just saying something really nasty to him. And then he goes away, and he comes back in a later episode, but we don't actually do that much together.

"But the night before I remember even more — I dyed my hair. I'd had it all cut off because I used to have really long hair and I just thought, 'I'll give it a bit of a lift'. So I went to Sainsbury's and bought, God knows what, conker hair dye or something, and it was just horrific. It was all matt, and because I hadn't washed it out properly, it was all stiff. The poor make-up lady was trying to do my hair which was just an awful thatch."

Other early scenes for Chloë Annett involved a different hairstyle and a much less comfortable working environment. She had to be suspended in the air for the two scenes where she falls down between the separated parts of the walkway between two dimensions: the first where she is suspended from Lister's dental floss, and the second where Lister harpoons her through the leg to save her from falling into infinity. For the actress, this involved hanging around in a harness ten feet up in the air for most of the day.

Lister's dental problems, incidentally, were inspired by Craig Charles' real-life adventures with his tooth cap which, when it dropped out, he foolishly decided to glue back in with superglue instead of consulting a dentist.

The arrival of Kochanski marks a seismic change in the direction of the show. *Red Dwarf* had always been about the last man alive, stranded three million years into deep space with a small all-male crew. With a woman on board, the chemistry was about to change, especially with the temporary departure of Rimmer. Even Kryten doesn't like it, and that was a deliberate ploy in the writing of the script. "Kochanski comes aboard and the fans' reaction is going to be 'uh oh, we don't like this as an idea at all, we're not behind this at all, this is a terrible idea," said Doug Naylor. "I thought if Kryten voiced that from the second she was there, it would help them relax a bit and go 'oh we're not the only ones who's thinking this'. Because it will take time for people to like her."

It produces some very funny scenes of Kryten being jealous, with the highlight arguably his conversation with Lister where he suspects Lister will prefer having sex with Kochanski than folding sheets with him.

These scenes were a favourite with actor Robert Llewellyn too. "He's judging her on the effect she has on his mates, so therefore it takes it into a whole new realm," he said. "Because it's an asexual character dealing with a woman, his reactions to her aren't sexist. He's not horrible to her, he's very two-faced, he's like an embittered ex-wife or a jealous mother. It was great because the chances for a man to play that sort of role don't exist unless you're in a dress pretending to be a woman. So essentially he's become a woman in some of the scenes and a very embittered and vicious one. And Lister puts up with it, is tolerant in the way a man would be with his mother, he has to listen to this whining and winging. I've seen a couple of those scenes played back and it's very funny indeed and very peculiar, it couldn't exist anywhere else outside this series."

Although *Ouroboros* introduces Chloë Annett's Kochanski into

Red Dwarf, it is ultimately about Lister and his origins. It was first revealed in the third series episode *The Last Day*, that Lister was an orphan who never knew who his parents were because he was abandoned in a box under a pool table. The episode begins with that scene with a baby in a box, played by Danny John-Jules' nephew, Alexander John-Jules. Danny suggested using his brother's baby because he thought he looked a little Lister-like with chubby cheeks. During the course of the episode, Kochanski and Lister make contributions to a test tube to produce a baby which will grow up to be Lister. So he becomes his own father and is the one who abandons himself in a box under the pool table, explaining the meaning of Ouroboros, the circle of life.

Of course, the people who found him thought the writing on the box meant that the baby's parents couldn't decide whether to call him Rob or Ross (our Rob or Ros), which probably explains why he ended up with a name like Dave.

Episode Four: Duct Soup

Written by... Doug Naylor

<u>GUEST CAST</u>
None

Story

The generators break down on Starbug and the crew are trapped. The only way to solve the problem is to crawl up into the service ducts, get to the generator and start it up again. There are just two problems: the generator is a long crawl away and Lister is claustrophobic. As Lister gets worse, Starbug gets hotter and it appears they are off course and heading for the sun. Only then does Kryten reveal that the generators may have had some help shutting down in the first place...

Funniest Moment (arguably)

Kochanski walks into the mid-section of Starbug with a white sheet wrapped round her, wearing earmuffs. 'Ah look,' says Kryten, 'it's Princess Leia.'

Behind The Scenes

Duct Soup was a script that came out of necessity. It replaced another script which had been written in pre-production by John McKay. *Identity Within* was going to be a Cat episode where the Cat had to have sex, or he would die. But it was an elaborate set-up and too expensive, especially after the extravagances of *Tikka to Ride* and *Stoke Me a Clipper*.

Doug Naylor needed a replacement script and it needed to be cheap. So the pressure was on. "He's a genius, there's no other word for it," said Robert Llewellyn. "He really is extraordinary. I think, as a writer, I know those walls that you hit and I know that Doug said for the last one we recorded, he was sitting in his room alone with a screen and everyone was going 'oh Doug can do it, he's great, he can just write one when he's under pressure' and he was just sitting there going 'I haven't got a fucking clue, how can I write under pressure, what can I write?' Particularly in circumstances with a cast and crew sitting in the studio going [whistling and tapping their fingers] 'come on then luv, when you're ready'. Oh, I couldn't do it, it must be awful."

The result was *Duct Soup*, a script title which references the Marx Brothers' 1933 comedy film, *Duck Soup*. It required no monsters, no guest stars, no location shooting and minimal sets and effects. It was the last episode of the run to be shot and, as it focused on the characters, it became a cast favourite.

"It's the best episode we've done," said Craig Charles. "I think it looks better, it's lit better, and the acting's better. It's all round better… It's very different. It's very much more character-led. I quite like those ones, I like the character-led ones."

It begins with Kochanski trying to get some sleep while being constantly interrupted by gurgling pipes. She takes this personally and not only shouts at the pipes, but bashes them with a spanner, even though any sane person would know that isn't going to do any good. It allowed the actress to play another aspect of the character. "It was a nice one for me," said Chloë Annett, "because that's when she goes completely mad and breaks down."

It also reflects something of Chloë herself. As it was the last episode to be written and filmed, Doug Naylor was able to incorporate a little bit of the actress into the character. "She is strong, she likes to boss them around, but only because she knows what to do," said Chloë of Kochanski. "She's horrified that they're so terrible and so lazy and don't know what the hell they're doing, but at the same time she's got these neuroses. They're probably from me, Doug put in tiny parts of me and exaggerated them. I saw what he'd done and

I thought 'oh he's clocked onto something'… Kochanski doesn't try to be funny, she doesn't think she's funny at all. She is just trying her best to get things together and to go home."

Things get worse for the Starbug crew when the generator and the back-up break down, and the doors seal shut as a precaution. The only way to reach the generator and to re-start it is to crawl through the maintenance ducts. The set for the ducts was small and enclosed and, because water had to be squirted into it, was taken outside into the carpark at Shepperton Studios. The effect was achieved by using high-pressure hoses and turning them on the cast.

"I thought, 'this is it, I'm going to die on *Red Dwarf*,'" said Robert Llewellyn. "If you set your VCR and pause it you can see Chloë in the middle acting and either side of that there's two men who are actually drowning!"

"God, I was a bit of a girl about that, actually," said Chloë. "I was saying, 'Oh, do you think it's going to hurt?' And they were going, 'For God's sake shut up!' Robert was very sweet about it though, and I've become really good friends with all of them. It was like having four elder brothers that would take care of you."

"I had three sheets of water just pouring down my face:" said Craig Charles. "I couldn't breathe, and when I did it went all up my nose. I was coughing and spluttering."

Kryten's costume was so battered by the water, it was virtually destroyed. He was also carrying a map which was so soggy it fell to pieces. That sort of thing, he said, shows how complicated it is to film *Red Dwarf*. "You go into a scene and you go, 'so I go in there and I get the thing and I give it to Craig' — but hold on I've got a bomb in my hand and I've got my leg up my arse and my head's about to explode! Everyone's going 'oh fuck, how do you do it?' When in another sitcom you'd come in with a cup of tea and sit on the sofa and you go 'well Dad…'; this one you come in through the wall at a hundred miles an hour and your head explodes!"

The final scene to be shot for *Red Dwarf VII* was where the cast are forced up against a series of bars at the end of a duct by the force of the water gushing in behind them. It's a long way from coming in with a cup of tea and sitting on the sofa. "What happens in *Red Dwarf* as far as visuals are concerned knocks other shows out of the park," said Danny John-Jules. "There's one scene in *Duct Soup* you ain't going to believe! We're sitting in a duct and the water's going crashing past and we're doing a scene. It's just tonnes of water flying past us. And the next thing we're sitting on like a surf board being funnelled down this duct. It looks mad!"

Not bad for an episode which had to be done on the cheap.

Episode Five: Blue

Written by... Kim Fuller & Doug Naylor

<u>GUEST CAST</u>
None

Story

As Kochanski chases the rift she hopes will take her back to her own dimension, Starbug is damaged by the debris from a comet. Lister asks the Cat to come help him fix it, but calls him Rimmer by mistake. It makes Lister think of all the 'fun' times he and Rimmer had together. He even dreams about him, about how Rimmer would return and they would kiss, and wakes up screaming. There's only one thing for it, decides Kryten, they have to be reminded what Rimmer was really like...

Funniest Moment (arguably)

Rimmer, Lister and Kryten playing golf on a desert planetoid.

Behind The Scenes

Blue, or *Heartache* as it was originally titled, was one of the episodes which came from an outside writer. There were a number of problems using people from outside the *Red Dwarf* stable to write episodes, not least that they didn't know the show as intimately as people who had been working on it from day one. But Doug Naylor thought Kim Fuller had come up with some interesting ideas surrounding Lister's feelings for the departed Rimmer.

It was an episode that was deliberately more low-key and more character-based. The idea of Lister missing Rimmer provided a seamless chance to keep Rimmer in the show, even though he had technically left, but at the same time acknowledge that he was gone and it was time to move on.

The first flashback saw the cast visit a nearby quarry where clever editing made it look like Rimmer was a far better golfer than Chris Barrie actually was. The second flashback saw Rimmer and Lister playing the locker game back on Red Dwarf where they would break into lockers belonging to the dead crew to see what they would find. Rimmer has the bad luck to find a locker that shoots a plume of flame into his face in a shot impressive enough to make it into the opening titles. The effect was achieved live in the studio with a real flame firing off-camera and its image reflected using a semi-silvered piece of glass so it looked like the two things were happening in the same space. Continuity buffs will notice that Rimmer shouldn't be wearing his blue hard-light costume in this scene because he didn't get his hard-light drive until after they had lost Red Dwarf in the sixth series.

Rimmer's next appearance wasn't in a flashback, but in Lister's dream where he imagines Rimmer has missed him so much that he returns. The pair embrace with a full-on kiss. Both actors, by all accounts, approached this scene with due professionalism.

"We get one of the most passionate on-screen snogs of all time — a*rrrghhh!*" said Craig Charles. "I just thought it was a laugh, the idea of Lister snogging Rimmer is an anathema to both our characters."

While Lister is getting worried about his homo-erotic dreams, Kryten is having more problems with Kochanski. Everything she does irritates him, even when it comes to taking the salad cream out of the fridge and putting it on the shelf. "I've really enjoyed doing the scenes of Kryten being jealous," said Robert Llewellyn. "He's insanely jealous of this new girl that comes on board. It was a great way of dealing with the fact that there is a new character on board, that she's actually loathed to death by one of the other characters. He [Kryten] says all of the things that viewers potentially could say, like 'Oh Rimmer was much better, I liked Rimmer much more, even though he was a git, she's rubbish.'"

Chloë Annett, as Kochanski, also found this aspect of her character something she could get her teeth into. "It's just brilliant to play," she said. "She has this relationship with Lister and there is this sexual chemistry there which I think is nice and important — will they or won't they get it together? But on the other hand, she thinks he's a complete loser. The Cat, she just doesn't really give the time of day to, she's like 'for God's sake!' and the Cat's trying to impress her. And Kryten is a joke. This mechanoid, who's supposed to have no feelings whatsoever, has suddenly become a totally neurotic mess and really childish too. So I think she's turned everything upside down."

Blue is the episode where Chloë got a bit of a costume change and, to explain it, is seen working at a sewing machine. Her original look, pitched along the lines of Diana Rigg's sexy catsuits in the 1960s TV show *The Avengers*, led to her wearing tight PVC trousers. Doug Naylor insisted the costume decision was not his. "I remember reading in *Time Out* where I was blamed for that costume, the red PVC job," he said. "Not me! I said, 'maybe red as a colour', but I didn't say PVC. So her bum looked like an over-ripe tomato."

The red PVC had some admirers, but Chloë wasn't one of them. She was happy to quietly swap to a more combat-trouser look. "She doesn't have many sets of clothes: she has two sets," said Chloë. "She starts off in these PVC trousers which we got rid of quite quickly, as they were rather hot. Then she has this sewing machine which is established in the plot because suddenly she's getting these new clothes and people would be wondering where they came from otherwise! There's actually a scene [in *Blue*] where she's running up this scarlet number."

By the end of the episode, Kryten's fed up with Lister's melancholy and decides something needs to be done. He puts together a little tribute to Rimmer, just to remind everyone what he was really like — The Rimmer Experience.

The filming of these sequences led to one particular day being known as 'Black Wednesday' (or was it 'Black Monday' or 'Black Thursday? No one quite remembers) where they were all sitting in a car from a fairground ride being wheeled through the doors into the Rimmer Experience. They had nothing to do but sit there while technical things went wrong. As they went through take after take, they were wheeled back and forth through those doors umpteen times.

The result was one of the most memorable scenes of *Red Dwarf VII* — not least because of the fiendishly catchy Arnold Rimmer munchkin song. The lyrics were written by Kim Fuller and Doug Naylor and were sent to *Red Dwarf* composer extraordinaire, Howard Goodall, to set to music. Chris Barrie has since said he would have liked to have had a go at singing the song himself, but Howard Goodall's recollection is that Chris didn't want to attempt any singing, despite Howard being willing to coach him through it. Either way, the voice which can be heard singing on the episode is Howard's. Chris Barrie mimed to the song in front of a blue screen, so his head could be electronically put on top of the little munchkin Rimmers which were made out of soft toys wearing miniature Rimmer costumes run up by Howard Burden's costume department. The special effects team say this was one of the most enjoyable days filming of the series for them, and they spent the next few days humming that very catchy song.

Episode Six: Beyond a Joke

Written by... Robert Llewellyn & Doug Naylor

GUEST CAST
The Simulant... Don Henderson
Mrs Bennet... Vicky Ogden
Jane Bennet... Alina Proctor
Kitty Bennet... Catherine Harvey
Lydia Bennet... Sophia Thierens
Mary Bennet... Rebecca Katz
Elizabeth Bennet... Julia Lloyd

Story

Kryten is driven to distraction by the rest of the crew. Not only do they disappear off to Pride and Prejudice Land when he has cooked them a special dinner, but when they return, Lister insists on having brown sauce on his lobster. It's too much for Kryten, and his head explodes. The others visit another ship to get a new head for Kryten, where they encounter a simulant who double-crosses them and steals Kryten for himself. The simulant orders another mechanoid, the otrazone-addicted Able, to fix him. As they escape, Kryten learns something about his past that shocks him and Able learns the truth about what it means to be a brother.

Funniest Moment (arguably)

Kryten turns up in a tank and blasts the Bennet sisters to smithereens.

Behind The Scenes

Red Dwarf VII was the first series to use writers other than the original creators, Rob Grant and Doug Naylor, and *Beyond a Joke* was the only time a member of the cast was allowed to contribute a script.

"I begged, pleaded and cried at Doug's door," said Robert Llewellyn. "The amount of time we've been doing it — it sort of goes a bit hazy — but we've been talking about it for a long time and I've written whole storylines in the past which they've never used — and rightly so, they were really awful. I did go off and write half a dozen storylines until we found one that started to hang together. It was very much done in conjunction with Doug and I think the end result that you see on screen is seventy/thirty Doug's, if not more.

"I just found my *Red Dwarf* file on the computer the other day and I'd forgotten there's thousands of documents on it, with openings of scripts," said Robert. "When I eventually wrote the storyline that we had — about thirty-five pages of the script — and showed it to Doug and Ed, they laughed and said 'good, funny, finish it.'"

Looking at the episode, which features Kryten's 'brother' and discovering the truth about his creation, casual viewers might think the actor had deliberately written in things that he wanted Kryten to do, but that was not the case. In the first draft of the script, Robert tried to do the exact opposite and wrote Kryten out of most of the episode. "This is the cruel twist of fate," he said. "What happens in the first scene is Kryten's head blows up. I thought I'd be sitting there with no head on, so I wouldn't have to wear my head, no lines, and all the others do all the talking… I had this dream that I could do one where I only have two scenes at the beginning and two scenes at the end."

But it was not to be. "I kept trying to write myself out and Doug kept saying 'No, you're not getting off that easy' and he was writing me back in! So that's how it was written and then it gradually changed over the months until his brother came in and I played his brother, so in the end I had more masks and I was doing more lines. I really paid the price! But Kryten doesn't feature in it a great deal. I think it's Lister who's in it the most. It was a very important thing that I didn't write a story that was just about my character and nothing else."

The scripts written by outside writers for *Red Dwarf VII* really went through the mill. There were many calls for re-writes and Doug Naylor was hands-on with his input, and re-wrote many of them himself to give the series an overall feel. "It was a hell of a lot of time I spent with Doug writing that," said Robert. "When I finally started to write the script it was fun, and it worked and it was funny and it had lots of funny lines in, but it was really for Lister-Craig and Cat-Danny, Kryten-Robert and Chris-Rimmer — it was us! They were very much the people that I knew and that was my problem with it. I was too close, I now realise. So it was an experiment from that point of view. I'm really pleased I got the chance to do it and I'm very pleased with the episode that's come out of it. I think it's good and I'm proud of my input."

One of the elements which survived Robert's original draft was the virtual reality visit to *Pride and Prejudice World*. Everyone got to dress up, but Craig Charles felt he drew the short straw. "There were six available women with the Bennet sisters — and Robert managed to write me in as a vicar!"

"Yeah," laughed Robert. "That was one of my ideas that got through. Craig's got to be a vicar — he doesn't get any!"

Meanwhile, Chloë got to be all girly and the complete opposite to her Kochanski character. "I loved the *Pride and Prejudice* one because I got to wear this ridiculous wig. Kochanski [normally] wears this wonderful, striking combat outfit and suddenly I had this yellow period dress and I decided to have this blonde wig just so it would be a complete contrast. I loved the dressing up — Kochanski thinks it would be fun, but they [the rest of the Starbug crew] don't. And in real life I think it would be fun, too, but they [the other members of the cast] don't. To go into virtual reality and meet all the Bennets and walk around, that's their idea of a complete nightmare!"

Danny John-Jules' costume was probably the most outrageous,

as he was dressed as some sort of cavalry officer with strikingly large hair. "I had extraordinarily tight pants," he said. "He just looks like Mr Darcy. He's geared up, but the Cat has done his hair in the wrong period, so he's Mr Darcy from the neck down and from the top up he's like Amadeus! He's crossed both centuries there, I think, and it went down a treat."

But it was an anxious day out on location for Danny John-Jules, because the day *Red Dwarf* went to *Pride and Prejudice World* was the day he lost a pair of his distinctive Cat teeth. "Something crazy happens every day on *Red Dwarf*," said Danny. "I lost my teeth on a tea break — and I only had one set because the second set was still at the dentist being made! I ended up finding them in the dustbin."

He threw his teeth in the *dustbin*? "I took my teeth out to eat these bunch of grapes," he explained. "So you throw the pips in the bin, obviously, so I must have thrown my teeth in the bin! We were looking round in the middle of shooting — and no teeth! And then after losing them and finding them again, I really lost a set. They had to bike a pair down in the morning, it was madness! I had so much bad luck with those teeth. I went to a fitting and during the fitting — blink! — the dentist broke one in my mouth. So it was a year of bad teeth for the Cat. The whole show at one point was resting on teeth, 'where's the teeth?'. It was really getting to me, every time I had a make-up check, 'got your teeth in?'. Three and a half months of 'where's your teeth?' and 'have you got your teeth in?'. In nine years this was the first set of teeth I lost."

The idea of visiting a Jane Austen-inspired location came from the prevalence of costume dramas being produced in Britain at the time. The BBC's production of *Pride and Prejudice* had been a huge success in 1995 and came off the back of other successes like the Merchant Ivory films and other TV dramas. Robert Llewellyn was getting a little tired of seeing them everywhere. "I think I was sick to death of long dress stuff," he said. "I mean, I was in Australia in

February which is as unlike *Pride and Prejudice* as you can get — and every telly had *Pride and Prejudice* on! I was going, 'oh God, that's all we ever make in this bloody country!'"

So he was able to take his revenge and turn up in a tank as Kryten and blow the whole of the *Pride and Prejudice* cast to smithereens. "Yes!" said Robert. "It's one of those silly, giggly jokes that took on a shape."

The tank itself had already made a name for itself in showbiz and was borrowed from the James Bond stage at Leavesden Film Studios (where *Goldeneye* was filmed in 1995). It merely had to travel a little way out of the lake where Kryten would supposedly hit the controls to fire the cannon. The resulting explosion of the little gazebo, which had been built especially for the episode, was rigged by the special effects team using explosive ribbon. The explosion was huge and far bigger than people had been expecting. There was nothing left of the gazebo apart from pieces of flying debris.

"That got us into a lot of trouble," said Craig Charles. "It was the biggest explosion I ever witnessed and we were about half a mile back and we could feel the blast. Robert was filming it on his camcorder and almost dropped his camcorder!"

The problem was that nobody had told the neighbours. This was on advice from the military who owned the piece of land and never felt the need to tell people living nearby when they were carrying out loud military manoeuvres. The *Red Dwarf* special effects team, it turned out, were louder than the army and the huge bang they created caused, it is claimed, some people to call the police. It was also a lovely day in August and many people were enjoying the sunshine in the garden when pieces of gazebo fell from the air. It was not the best day for public relations.

But it was one of the best days for *Red Dwarf*. Robert Llewellyn, in particular, had fond memories. "The most exciting moment was seeing all the actors dressed up in nineteenth century costume. That morning I actually had a late call which was very unusual for me, I wasn't there first, and when I saw Danny and Craig walking across a beautiful forest in the sunlight in the morning and Craig dressed up as a vicar and Danny in a cavalier costume, I was just in hysterics. And then six women in long dresses walked behind them and got on a minibus and drove round the corner to get blown up. I was really thrilled because that was the one that I wrote and my thoughts were behind that originally. They looked so brilliant, make-up and costume had really gone to town. That and the tank — those two moments — that day was a highlight of series seven."

Episode Seven: Epideme

Written by… Paul Alexander & Doug Naylor

GUEST CAST
Caroline Carmen… Nicky Leatherbarrow
Epideme… Gary Martin

Story

The crew of Starbug find a woman frozen and barely alive aboard the starship Leviathan. But when she wakes up, it seems the only thing that kept her alive was a virus. She survives long enough to attack Lister and give him the deadly Epideme virus. The manmade Epideme was built with intelligence, and so Kryten devises a method of communication in the hope Lister will be able to reason with it not to kill him. Epideme refuses and they embark on a more drastic plan to draw Epideme into Lister's arm and cut it off. But when the virus survives even that, they have to take the ultimate step — to kill Lister before the virus can infect anyone else.

Funniest Moment (arguably)

Kryten and Kochanski exit the medical bay, chatting happily over how they managed to defeat Epideme — only to suddenly realise that Lister is still dead.

Behind The Scenes

The idea for *Epideme* came from writer Paul Alexander who had once written a sketch for Jasper Carrott where he imagined what it might be like to communicate with a virus. He brought this idea with him when he was asked to write for the series, and exaggerated it in a *Red Dwarf* way. Originally, the virus was to be more serious and darker in its mission to kill Lister, but the episode was considered dark enough already and so more levity was incorporated into the character of Epideme. Instead of booking a serious actor to do the voice (Patrick Stewart was one idea for the role), it went to Voiceover Artist extraordinaire, Gary Martin, who injected a liveliness into his delivery. With Ed Bye's suggestion to turn the virus into something more visual by projecting it onto the screen, the character was created.

It was one of many changes to be made to the script, which was first written a long time before production started and before Chris Barrie's decision to return for only a handful of episodes. The finished episode saw Kochanski trick the virus into infecting the dead arm of Caroline Carmen (albeit pumped with blood and adrenaline to appear alive), and destroying it. In the original version, the virus was tricked into infecting Rimmer who then turned off his light-bee, allowing Epideme to be blasted out of the air with a bazookoid. Another change was a scene in which Lister tried to find a solution by consulting with some of history's greatest thinkers in virtual reality. This idea got as far as casting and costume before it was ditched and the scene deleted.

The filming of the episode saw an impressive use of location once again. The crew returned to the same engine testing facility outside Farnborough which had provided such a visual treat back in *Tikka to Ride*. This time, they went to a disused area of the complex which set designer Mel Bibby made to look like the frozen interior of The Leviathan by spraying frosting all over the various metal pipes, walkways and equipment. It looked fantastic, but with lots of low metal beams all over the place, gave ample opportunity for people to bang their heads. "We went to some weird places," said Chloë Annett. "We ended up in this enormous factory where they test Concorde engines. That was really eerie and everyone had to wear hard hats, apart from the actors who couldn't wear a hard hat. That was something that crossed my mind: '*You* have to wear them because it's dangerous — what about *us?*'"

When the Starbug crew leave The Leviathan, they bring with them the barely-alive body of Caroline Carmen. It is her zombified body that attacks Lister and infects him, a sequence which was extended at the suggestion of director Ed Bye who relished the idea of making a little bit of a zombie movie while, at the same time, putting a bit more action into the episode.

Lister's condition leaves the others uncertain as to what to do. The Cat gets to make some of his typical insensitive comments, while Kryten gets to make a fuss. It led to another scene of conflict between Kryten and Kochanski that Robert Llewellyn enjoyed filming. "Scenes like Kryten making Lister's bed when he's ill and Kochanski changing it because '*her* Dave has two pillows like that' and they have a row and they're fighting over him. It's like a scene between two women fighting over a man. It's very funny, very weird."

At the end of the episode, they have achieved a victory of sorts. Kryten has tricked Epideme into telling them a way to improve Starbug's engines so they can travel faster, and the virus has been destroyed. The only problem is, Lister is left with one arm.

Although not devised as a two-part story, the issue of Lister's missing arm provides a little teaser into the final episode, *Nanarchy*.

Episode Eight: Nanarchy

Written by... Paul Alexander, James Hendrie, Doug Naylor

GUEST CAST
Holly... Norman Lovett

Story

Lister tries to cope with life with one arm and finds he can't really cope at all. Even Kryten's attempt to fix him up with an artificial arm doesn't work. So Kryten sets co-ordinates for the planet of the Despair Squid where he last had his nanobots — which he hopes he can recover and use to re-grow Lister's arm. What they find is a planetoid which the scanners claim to be Red Dwarf. It turns out Kryten's nanobots were the ones who stole Red Dwarf in the first place and re-formed it into a planetoid. All Kryten needs to do is persuade them to turn it back into a ship.

Funniest Moment (arguably)

Kryten coaching Lister to use his new artificial arm to pick up a ball until Lister gets so frustrated, he punches Kryten in the head.

Behind The Scenes

Nanarchy was the episode which set fire to a special effects cameraman. This was not the intention of the special effects department when they set up a shot of Starbug lifting off from a planet. They did as they always had done and rigged airbrush canisters to blow gas out of the engine exhausts, creating four white jets thrusting down onto the planet surface. However, since the last time the team had filmed Starbug's jets, the manufacturers of airbrushes had stopped using the inert propellant gas Freon, because of the ban on CFCs, and replaced it with butane, which is flammable. A spark from a pyrotechnic ignited the gas, the jets caught fire, Starbug swung on its wires and landed on the back of cameraman Peter Tyler — still on fire! Other members of the crew were quick with fire extinguishers, and Peter walked away with only singed hair on his arms and head.

Nanarchy was also the episode which went through a lot of changes at the script stage to incorporate what was happening at the end of the series. The early drafts were written by James Hendrie, but as the production date got nearer, it was decided to make it the last episode of the series, which meant it had to include finding Red Dwarf. There was also a need to resolve the cliffhanger of Lister's missing arm. In the meantime, James Hendrie had moved onto other projects and re-writes were handled by both Paul Alexander and Doug Naylor.

The concept of nanotechnology (manipulating matter at a minuscule level) featured heavily in James Hendrie's original drafts and stemmed from his research into current scientific advances. Much of the plot had to do with the ways the nanobots attempted to 'improve' Lister's body after growing back his arm. A lot of this was lost in the re-writes, but the basic idea of trying to give Lister a better body and getting it spectacularly wrong remains with his transformation into a muscular hunk. This was achieved by super-imposing Lister's head onto the body of genuine bodybuilder Terry Fisher.

It had always been the plan for the crew to catch up with Red Dwarf at the end of the series, and the nanobots provided an opportunity to do that in a novel way. Not only do they find the remnants of the craft, they rebuild it to be bigger and better than ever before. This allowed for the return of one missed element of the old *Red Dwarf* — Holly.

He was once again played by Norman Lovett. "I was worried initially when I spoke to Doug about me coming back," Norman told *Starburst* magazine. "We had this brief meeting and I said; 'gags! Gimme gags!' I'm pleased to say that the gags were as good as any

I'd done in the past. I'm delighted… I went back in a professional way and did the job."

In a way, *Red Dwarf* had come full circle and was back to where it had started, on board its original ship with its original Holly. It was enough to set the scene for a whole new series.

Red Dwarf VIII

Executive Producer... Doug Naylor
Written by... Doug Naylor with Paul Alexander
Produced & Directed by... Ed Bye

Rimmer... Chris Barrie
Lister... Craig Charles
Cat... Danny John-Jules
Kryten... Robert Llewellyn
Kochanski... Chloë Annett
Holly... Norman Lovett

Recorded: September-November 1998
First broadcast: February-April 1999

The crew of Starbug finally caught up with Red Dwarf at the end of *Red Dwarf VII*, but it had to be converted back into a spaceship by the nanobots. And, as Cat was heard to say before the end credits rolled, 'we got a problem' because they had somehow turned it into something much larger than the original. They had also resurrected all the crew, so it is a much more crowded Red Dwarf than people were used to.

"There's a lot more big group action and brilliant extras that have been annoyingly funny," said Robert Llewellyn, who was back as Kryten. "So that's been great, there's been other characters to interact with and be beaten up by. So it has changed a lot."

It was a big departure from *Red Dwarf VII*, but in other ways the eighth series was very similar to the style of the original show, as they were back on Red Dwarf with Chris Barrie as Rimmer, Norman Lovett as Holly and recording the episodes in front of a live studio audience.

"We've done it in a slightly different way," said executive producer and writer Doug Naylor. "Marrying the way we did it last time to the way we did it in the past. Also, I think the series is stronger than the last one because we weren't able to make the series in the way I really wanted to make it last time. When [co-writer] Rob [Grant] left; there was no Rob, there was no Norman, there was no Chris… A lot of the strength of *Red Dwarf* is the Lister/Rimmer kind of scenes and we weren't really able to do that last time. It was something I always wanted to get back to, and we've done much more of that in this series and — certainly in terms of audience reaction — they've done very well."

The old-style bunk scenes were made possible, not by putting Lister and Rimmer back into their old quarters, but locking them up in jail together. In the opening episodes, the main characters are charged with stealing Starbug and sent to serve their sentence in 'The Tank', a prison complex located on Floor Thirteen. It separates Lister and Rimmer, who share a cell, while Kryten and Chloë Annett's Kochanski share a different cell. It was never revealed who Cat was sharing a cell with.

"The sleeping quarters scenes we've got back with Lister and Rimmer have been great fun," said Chris Barrie. "It's great to have

Norman back. Chloë is excellent and the boys are the boys and we're all happy. It's the eleventh or twelfth year of doing this show now, so we're cracking jokes about *Dad's* Army-in-space and everything, coming to cover up all the old grey temples and that kind of stuff. So it has a great feeling of 1988, or 1987, or whenever we started and the new moving forward generation. We hear people abroad are taking to it and everything, so it's just a good feeling to be in a good, successful show."

Rimmer's return to the fold was something the actor had considered very carefully. Following his disquiet over the sixth series, he had a lot of fun filming the bits he did in the seventh series — escaping from Nazis, wrestling crocodiles and jumping out of an aeroplane — and decided *Red Dwarf* was where he belonged. "I thought about it after the seventh series," said Chris. "And thought that, as the years go by, it's increasingly unique on television. At the time, I was looking at other stuff I was thinking about doing and you're never going to get the same sort of script material — for the kind of show that it is — anywhere else, so I thought I just want to see it through. I thought I may as well stay right until the end because it probably — for certainly the first part of my life in this business — will go down as the thing I was best known for, so I just wanted to do it again. Plus, I did enjoy doing the couple of episodes I did in the seventh series, I just wanted to get back into it. The vibe I got from inside and the fans was that the balance of the show wasn't quite there without Rimmer, [but] mainly it was a personal thing of just missing such inventive scripts."

Rimmer changed slightly in the eighth series, as he was no longer a hologram. He was resurrected along with the rest of the crew and, therefore, is the Rimmer of old; a weasely character who dreams of becoming an officer.

Holly, meanwhile, is just as senile as ever, with Norman Lovett back playing the role full-time. "There are a couple of shows where he's not in it as much as I would have liked him to be in," admitted Doug Naylor. "That's partly because the cast now is six, and getting everyone to have a really good part isn't always possible, but Norman's just been fantastic in the series. I'm not a bit surprised. He's an absolute joy to write for and his timing is so wonderful and the audience love him, so you can't really go wrong with him around. So I wanted him back full time, desperately."

"It's good," said Norman Lovett. "It's good to be back, enjoying it very much. It's just more lavish, more room, more dough — not for me — but more dough around. It's just more professional, and better than ever, really. That's my experience of this series, very impressed with it — and I'm not just saying that."

It may have appeared there was more money around in *Red Dwarf VIII*, with a larger cast and sets which had moved away from the cardboard-painted-grey look of the first series, but money was actually pretty tight. Many production decisions were over-shadowed by financial considerations and had to be scaled back. This was most obviously felt in the decision to extend some stories to two or three episodes, and to abandon plans to go back to Earth in the final episode.

"Our budget is less than *dinnerladies*, the Victoria Wood sitcom," said Doug Naylor.

That's the very conventional (and very funny) comedy filmed on one set in a factory canteen with no location filming or special effects.

"Yeah," said Doug. "And people just go 'oh….'"

This is one of the things Ed Bye had to wrestle with as he was producing and directing the series. "It's mind bogglingly difficult," said Ed. "In the old days people used to forgive *Red Dwarf* for its wobbly sets and its total lack of realism, but it was a comedy show. But you've got to keep up a bit with technology, which we do. So it's cheating, that's all I can tell you. We cheat like crazy, we get all the possible technology that we possibly can and use it just as cheap as possible to get the maximum result. So there's things like now there is computer software that can create effects. There's a guy who works on *Red Dwarf* now called Simon Birchwood who's got his own computer in his house, so while we're editing, he's rendering effects in his house, which he then brings to us on a piece of tape which we then stick in and lay on top of the pictures. We try every kind of cheap trick you can do because if we went to a facilities house and got some of the effects done, we just couldn't afford anything.

"It's how you use your money, I have to be honest with you," Ed added. "It's difficult, it really is. For instance, we use a lot of green screen and stuff like that because a green screen, a green cloth, doesn't cost very much. You can plonk someone in front of that and light it and then they can be put on a different background, and that background doesn't have to be in the studio, you can take a shot of it somewhere else. We use models a lot, model sets. I'm not going to tell you which one — it's a quiz! — which shot is a model. And if you shoot it right, then it looks like a huge 161 or whatever, but it's not, it's a model. These are shoots that you have to do. Yeah, if you were doing a great big movie, you'd go to the great big NASA hangar and have your thing. There's always things I would love to do, but we just couldn't afford it."

Other technical constraints were put on making the episodes because of the nature of filming in front of a live audience. It was one of the reasons why, in the previous year, the audience was jettisoned in favour of filming the show like a drama. For *Red Dwarf VIII*, the audience was back, a move which was not popular with everyone. "There were people that needed persuading," said Doug.

"The great thing about having an audience there is you get feedback," he continued. "If they don't laugh, you know it's not working. And the other advantage is the audiences give you a higher energy level when they [the cast] know there's a performance in front of an audience. When you're shooting single camera and it's the fourteenth day, everyone can get a bit down because it's such an exhausting shoot and you only realise when you get in the edit… It is much harder to make it look good when you've got the audience there and you can't light every shot, you have to light the whole scene. But, in the end, it's a comedy show — more this series than in the recent past — and I very much wanted to remind people that 'look, I want to get as many laughs as we can from this series' and that's what's most important."

For the actors, to have their performances peppered again by laughter gave them a huge boost. It helped their confidence and allowed them to get a feel of how the material was being received. "I think Doug Naylor's on excellent form, the funniest scripts," said Craig Charles, who was back playing Lister. "I'm talking about getting rounds of applause in the middle of scenes. You've got to act your way through it, you've got to wait to deliver your line while the audience stop clapping. There's been a lot of rounds of applause, big laughs… It's nice to have a studio audience back because sitcoms need to be played to an audience so you can gauge and judge the laughs better and pitch the performance."

The eight episodes of *Red Dwarf VIII*, rather than the usual six, matched the eight episodes of the previous year and were a ploy to bring the total number of episodes up to fifty-two. The idea was to boost foreign sales because it meant TV channels could run the show every week all year round if they wanted to.

Another inheritance from the previous year was Paul Alexander. After the departure of co-creator of *Red Dwarf*, Rob Grant, Paul was part of a team of writers called in to work on the scripts. Although this was not an entirely successful venture, Paul stayed to become script associate and he is credited as co-writing two of the episodes. "Generally what's happened is I've written the script and he's come in," said Doug Naylor. "We'll come in, and Ed will be here, and we'll chat about what direction we want the series to go in and I might have an idea or Paul will go off and write it or whatever. It's hard to define.

It's certainly been very good the three of us knocking ideas together."

It shows how much Ed Bye's role had changed, from being 'just' the director at the beginning to producing the show as well. "In the early days I used to be more like a regular TV producer and just go 'where are my scripts?! I haven't got any scripts, I can't shoot this!'. I basically would get finished scripts from Rob and Doug and then work on them from there. Sure, in the process of shooting it, it was my job to say 'I don't think this works', or 'let's change this bit', but not as much as I do now. We sit down at the beginning of the series and sort it out, decide what we want to do and how we make it better."

The result was a series of *Red Dwarf* which certainly met the approval of the cast. "It's more fun, I think," said Craig Charles. "I think we're all much more settled in ourselves and more mature. I think we all genuinely get on. Over the years there's been fallings out, but when you're stuck together in a room with creative people all that time they're bound to get on your nerves, but this time it's been so easy and painless. It's the most enjoyable *Red Dwarf* experience I've had, really."

Chris Barrie agreed. "Something obviously happened to me in the last couple of years, but this time I think this is the most comfortable series to do ever. It all feels very different, we work really well together. I don't know what happened, but there's a good balance now between studio audience and location and rehearse/record and I think the episodes have got a good balance of funny dialogue, or character dialogue, and visual effects. I think it's all come together wonderfully, and the studio audiences are just wonderful."

Episode One, Two & Three
Back In The Red

Written by... Doug Naylor

<u>GUEST CAST</u>
Captain Hollister... Mac McDonald
Chen... Paul Bradley
Selby... David Gillespie
MP Thornton... Karl Glenn Stimpson
Doc Newton... Kika Mirylees
Dr McClaren... Andy Taylor
Panel Woman Officer... Jemma Churchill
Second Woman Officer... Sue Kelvin
Last Woman Officer... Genevieve Swallow
Doctor... Geoffrey Beevers
Ackerman... Graham McTavish
First Ground Controller... Yasmin Bannerman
Second Ground Controller... Jeillo Edwards

Story

Starbug crashes into the resurrected Red Dwarf, depositing the occupants into a whole heap of trouble. The original crew have also been resurrected by the nanobots and Captain Hollister puts Lister, Kryten, Cat and Kochanski on trial. Through a series of adventures, they make their escape, only to find out their attempts were for nothing — as they all happened inside artificial reality with the Captain watching. It proves that their story about where they came from and about the nanobots is true, but it also incriminates them for using confidential files of the crew and they are all sentenced to two years in jail.

Funniest Moments (arguably)

Episode One: Kryten's psychiatric examination, during which he reveals he was made in the future where the psychiatrist died and was brought back to life again.

Episode Two: Rimmer, having taken some of the sexual magnetism virus, is seduced by the female officers, one by one, during a dinner with the Captain.

Episode Three: Rimmer edits all reference to his own double-dealing out of the virtual reality record while Lister, Kryten, the Cat and Kochanski are inside — so they experience bits of missing time and jump from one moment to another.

Behind The Scenes

Back in the Red begins with Rimmer and Lister already in jail, where the two of them inhabit a bunkroom reminiscent of their bunkroom on Red Dwarf and the style of the early *Red Dwarf* stories. Most of the episode is told in flashback to reveal how they got themselves in that predicament, so the opening bunk scene serves as an indicator to the audience that the style of some of the best-loved moments of the early series was back.

The inspiration had come, partly, from a project writer Doug Naylor and director Ed Bye had worked on the year before, re-mastering the first three series of *Red Dwarf* for a DVD release. They found themselves watching the old episodes and realising some of the things which had made them successful.

"One of the worst things was looking through the rushes of stuff we'd shot eleven years ago and seeing myself directing people thinking, 'who's that kid?' — it was me!" said Ed Bye. "I have to say, one of the things I got from that — and I think Doug did as well — was that some of the stuff that we did then, particularly in the bunk scenes, were really good… That was something we were really keen to bring back in… So we made a deliberate policy to try and set that up…

That's true, that came from the re-mastered."

This was made possible by the return, full-time, of Chris Barrie as Rimmer. The difference is, this time he's alive. The change was a calculated move by writer Doug Naylor.

"The relationship is different," said Doug. "This isn't going back in time and saying, this is the old Rimmer and the old Lister and their relationship is the same. This is a different relationship because Lister is older, Lister is more mature than he was, he's had the experience of knowing Rimmer that Rimmer isn't aware of, so he knows a lot of his backstory that Rimmer hasn't told him. Then, equally, he knows the mistakes that Rimmer is going to make, so in a sense he could manipulate him in a way that he wasn't able to do [before]... So no, Rimmer isn't dead, but in the end, Rimmer was neurotic before he was dead and he had a lot of the angst of being dead and we have seen a lot of that and explored that area. And so to explore a new facet is like a new opportunity to see Rimmer, I thought might be interesting."

But even though he didn't wear an 'H' on his forehead, Chris Barrie didn't feel being alive was a major departure for Rimmer. "I think his character developed quite a distance from the cornerstone of being dead. I think if you see this series of the whole crew resurrected, it's not a change that you miss that much. Obviously he's not moaning about the fact that he's dead now, but he finds a hell of a lot of other things to moan about. Being dead was the ultimate downside of life, wasn't it? For us all!"

These scenes went down well with the studio audience. It had been a long time since *Red Dwarf* had been performed in front of a live studio audience and, despite the pressure of getting it right on the night, there was certain amount of relief from the cast when they stepped out in front of the cameras for *Back in the Red*. "It was such a joy to do the first one in front of an audience again," said Robert Llewellyn, "because it reminded us of what the show can do because we were kind of working in isolation in the last series and I kind of missed the audience, although we then discovered lots of other areas that we could do, which we could never do before. But that immediate blast from an audience was really great and we all raised our game for it, we were lifted by that. And also from my point of view, I'm only in a mask for four hours as opposed to twelve, you only put it on at night and it was great fun. It reminded me of where the comedy in that show was and how strong it was and the audience reacted to it, it was absolutely phenomenal."

Doug Naylor agreed that having the audience back made a real difference to everyone's performance. "There is something else that happens when the audience is there," he said. "There's a great example of that at the beginning of episode two [of *Back in the Red*]. Rimmer is trying to impress Captain Hollister and he comes in and he does — it says in the scripts — 'a really long Rimmer salute'. In rehearsals Chris does all this [waving his arm] for quite a long time and then he does this thing and it's like a piece of paper dropping with his hand, and it goes back to his side. I laughed a lot at this. And the more he did it, and the longer he did it, the more I laughed. It wasn't just me, but I thought it was just so funny. And then on the night he did it longer than he did it in rehearsals, and not only did he do that, he did another one which wasn't scripted at all which was longer and more elaborate and he would never have done that if it was single camera. It is one of the highlights of the series for me and every time I watch it makes me laugh. Obviously, if he had done the salute and nobody had laughed, he would not have done it, or he would have stopped, but the audience, there was just this huge rolling laugh, which goes on for about fifteen or twenty seconds and he milks it for everything. You could say that it's completely self-indulgent, but personally I think it was inspired from Chris and was absolutely wonderful. And that's one of the glories of doing it in front of the audience."

As always with *Red Dwarf*, not everything could be done live.

Anything on location had to be filmed ahead of time, along with anything which required complicated effects. The most complicated sequence in *Back in the Red* — and, in fact, the whole of *Red Dwarf VIII* — was the Cat dancing with Blue Midget. Or, as Danny John-Jules put it: "a dancing thingamajig, *à la* Will Smith with the alien. It's a bit of a send-up of that."

The technically difficult idea came out of the mind of Doug Naylor, who decided to run it past Ed Bye before writing it into the script. "My first thought was 'that's great, a fantastic idea!'" said Ed. "My second thought was 'shit, we're never going to be able to do this!' Several times I've turned round and said to Doug '*easy* to write, *easy* to write!' We both knew what we were letting ourselves in for, it was a really tough thing to do, right from getting the music, working out the moves, getting it all sorted out, shooting it, compositing it, shrinking the creature, getting the CGI in, colourising it, making it work, matting it in, getting the timing right and then dubbing it. Just a nightmare, but it was worth it, very funny. I've never seen anything like it before."

Danny John-Jules learnt the dance routine with help from Charles Augins (who had played Queeg and worked on the *Tongue Tied* dance routine in the second series) as choreographer. It turned out to be quite difficult dancing with an invisible dancing partner, so a second dancer was hired for rehearsals to play the part of Blue Midget. For the filming, Danny performed on his own and a computer-generated Blue Midget was added later.

"It's a model, a real model, but it's ported into a computer, wire framed and turned into an animated creature, or animated ship," said Ed Bye. "So, basically, you can do whatever you like, within reason. We got Danny to do a dance routine which we shot against green. I shot him basically head to toe or in mid-shots on green and then the whole picture was manipulated so that he has a dance routine with Blue Midget. Then we introduce other Blue Midgets into it as well, so it's a big musical number with Danny and Blue Midget."

With so many elements of the final piece missing during the initial filming, it was a bit of a headache for everybody. "It was the most complex thing to do," said Ed. "Because when you're shooting it, you're just shooting it against green cloth, so you have to get all the angles right so when he's shrunk down to match, he's dancing next to this huge spaceship that's doing the same thing as him... I had to plan all the shots and just hope that it would all work. I was fairly confident it would work, but when we were actually shooting it, me and probably the director of photography Peter Morgan, were the only two people who knew what the bloody hell was going on. The rest of the crew just stood around thinking 'we don't know what's going on'. And there were moments when I thought 'I don't know what's going on' and there were moments where I'm sure Danny didn't know what was going on! But we got it all together and it all matted in perfectly, it was edited beautifully, it was rendered beautifully, Chris Field did a fantastic job [with the CGI] and it's turned out really, really well. But it was the most complicated thing we've done because you just couldn't see any of it, none of it existed... That was really hard, that, and I did think at one stage, I really didn't know if it was going to work."

Two other large effects sequences made it into the first episode. First was the giant rat that Starbug followed through the bowels of Red Dwarf, which was clearly a CGI construct, and the second was the demise of the Starbug craft itself. The sequence is quite meaty with Starbug breaking into two, bouncing into the Red Dwarf hangar and crashing. But it wasn't that way in the script. It was Ed Bye who suggested giving it more impact. "Doug will very often do a first draft and that gives me something to work with, so I sit down and do a breakdown of it. I remember... I got to the point where I went 'ooh, there's a moment where they crash' and it went, 'well that's that part of the story and we move on'. And I thought, no I think this crash should be huge because it's farewell to a very famous craft, so it should go out with a bang. And it does! I've never seen anything like it."

Back to the Red was originally written to be a one-hour special. However, as filming of the series continued, it became obvious that the budget was being squeezed beyond capacity. Some scenes — such as the Rimmer salute scene — were longer in their finished form than they had appeared in the script so there was a lot of material to work with. It was decided to turn *Back in the Red* into a three-parter. This involved going back and doing some re-shoots, and adding in some extra scenes in order to bring it up to length. This is probably why some scenes seem like a series of sketches, two of the best being Kryten's interrogation by the 'lovely' psychiatrist, and Captain Hollister in the medi-lab enjoying the funky rhythm of Cat's heart and pulse. The three episodes were later edited into a single one hour and twenty minute special and included on the DVD release, which many people felt worked much better.

Episode Four: Cassandra

Written by... Doug Naylor

GUEST CAST
Cassandra... Geraldine McEwan
Captain Hollister... Mac McDonald
Ackerman... Graham McTavish
Kill Crazy... Jake Wood
Warden Knot... Shend [Chris Harz]
Guard... Ian Soundry
Blood Drinker... Joseph Crilly

Story

Lister signs everyone up to the Canaries, a prison commando squad, whose first mission is to board a ship under water on an ocean moon. There, they encounter Cassandra who can see into the future, and she reveals that Rimmer is soon to die. Rimmer tries to cheat the prediction without success, but cheers up when he hears his final moments are to be while making love to Kochanski. He accepts his fate, but it seems Cassandra was lying because what she had really seen was her own death.

Funniest Moment (arguably)

Kill Crazy launches himself into the mission with great gusto — only to hit his head on the doorway and knock himself out.

Behind The Scenes

Cassandra is the first episode where the crew are firmly ensconced in jail. The advantage of the new format is seen from the outset in another bunk scene with Rimmer and Lister, who are forced to share a cell with all the tension that brings.

Putting all the characters in jail was an idea writer Doug Naylor had always planned to do. "Rightly or wrongly," he said, "it was there from the end of the last series. I wasn't sure how long the prison thing was going to last and I thought we'll write a few episodes, see how it goes and it might get 'urrgh, are you going to do this for the whole series? Because it's going to be really boring and we're not interested.'"

Once Lister, Rimmer, Kryten, Cat and Kochanski are signed up to the Canaries, it gives them a chance to go out on dangerous missions together. Had they been absorbed into the general crew, it would have been difficult to explain why they were always the ones leaving the ship to explore whatever Red Dwarf discovers.

"I also had an idea for a film," said Doug Naylor, "which actually turns out to be the same pitch as *Armageddon* — which was *The Dirty Dozen* in space — and that's what happens in the middle of the series, where they join this convict army on suicide missions where they're not in control in the way that they used to be. I thought it would be good to get authority figures in, people who they could rebel against."

In typical senile Holly style, he announces to Lister that he has found a way for him to serve his two year sentence in just fourteen weeks. He needs to become a dog because dog years are shorter. "There's some smashing lines," said Norman Lovett. "It's a strange form of acting to do that role, but I like it… On the night I sit on my little chair with the lighting. I've got more lighting for this series than I ever had before. They just had a candle in the first and second series. No candles now, electricity and everything! It was candles and camcorder in the early series, now it's the real thing, it's great — that's just a little joke!"

It is Holly who suggests Lister volunteer for the Canaries. Lister, believing it to be a singing troupe, signs everyone else up as well. They gather for inspection in a space which is the on-board equivalent of the prison yard, a location which was used several times for the series. It was all filmed in the old Guardian building which, by all accounts, was not a particularly pleasant place to be. "We've gone to some awful locations, the pits of the world," said Craig Charles. "We've been doing a lot of stuff in the old Guardian building which was blown up in the Docklands bomb: dirty, cold, cavernous."

The Canaries' mission, which leads them to encounter Cassandra, sees Kochanski get involved as one of the team. This is the new-look Kochanski: not only has she lost her red outfit, but her antagonism has also disappeared. "She's calmed down and accepted what's going on and it's much more action girl as opposed to snooty boots," said Chloë Annett. "Before, she was so anxious to get out, [be] more aggressive, and she's less so now. It's nice because I have a lot of scenes with Robert, which are great, and with Rimmer, which I'd didn't have before, so there's a new relationship there which is not a good one."

Indeed. After Cassandra makes a prediction that Rimmer will die making love to her, Kochanski takes the fortune teller at her word and prepares to accept her fate. Rimmer jumps up and down excitedly on the mattress, while she stands in dread at the side of the room. When an accident with the tap causes a pipe to squirt water all over her, soaking Kochanski to the skin, the audience realises what is going to happen. Naturally, she ends up naked under a blanket while Rimmer — in contrast to his sexual encounters in *Red Dwarf V* — doesn't even get to take his shirt off.

Episode Five: Krytie TV

Written by... Doug Naylor & Paul Alexander

<u>GUEST CAST</u>
Kill Crazy... Jake Wood
Ackerman... Graham McTavish
Man in Film... Mark Caven
Woman in Film... Sarah Wateridge
Guard... Clifford Barry

Story

Kryten is captured and reprogrammed by some of the other inmates to use his status as a 'woman' to secretly film the female prisoners in the shower. Kryten — now without his inhibitions — turns this into 'Shower Night', replacing the men's usual movie and making them pay to watch a bit of foam and flesh. Krytie TV is such a hit that Kryten sets up Lister and Rimmer to trash the warden's quarters in the belief they are sabotaging Kochanski's date — whereas, in fact, he is secretly filming them. Meanwhile, Lister launches an appeal which Rimmer believes is to get them an early release, but is really a request for Lister to be allowed to have strings on his guitar.

Funniest Moment (arguably)

Kryten in the communal shower surrounded by naked women, trying to read his book while keeping dry under an umbrella.

Behind The Scenes

This was the episode where Chloë Annett spent the day of the studio recording at home in bed. "I had a kidney infection so I missed it," she said. "I had to be sent home. I was really ill — I walked in yellow!"

The show was recorded without her and Chloë had to come back and do her scenes later. The place where this is most obvious is in the scene towards the beginning of the episode where the Canaries are in the transport coming back from a mission. She has a couple of lines where she appears in close-up, while eagle-eyed viewers will spot she is missing from the wide shots.

The idea for *Krytie TV* came from the *Game for a Laugh* and *You've Been Framed* type of hidden camera shows which were popular in the 1980s and 1990s, often presented by the late Jeremy Beadle. The bearded 'disguise' which Kryten wears when he greets Lister coming out of the warden's quarters is clearly meant to be Beadle-esque. This plot thread came from scriptwriter Paul Alexander, while the subplot regarding Lister's appeal came from the pen of Doug Naylor.

The two strands of the episode reflect the new format of the show where Lister and Rimmer are locked together in one cell, while Kryten is forced to be with Kochanski in the women's wing. It was a deliberate decision to explore those two dynamics. "The original idea was to have two relationships," said Doug. "One was a Lister now maturer than he used to be with the original Rimmer and be able to come in with that relationship at a different angle. I thought Lister could almost be Rimmer's mentor in some respects, to know how he irritated him in the past and also be able to influence him — being able to give him information about Starbug and the confidential files and things like that — so you could use him in that way. And also a relationship between Kochanski and Kryten because Kryten is classified as a woman — because he's got no genitals — because they don't get on. To have those two things going on simultaneously, with the Cat pinging back and forth."

It did leave the Cat, sadly, with not much of a part in many of the episodes. In *Krytie TV*, the Cat gets some reaction shots in the transport where Kryten is talking about having to shower with the women, and only a few lines when he's with the rest of the inmates watching Shower Night. But Danny John-Jules didn't seem to mind.

"I've never really had a lot of lines," he said. "The character's not essential to the plot, usually. He's the relish and the tomato ketchup on the egg and chips."

Shower Night itself was filmed in some real communal showers. As it was a pre-recorded sequence, Chloë Annett was there along with seven extras, and Robert Llewellyn in his naked Kryten suit with an umbrella and a book. "I got to shower with eight semi-naked women in a rugby club," said Robert, trying to sound impressive. "I have to say that a rubber head has a very limiting effect on the libido."

The success of Krytie TV gives Kryten a degree of money and power in prison, and he is seen wearing gold jewellery somewhat like a king in his adorned cell. It is very reminiscent of the character Grouty (played by Peter Vaughan) in the BBC's 1970s prison sitcom, *Porridge*. As the original idea of *Red Dwarf* had been to do a sort of Porridge-in-space, complete with the bunk beds, it seemed somewhat appropriate.

The episode, as one of only three self-contained half hours in the series, was one of the more successful ones, and got one of the best reactions of the run from the live studio audience. "[It] was just astonishing," said Robert Llewellyn. "It was one of the best live performances I've been involved in, including stage and everything. It was really explosive. And scenes doubled their length because we had to stand round while people were clapping."

Episodes Six & Seven: Pete

Written by... Doug Naylor & Paul Alexander

GUEST CAST
Captain Hollister... Mac McDonald
Ackerman... Graham McTavish
Mex... Andrew Alston
Young Kochanski... Holly Earl
Young Cat... Perry Michael
Baxter... Ricky Grover
Birdman... Ian Masters
Warden Knot... Shend
Kill Crazy... Jake Wood

Story

Lister and Rimmer are repeatedly causing trouble and being called to the Captain's office to explain themselves. As punishment, he puts them in 'The Hold' where they meet an old man with a pet sparrow he calls Pete. When they escape — with help from Bob the Scutter — they meet up with Kryten, Kochanski and Cat who have acquired a timewand from a recent Canary mission. They think they can use it to speed up time and get their prison sentence over with. But when Kryten tries to bring Pete the sparrow back to life, he accidentally reverses evolution and turns him into a Tyrannosaurus Rex!

Funniest Moment (arguably)

Lister and Rimmer are beaten up by two Canaries, but their bodies don't feel the effects until they are in the Captain's office — when they appear to get beaten up by two invisible people.

Behind The Scenes

Pete, the dinosaur episode, was conceived largely because *Red Dwarf* was now using CGI effects and programs to create dinosaurs already existed. It was a way of using an impressive monster without the expense of designing one from scratch. Even the close-ups of the head, which were a physical model, had been made for a different production, and were therefore relatively cheap.

Money, however, was still tight which is why the script stretched a little to become a two-parter. A subplot from an earlier episode — *Cassandra* — was also moved across to become part of *Pete*. This thread involves Kryten's desire to be designated a man and his solution to make himself a penis which he calls Archie. Unlike the rest of the inmates, Kryten's penis finds it easy to escape, and spends most its time zipping around the cell or wrestling inside Cat's top in a spoof of the *Alien* movie. Needless to say, Archie was employed for a very modest fee.

Reminiscent of *Back in the Red*, *Pete* is almost a series of sketches as Lister and Rimmer take part in a chain of escapades which increasingly irritate Captain Hollister. Most of this is thanks to one of the scutters, Bob, whom Lister has befriended.

Bob gets Lister a stiffening solution for the basketball game which causes the men on the guards' team to have an issue in the groinal region. Bob also supplies a programmable virus which helps Lister and Rimmer carry out their potato-peeling duty with ease. Unfortunately, the virus is a little over-keen and eats their clothes and hair as well, leading to a naked visit to the Captain's office. This meant Craig Charles and Chris Barrie had to get their kit off for real, wearing only bald caps to hide their hair.

The scutters were always popular with viewers, but were a headache for the production team. The radio-controlled robots were notorious for ignoring the instructions of their operators and going off to do their own thing. In the intervening years since their first appearance, technology had improved enough to make them a little more reliable. "They're much better behaved," said Robert Llewellyn. "They still go wrong a staggering amount of times, it's amazing how many things can go wrong with them. There's usually a man fiddling about inside of them. But they've been very good, they've had some good comedy moments, Bob and Madge."

Meanwhile, Kryten, Kochanski and Cat have returned from a Canary mission with a timewand. This is what turns a dead little bird into a living and scary dinosaur. It was so big, it needed somewhere large to house it. This sent the location scouts out to Bedfordshire and the village of Cardington where two sheds were built in the early twentieth century to house airships. "That is the biggest building I've ever been in," said Craig Charles. "There's been some immense places. But *Red Dwarf* locations are never great, they're supposed to be dingy."

Ironically, despite filming in a hangar big enough to house a dinosaur, it wasn't actually there. It was added later using CGI, meaning the cast were acting with nothing but their imaginations. "We've had to do a lot of looking at huge things that aren't there," said Robert, "which is one of the prop men with a stick with a white cross on the top."

"It's weird working on green screen for hours because you're not quite sure what's happening," said Craig. "So it can be a bit disconcerting, but we've done a lot of blue screen stuff before, it just looks better now because the technology's moved on… The dinosaur is going to be awesome. It's like Spielberg!"

It's while battling the dinosaur with the Canaries that Lister and Rimmer get into a fight with Kill Crazy and Baxter. But, having been zapped with the timewand, their bodies are on a different time stream and don't feel a thing. Until they are, once again, ordered to the Captain's office. As they stand there being told off, the effects of the fight hit home and they are thrown around the office. "I get put through the mill, it's always the case," said Craig Charles. "Being thrown through walls, diving off trampettes and some quite physical stuff which I quite enjoy because it can be a bit boring doing the acting bit. You do the acting bit, do the lines, then someone [else] has all the fun jumping around on trampettes, flying on wires and things like that — I mean, that's the stunt man." But in this sequence, Craig did his own stunts. "That's the fun work, a bit of stress relief."

Episode Eight: Only The Good...

Written by... Doug Naylor

GUEST CAST
Captain Hollister... Mac McDonald
Ackerman... Graham McTavish
Talia... Heidi Monsen
Dispensing Machine... Tony Slattery
Baxter... Ricky Grover
Big Meat... David Verrey

Story

An escape capsule from the SS Hermes arrives, bringing the Captain's spiritual advisor, Sister Talia. But it also brings a virus which starts to eat through Red Dwarf. Kochanski suggests finding an antidote in a mirror universe where the virus's opposite will exist. Kryten rigs a machine to break through the dimensional barrier and Rimmer enters into the mirror version of Red Dwarf. When he returns with the formula, the others are missing and the ship is falling apart. The formula was also reverted to that of the original virus when he stepped back through the mirror. As the piece of paper it is written on catches fire, Death comes for him. But instead of accepting his fate, Rimmer kicks Death in the groin.

Funniest Moment (arguably)

Cat as a professor in the mirror universe.

Behind The Scenes

The original plan for the end of *Red Dwarf VIII* was to have an episode where they go back to Earth. However, this was an expensive plan and one it would be difficult for the cash-strapped production to afford. So, sadly, it was dropped in favour of something cheaper and more ship-bound.

The episode begins with the Dwarfers on probation and Rimmer asking Captain Hollister if he has the potential to become an officer. Hollister tells him he is not officer material, but when Rimmer later enters the mirror universe, he is not only an officer, but also Captain of Red Dwarf. It led to Chris Barrie's favourite line of the series as Rimmer kisses the captain's spiritual advisor, Sister Talia, not realising she is a nun. "I think my best line has to be 'I'm giving you a big wet snog with oodles of tommy tongue,'" he said. "There's so many excellent lines, the scripts have been really good."

His foray into the mirror universe is one of a handful of science fiction ideas that appear in *Red Dwarf VIII*, which had been much less action-driven than episodes in the fifth series, for example. But *Only the Good…* was based on a complicated theory which had the cast scratching their heads. "There's some plot lines that are quite hard to get your head around," said Craig Charles. "Especially when you're talking about parallel universes and mirror worlds and things like that, and everything's got to happen back to front. I think Doug finds it difficult to get his head around it, we're on set and we're going: 'oh no, we can't do that can we?' so you have a process of working it out as you go along and trying to maintain a certain amount of continuity which has always been a problem with this show."

The mirror universe was originally going to play a much larger part in the episode, but a lot of it was lost when a last-minute decision was made to change the ending. There was a concern that the first ending wasn't a cliffhanger and, by rounding up the story, there was less chance of getting another series.

The original ending saw Rimmer entering the mirror universe — as in the broadcast version — and becoming trapped when Kryten's dimension device short-circuits. The point when Rimmer is finally able to return through the mirror, is the point where the two versions diverge.

In the original version, Kryten is seen to have repaired the dimension device and Rimmer returns to find the others still there and the ship intact, but with a formula which has reverted to that of the virus. He then steps back through the mirror to read and memorise the antidote formula. Except, he can't remember it and has to keep going back to read it before finally being able to return through the mirror and recite it correctly.

Kryten makes up the antidote, spreads it around Red Dwarf and the damage is reversed. In the meantime, Captain Hollister and all the rest of the crew have boarded the escape pods and are moving away from the ship. Rimmer tells Kryten to let them go, leaving the main characters alone once again on the ship. Savouring his victory, Rimmer decides to pay the dispensing machine back the coin he owes it, only for the machine to have its revenge by spitting out a drinks can, knocking Rimmer out.

Other moments from the mirror universe had also been deleted, notably a whole scene where Rimmer meets an alternative Lister sporting an impressive military moustache. Other things to have hit the cutting-room floor were moments when Rimmer first arrives in the mirror universe and realises everything is backwards, and a moment where two crew members greet him with a Rimmer-style salute. An earlier scene, where Hollister tells the prison population that they were not going in the escape pods, was also severely trimmed. The middle of this scene originally saw Lister granted space in a pod (presumably for telling the Captain about the virus), but rejecting it so that Kochanski could have his place — in the end, neither of them book passage as Lister is pressured into giving it to Baxter.

Had these elements been allowed to stay, it would have given a lot more balance to the story, allowing much more of the episode to deal with the actual plot. There would also have been a lot more fun in the mirror universe itself and it would have set the scene for the characters to be alone on the ship for a possible next series.

The new ending, which featured in the broadcast version, was hastily pulled together after the rest of the series had been filmed, and involved getting a small crew to come back to Shepperton Studios, along with Chris Barrie. Ed Bye stood in to play Death and a costume was quickly put together by costume designer Howard Burden, who literally begged another production at Shepperton to let him borrow a black cloth. So — instead of returning to a ship with Lister, Cat, Kryten and Kochanski — Rimmer is left alone, faces Death and decides to stand up for himself by kicking Death in the groin.

It could be considered more of a cliffhanger ending than the original, but it turned out not to be needed. Because the BBC decided they didn't want any more *Red Dwarf*.

Red Dwarf IX

Back to Earth

A three-part special for digital channel, Dave

Written and directed by... Doug Naylor
Producers... Jo Howard, Helen Norman
Executive Producers... Charles Armitage, Doug Naylor

CAST
Rimmer... Chris Barrie
Lister... Craig Charles
Cat... Danny John-Jules
Kryten... Robert Llewellyn
Katerina... Sophie Winkleman
Special Guest Appearance by Chloë Annett as Kochanski
Woman (in TV shop)... Karen Admiraal
Man (in TV shop)... Jon Glover
Salesman... Tom Andrews
Noddy... Jeremy Swift

Swallow... Richard Woo
Simon Gregson... Himself
Michelle Keegan... Herself
Creator... Richard O'Callaghan
Bus Driver... Julian Ryder
Oracle Boy (boy on bus)... Charlie Kenyon
Oracle Girl (girl on bus)... Nina Southworth

Recorded: January-March 2009 (in three separate blocks)
First broadcast: April 2009

Story

On Red Dwarf, the crew are gone, Kochanski is dead, Rimmer is back as a hologram and there are problems with their water supply. The reason appears to be a giant squid residing in their water tank. Lister, Kryten and Cat take a diving bell to investigate and kill the squid.

A new hologram who outranks Rimmer, Science Officer Katerina Bartikowsky, takes command to make sure Lister, as the last man alive, revives the human race. She accesses another dimension, the others fall through and find themselves in a department store in London, with *Red Dwarf* playing on every television set. It seems they are fictional characters in a TV show, with only one episode left to run. Their mission becomes to find their creator and get him to write more episodes to extend their lives.

Their creator refuses to help them and says he will gun them down in a *Blade Runner*-inspired chase through the streets. But Lister, feeling his 'life' is meaningless, turns on the creator and kills him. Only then does Kryten realise the origami shapes Cat has been making are representations of the squid and the world in which they are fictional characters is an illusion, created by the ink squirted all over them when they killed the squid back on Red Dwarf. They all return to reality, apart from Lister who decides to stay and have another chance with Kochanski — until he realises he's cool enough and brave enough to return to the real world and win her back for real.

Funniest Moment (arguably)

Lister sits at the creator's typewriter and whatever he types happens around him, including Kryten repeatedly stepping on a garden rake and getting hit in the face.

Behind The Scenes

Red Dwarf VIII did good business for BBC2, but the channel wanted to move on and do different things, so they declined to recommission *Red Dwarf* for another series. The much talked about *Red Dwarf* movie had failed to materialise so it looked like it was the end for Lister, Rimmer, Cat and Kryten unless executive producer Doug Naylor could pull a rabbit out of a hat. This he managed to do by sweet-talking the British digital channel, Dave.

Dave, describing itself as "the home of witty banter", had been showing *Red Dwarf* re-runs for years, with some success. If anyone was going to get out their wallet to finance a new series, it was going to be Dave. They were already investing in original programming, such as comedy quizzes, but financing a scripted show was a new departure for the channel.

Money, it is fair to say, was tight. It was the sort of shoestring budget which made the old days back at the BBC seem halcyon. The first casualty was live recordings in front of an audience, as the production couldn't afford to pay for a week's rehearsal time on top of location filming and an evening's performance. The second, sadly, was the loss of Norman Lovett's Holly. Scraping together enough cash to pay the main cast in the first place hadn't been easy and there was a question mark over whether the budget could stretch to another performer. Norman was approached to pencil in a few dates for filming in the hope he could make an appearance, but he asked for a definite decision one way or the other and, as he hadn't been written into the script, the answer had to be 'no'.

Ed Bye, *Red Dwarf's* long-standing director, also failed to return. It was announced in June 2001 that he had dropped out of the ill-fated *Red Dwarf* movie project and Doug Naylor was planning to direct on his own. This became the set-up for *Back to Earth*.

Financial restrictions also meant that a vast array of sets could not be built. However technology had improved immensely since *Red Dwarf VIII* had used virtual sets, whereby the actors are filmed against a green screen and a different background is keyed in later. *Back to Earth* embraced this technology with welcoming arms, producing some impressive-looking scenes such as Lister in the memorial garden, the hangar which houses the diving bell and many of the long corridor scenes. Equally impressive was Lister and Rimmer's sleeping quarters on board, which were built for real in the studio. This was courtesy of production designer Mark Harris, who was hired for the series after the untimely death of the show's long-standing set designer, Mel Bibby in 2002. In fact, a photograph of Mel can clearly be seen in the Memorial Garden next to the photo of Kochanski and under the headstone which reads 'to those we've lost'.

Location filming took place in a variety of places close to Shepperton Studios where the production was based. Scenes in the TV shop were filmed at John Lewis in Kingston-upon-Thames, scenes in the comic shop were filmed in a real comic shop called *They Walk Among Us* in Richmond (which was sold to become *Ace Comics* in 2009) and many 'locations' such as the bus stop, the creator's house and the *Blade Runner*-esque street scene were parts of Shepperton Studios in disguise. The most unusual location shoot was on the set of ITV's long-running northern soap opera, *Coronation Street*. Craig Charles had been part of the cast of 'Corrie', playing taxi driver Lloyd Mullaney, since 2005. The producers agreed to allow *Red Dwarf* access to the street itself and the iconic pub, the *Rovers Return*, in a bizarre plot twist which saw Craig playing himself as well as the fictional Lister.

The *Coronation Street* shoot took place on January 31st 2008, a good two weeks before the rest of the episode. As revealed in the *"Making Of..."* documentary which was filmed at the time and also broadcast on Dave, things did not get off to a good start. After the Dwarfers' snazzy little smart car version of Starbug arrived on set, it was discovered that someone had locked the keys inside. There was a lot of standing around while the producer rang the AA. In the end, one of the crew used a hammer to break through a small pane of glass and retrieve the keys so shooting could get underway. The car itself looked amazing, having been customised by the production team to look very like the space-faring Starbug. As the production could not actually afford such an expensive prop, Doug Naylor — desperately keen on the idea of a Smart Car Starbug (or 'Carbug') — bought the vehicle with his own money.

The rest of *Back to Earth* was filmed in two blocks, February 16th -27th and March 6th- 8th 2008. It was first shown on Dave in three episodes over the Easter weekend in 2009 (April 10th-12th). The original idea had been for a two-part story and a third 'unplugged' show filmed in front of an audience, but the latter was dropped in favour of the three-part story.

One scene sadly cut from the finished programme was a dialogue sequence with Lister and Rimmer lying in children's bunks in the furniture section of the department store, and very reminiscent of the bunkroom scenes on Red Dwarf. This was designed to open the second episode, but was cut when the first episode ended at a different point than had been scripted. A late addition saw Chloë Annett return as Kochanski in a move which was a closely-guarded secret. Chloë didn't even tell her friends she was back.

The result was a hit for Dave and *Red Dwarf*. It generated a lot of publicity and high viewing figures for the digital channel. It was such a success that Dave came back and asked for more.

Red Dwarf X

Written & Directed by… Doug Naylor
Executive Producers… Charles Armitage, Doug Naylor

Rimmer… Chris Barrie
Lister… Craig Charles
Cat… Danny John-Jules
Kryten… Robert Llewellyn

Recorded: December 2011 (2 episodes) & January 2012 (4 episodes)
First broadcast: October-November 2012

The return of *Red Dwarf* for its first proper series for thirteen years was hailed as a triumphant comeback by fans and critics alike. Although it's not possible to please all of the people all of the time, *Red Dwarf X* made a damned good attempt. It was "a real return to form," according to David Brown writing in *The Radio Times*: "What writer Doug Naylor has done is to remember what made *Red Dwarf* so enjoyable in the first place: namely, the bunkroom sparring between

Lister and Rimmer, and the essential sense of loneliness that befits a show centred around the last human being alive."

"It proved that *Red Dwarf* still has it," said Dave Golder in *SFX*. "It proved that *Red Dwarf* is not past it. And it proved that there's still a lot of love out there for the *Dwarf*, because — if the reaction on Twitter was anything to go by — instead of disgruntled fans going in with a 'go on, impress us' attitude, looking for hairs to split, people wanted it to be good and were downright deliriously happy that it was."

But it wasn't easy to get it made. It was commissioned by digital channel Dave, who had also paid for the *Back to Earth* specials (retrospectively referred to as *Red Dwarf IX*), netting them record-breaking audience figures. The success of those specials and the high level of publicity they generated made both Dave and Grant Naylor Productions keen to make a proper series. There was just the matter of negotiating the details and getting the cast back together, a task which led to a three year gap between *Red Dwarf IX* and *Red Dwarf X*. Craig Charles, in particular, had difficulty getting time off from his role in *Coronation Street* to play Lister again.

Writer and producer Doug Naylor insisted any new *Red Dwarf* revisited the tried and trusted sitcom format of six half hour episodes. That's six episodes which last half an hour, as they had done on the BBC, not a commercial half hour which includes adverts. Doug Naylor told *The Radio Times*: "I didn't want to write 23-minute episodes because *Red Dwarf* episodes are quite complicated — with 23 minutes you end up having to spread the story over several episodes. I don't think it's as satisfying as getting a whole story in one episode."

The other thing the producer wanted to do was to film the series in front of a live studio audience. This was something Dave was understandably wary of because it could mean the plots and all the best jokes ended up being leaked before the broadcast. So it was agreed that audiences would be sworn to secrecy. It was a bit of a gamble, but it seemed to pay off. "Certainly, when we did the last live recording in front of an audience in 1998 there wasn't *Twitter*, *Facebook* or any of that," Robert Llewellyn told *Wired*. "I think the fear we had was that everyone would post story lines, spoilers and things like that, but no one did and that was really fantastic. I mean Doug threatened them with death obviously, but the fact that no one did means the ones who did see it and really enjoyed it didn't want to spoil it for anyone else, as opposed to being told not to. I mean anyone could have posted spoilers but they didn't, which is really encouraging."

For a group of four comedy performers, having the audience there was considered essential. "It's so effective to your performance doing it in front of a live audience," Craig Charles said in an interview with *Digital Spy*. "It brings you up an extra notch. You've got the adrenaline running, you've got the excitement and it's brilliant for your timing because you can't talk over the laugh."

A sentiment echoed by Robert Llewellyn at the press launch for the series. "*Red Dwarf* is a sitcom which should be recorded in front of an audience," he told *Digital Spy*. "That's its core, that's its real soul and that's really what came back doing this show. Doing it in front of the audience was amazingly important for us, and it really makes a difference, [it] really raises our game, raises our performances."

Not that it didn't come without its problems. Doug Naylor had holed himself away for six months to work on the scripts for the series, only to find he had to do a lot of rewriting at the last minute. As well as having to deal with the usual production issues like the availability of guest cast, two weeks of location filming had to be scrapped at the eleventh hour when a massive hole was discovered in the budget. "Originally the audience wasn't part of the budget, for some reason that got overlooked," Doug told *Den of Geek*. "As a consequence, we lost two weeks of location filming so in a way that forced the series to be even more retro. We had one half-day shoot in a forest and that was the only time we left the building. Even on series two, we were able to go to quarries but we couldn't afford it for this one. It's a sorry state of affairs when a science fiction show can't afford go to a quarry!"

This impacted on many of the episodes, particularly one which involved a visit to the circus. "There was some 'excitement' after we realised we had to lose the OB filming as there were scripts littered with situations that we had to abandon," Doug told *Broadcast Now*. "Bizarrely, the result is an early type of *Red Dwarf* series where we are based on just a few sets. We didn't plan it but restrictions can make you more creative."

It was this return to basics which seemed to be a hit with audiences. While *Red Dwarf VII* and *VIII* had experimented with adding a woman to the mix and resurrecting the whole crew, there was more of a sense of the old-style series in *X*. The fifth episode, *Dear Dave*, even has something of the first series about it, being entirely set on board ship with just the main cast, a couple of talking dispensers and a non-science fiction plot of Lister getting a letter from his ex-girlfriend.

If it seems a long way away from those abandoned grandiose plans to turn *Red Dwarf* into a movie, then it is interesting to reflect that parts of the movie script made their way into several episodes. Doug Naylor revealed during publicity for *Red Dwarf X* that he wrote 35 drafts of the film and recycled just a few of those ideas and dialogue sequences. "Most of the ideas are fresh but for the last episode I borrow things from the very early drafts of the film and explain what happened after the conclusion of series eight," he told *Broadcast Now*.

Another improvement for the series was the return to using real models for the special effects rather than everything being computer generated. CGI was still used for some shots and to provide some elements, but solidity was added to the space scenes by using miniatures, just like in the old days. "We always wanted to film the models," Doug Naylor told *Wired*. "I think the miniatures — certainly with the budgets we have — look better than [CGI] model shots."

Ratings for the series reflected the critical and fan acclaim. More than a million people tuned in every week (considerably more than that if repeat showings are included in the figures), which constituted a major hit for a digital channel like Dave. It seemed the public was glad *Red Dwarf* was back — and so was the cast.

"It's been great fun, enormous fun," Robert Llewellyn told *The Independent*. "I love my fellow performers, we get on really well, it's such a privilege to work with them. So that was all good and the scripts were brilliant and the experience of doing it was all fun. The actual day-to-day grind of being covered in rubber and plastic is less fun but it's outweighed by the fact that it's such great fun to be in the show."

"The writing is second to none," Craig Charles told *Digital Spy*. "It's some of the best sitcom writing this country's ever produced, I'd say. Plus the chemistry of the cast, the four of us, it's a peculiar chemistry that's very difficult to recreate."

"It's in its own world, *Red Dwarf*," said Chris Barrie in the same interview, "and shows like that don't really date that much... That, [and] the fantastic writing and the chemistry have kept it going."

Episode One: Trojan

Story

Lister is enticed by an advert for a stirmaster on the All Droid shopping channel and phones up to place his order. While Lister is on hold, the crew board the derelict Space Corps ship Trojan where they receive a distress call from the Columbus III — a ship where Rimmer's brother, Howard, is a both a hologram and the captain. Wanting to impress his brother, Rimmer gets the others to pretend he is the captain of the Trojan and they are his crew. The ruse is such a success that Howard gets resentment overload and it crashes the hard drive that controls his hologram. When Kryten drains his resentment, Howard admits he is really a vending machine repairman, and not a captain after all.

It turns out Howard's crewmate, a simulant called Crawford, was the one who attacked his ship. She threatens the others so she can steal the Trojan datafiles. But Lister can't let her ambition get in the way of speaking to All Droid, so he dives for the phone. Crawford shoots, but Howard takes the shot in order to protect Rimmer. Kryten and Cat download Howard's resentment into Crawford so she crashes — just in time for Lister to pick up the phone, only to hear the line go dead.

Rimmer feels he has finally put to bed his resentment of his brother Howard, knowing that both of them never rose above the role of vending machine repairman. Until a letter arrives revealing that, because of his heroic death, Howard has been awarded the Platinum Star of Fortitude.

Funniest Moment (arguably)

Lister's apoplectic insistence on picking up the phone, even though a simulant is going to shoot him.

Episode Two: Fathers & Suns

GUEST CAST
Pree... Rebecca Blackstone
Medi-Bot & Taiwan Tony... Kerry Shale

Story

It's Fathers' Day and Lister — being his own father — is making himself a card to be delivered to himself in a year's time, which he does every year. As he gets drunk to forget what he has written, the previous year's card arrives with a message from his dad (himself) to buck his ideas up, get his teeth fixed and enrol in the Jupiter Mining Corporation engineering programme. When Lister chickens out of getting his filling repaired at the denti-bot, his dad resigns from the crew and he becomes a former crewman.

Meanwhile, Rimmer and Kryten have initialised a new ship's computer with predictive behaviour technology. Prix, as she calls herself, decides former crewman Lister is no longer entitled to free oxygen and forces him out of an airlock. With no human left on board Red Dwarf, Prix decides it no longer has a mission and changes course to fly into a sun. Lister jet packs back on board to help, but they appear to be doomed as Prix launches an attack of laughing gas and remote controlled walls with deadly knives sticking out of them.

Lister has to persuade Prix he is not the member of the crew who resigned, but actually his son and use the medical records he started at the denti-bot to prove it.

Funniest Moment (arguably)

Lister being so drunk when he records a message to himself that he falls off his chair.

Episode Three: Lemons

GUEST CAST
Erin… Indira Joshi
Jesus… James Baxter
Uncle Aaron… Nicholas Richards
Man Who May Be Jesus and Judas… Tom Pepper
Waiter… Hormuzd Todiwala

Story

A delivery of a Rejuvenation Shower catches up with Red Dwarf, theoretically enabling the crew to restore their bodies to a younger state. But when a test goes wrong, it ends up sending them to Earth in 23 AD without the batteries needed to operate the remote control to send them back. Their only hope is to fashion some crude batteries using lemons, which they can find in India.

The crew not only find lemons in India, they also bump into Jesus. Jesus has got himself into a spot of bother with some Roman soldiers and the crew help him to escape to Red Dwarf. On board the ship, Jesus reads about all the religious wars which were fought in his name and returns to his own time determined to destroy his reputation and stop the Christian religion from being started.

As the others try to persuade him of the positive side of Christianity, Jesus reveals he is not Jesus of Nazareth, but Jesus of Caesarea, and is not the man featured in the bible.

Funniest Moment (arguably)

Jesus responds to Lister cussing his name: "Jesus!" "Yes?"

Episode Four: Entangled

GUEST CAST
Begg Chief… Steven Wickham
Chimp… James Baxter
Chimp Puppeteers… Nik Williams, Jun Matsuura
Professor Edgington… Sydney Stevenson
TV Character 1… Emma Campbell-Jones
TV Character 2… Nick Barber

Story

Lister takes Starbug to investigate life signs on a nearby moon and finds a community of Beggs (Bio-Engineered Garbage Gobblers). When he joins them in a game of poker, he not only gambles away Starbug, he also promises to hand over Rimmer. To make sure Lister lives up to his end of the bargain, the Beggs fit him with a groin exploder which will blow up if Rimmer isn't delivered to them.

Due to an experiment Kryten was running with crystals taken from the quantum rod in the Trojan, he and Cat have become quantum entangled and, coincidentally, keep saying the same things. Using their powers of coincidence, they find the space station where the groin exploder was developed in the hope of finding a way to dismantle it. Unfortunately, the space station is the home of the Erroneous Reasoning Research Academy where scientists specialised in getting things wrong — and the inventor of the groin exploder has mistakenly de-evolved herself into a chimp!

Kryten manages to reverse the evolution process and return Professor Edgington to being a woman. But because she specialises in getting things wrong, they have to do the opposite of everything she says to crack the code and release Lister from the groin exploder.

Funniest Moment (arguably)

Lister thinks Rimmer's description of the woman in stasis on the space station sounds like Kochanski — but she turns out to be a chimp.

Episode Five: Dear Dave

GUEST CAST

Dispensers 23 & 34... Isla Ure

Story

Lister is missing the human race. He reminisces that they were special, but Kryten insists he will, one day, meet another species that will make him just as happy. Lister seeks solace in a conversation with two vending machines, leading to a bizarre love triangle.

The arrival of a mail pod from Earth causes excitement, especially as it includes a letter from an old girlfriend of Lister's, revealing she is pregnant and he could be the father. So the search begins to find a second letter in which she's told him the result of a DNA test to determine if Lister or a bank clerk called Roy is the dad.

Rimmer orders Kryten to help him after discovering he risks being demoted for not reporting for duty in more than three million years. Kryten suggests bribing the medical computer to write a note to get him off. He gathers up a pile of toilet paper from the 2,143 rest rooms on board so he can move money from the supplies budget and fund a donation to the medical computer. It leaves Cat without the necessary bum-wiping material, so he finds some of the mail to use instead. But before he can wipe his derrière, Lister recognises an envelope from his former girlfriend. He takes the letter from Cat and opens it to discover whether he became a father and contributed to the propagation of the human species.

Funniest Moment (arguably)

The Cat uses charades to pass on the bad news that a mail pod has flown into his clothes drying on the washing line.

Episode Six: The Beginning

<u>GUEST CAST</u>
Hogesy the Roguey... Richard O'Callaghan
Dominator Zlurth... Gary Cady
Chancellor Wednesday... Alex Hardy
Chancellor Thursday... Colin Hoult
Lecturer Rimmer... Simon Treves
Big Simulant Advisor... Taylor James
Young Rimmer... Philip Labey
Wendy... Joanne Gale

Story

A rogue droid boards Red Dwarf determined to challenge Lister to a duel across time and space. Lister and the rest of the crew have had enough of Hogesy the Roguey's duels and suggest a cooking contest instead, but before they can begin a rogue simulant death ship launches an attack. Red Dwarf is holed, Hogesy is sucked towards the vacuum and Lister steals his gun, which turns out to be capable of destabilising the molecular structure of solid objects.

The crew escape in Blue Midget and hide in an asteroid while Rimmer is given the task of devising a military strategy. When he can't come up with a plan, he decides he might as well play his father's message. It reveals that the man he thought was his father, wasn't his father after all, and that honour belongs to the family gardener. It seems Rimmer was not descended from a great military family, but from working class stock. This lowers the level of expectation on his shoulders and gives him the impetus to come up with a plan to make Dungo the Gardener proud.

The crew allow the simulant death ships to surround Blue Midget and fire their photon mutilators. As the missiles hurtle towards them, Hogesy's gun is used to destabilise the molecular structure of Blue

Midget's hull. The photon mutilators fly straight through Blue Midget and out the other side where they hit the simulant ships and destroy them. The plan has worked and Rimmer is a working class hero.

Funniest Moment (arguably)

Hogesy the Roguey's attempts to challenge everyone he meets to a duel across time and space.

The Missing Episodes

Bodysnatcher (Red Dwarf I)

Written by… Rob Grant and Doug Naylor

<u>GUEST CAST</u>
None

Background

Had BBC technicians not gone on strike in 1987 and prevented the recording of the first series of *Red Dwarf* on the first attempt, *Bodysnatcher* would have been made and broadcast. As it turned out, all the episodes were rehearsed week by week and none of them were recorded. When cast and crew came back for a second try later that year, the writers had decided to drop *Bodysnatcher* and replace it with another episode, which became *Me²*.

The script (which didn't have a title at the time) was resurrected in 2007 for *The Bodysnatcher Collection* DVD release, which was a boxset of the first three series of *Red Dwarf*. For some reason, the script they dug up from the archives was never completed — which seems odd because the episode would have been rehearsed in 1987 before it was dropped — and the decision was made to finish it. Rob Grant agreed to be involved — for the first time since his split from writing partner Doug Naylor — and the pair of them sent the script back and forth until it was completed. Chris Barrie recorded an audio performance of the script — complete with impressions of Craig Charles' Lister and Norman Lovett's Holly — and it was illustrated by Neil Maguire in black and white storyboard form.

The result is classic *Red Dwarf* in the style of the first series. All of the action is kept on board ship and there are no guest actors, but the dialogue is on par with *Red Dwarf* at its best. It's impossible to separate the original script from the revised version which appears on the DVD, and which has clearly had some substantial polishing and a new ending. Nevertheless, it is an interesting bit of *Red Dwarf* history.

Story

Lister wakes to an emergency siren and staggers to the canteen to discover the alert is only Rimmer carrying out a roll call, even though he knows Lister is the only crew member left alive. Rimmer tries to impress upon Lister how horrible it is to be dead, much to Lister's disinterest, and then gets frustrated at the scutters' inability to write for him.

The next morning, Lister wakes up totally bald with bits of hair all over the bed. At first it seems the problem is stress, but it turns out to be Rimmer who secretly employed the scutters to steal Lister's hair. Rimmer's plan is discovered when the scutters return to pluck some of Lister's eyebrow hair to get the root which contains the DNA and RNA which Rimmer hopes he can use to clone a body for himself. Lister tells him it would be impossible, even for a Nobel-winning geneticist and puts Rimmer on notice that he will be turned off.

This gives Rimmer a chance to hide all the other hologram discs, so Holly cannot bring back Kochanski as a hologram. There is only one disc Rimmer forgot to hide — that of Lister himself.

Lister finds living with Hologram Lister unbearable. He decides that one of them has to go, he gets a flare gun and — rather than shooting himself in the head — fires at Hologram Lister. It sets the bunk on fire, but Lister can't find the fire extinguisher — he needs Rimmer! Hologram Rimmer is restored and finds the fire extinguisher the scutters had tidied away for him in alphabetical order.

The following morning, Lister is woken by emergency sirens. He staggers to the ship's canteen, only to discover Rimmer is launching an investigation into how the fire started. Lister bangs his head on the table in despair.

Dad (Red Dwarf III)

Written by… Rob Grant and Doug Naylor

<u>GUEST CAST</u>
Lister's baby

The first episode of *Red Dwarf III* was originally going to follow on from the cliffhanger at end of the second series where, in *Parallel Universe*, Lister discovers he is pregnant. Rob Grant and Doug Naylor started work on a script, which was eventually abandoned because they felt jokes about a man being pregnant were disrespectful to women. Doug had also recently become a father while Rob had yet to have kids, and they both brought totally different experiences to the script, which didn't help the writing.

Parts of the script that survived were resurrected for *The Bodysnatchers Collection* DVD, and again voiced by Chris Barrie with illustrations by Neil Maguire.

The episode opens with a long dialogue sequence in the bunk-room with Lister walking in heavily pregnant and complaining about his bulging belly and swollen ankles. Kryten later takes Lister to the science room while Rimmer and the Cat pace around outside like expectant fathers. When Kryten emerges, Rimmer has to explain to him about male genitalia before they can establish that Lister has given birth to a boy. A final scene takes place six weeks later where Lister complains that his son keeps waking up at night. Rimmer suggests Lister calls his son Arnold, but Lister prefers the name Barry. Rimmer points out that this would mean he'd be called B. Lister — Blister!

At this point, the script runs out. It's interesting to note that Lister gives birth to only one son — not the twins seen in *Future Echoes*.

Identity Within (Red Dwarf VII)

Written by... John McKay

<u>GUEST CAST</u>
Ora (a female cat)
Zural (a GELF)
Zural's cat alter ego
GELF extras

Background

Identity Within was one of the episodes commissioned from outside writers for use in *Red Dwarf VII*. Written by John McKay, it went through several re-incarnations before being dropped for budgetary reasons. The location filming and numerous GELF sequences were too expensive for a series which already included *Tikka to Ride* and *Stoke Me a Clipper*.

John McKay's original script was resurrected for the DVD release of *Red Dwarf VII*, read by Chris Barrie with illustrations by Neil McGuire. It's certain, even had the money been available, the episode would have changed significantly from John McKay's original if it had been made — it's too long for a start, running at more than forty-three minutes, and hadn't factored in the departure of Rimmer and arrival of Kochanski. Even so, it is the first glimpse of other members of the Cat race since the Cat Priest in *Waiting for God* and the only episode to focus on the Cat.

Story

Cat is sick. He has a toxin which can only be cured by a substance found in 'the business end' of a female cat. In other words, he has to have sex with a female cat, or he will die. Starbug is put on course to follow the trail of the Cat People.

Starbug lands on a planet and they enter a GELF village where Cat discovers a female Cat called Ora being kept in a cage. She doesn't believe he is a real cat because he doesn't smell like a cat and he has no poise or instinct. Cat blames his domestication by the others. He's also angry that the others had only ever been interested in finding other humans or Red Dwarf and never tried to find the Cat People.

After Cat attempts, and fails, to rescue Ora, the others go to a GELF gambling den to win enough currency to buy her from her captors. But their plan to cheat using Kryten is thwarted when a GELF called Zural joins the table. With his winnings, Zural doubles Cat's bid for Ora at an auction and takes her away. But Cat won't accept defeat, takes a sword from a nearby GELF and goes after them. Zural reveals himself to be a male Cat in disguise, Cat spears him with a sword and kills him. Ora and Cat kiss.

Cat drops Ora off at a planetoid and they swear they will never forget each other. But, when he returns to Starbug, he can't even remember her name.

Red Dwarf USA

The Pilot

The pilot for the US version of Red Dwarf *was never broadcast, although it was widely leaked. The story is similar to the first episode of the British version,* The End, *but with the addition of Kryten and some American gags.*

Executive Producer / Developed & Written by... Linwood Boomer
Directed by... Jeff Melman
Created by / Creative Consultants... Rob Grant and Doug Naylor

<u>CAST</u>
Lister... Craig Bierko
Rimmer... Chris Eigeman
Kryten... Robert Llewellyn
Cat... Hinton Battle
Holly... Jane Leeves
Christine (yes, they changed the spelling) Kochanski... Elizabeth Moorehead
Captain Tau... Lorraine Toussaint

Story

A robot called Kryten arrives on board the Jupiter Mining Corporation vessel Red Dwarf and asks for directions from two crew members, Lister and Rimmer, who clean the chicken soup machines. Rimmer is hoping to pass the astro-navigation exam, while Lister is getting dumped by Christine Kochanski.

Lister has smuggled a pregnant cat on board and, when it's detected by the ship's computer Holly, Kryten hides it for him. When the Captain asks Kryten to reveal where the cat is, he doesn't want to tell her, but it goes against his programming not to and he blows a circuit. Lister is put into stasis for breaking the rules over animals on board. Just before he is frozen in time, Christine Kochanski mouths through the glass; 'I love you'.

Three million years later, Lister is revived by Holly to discover the rest of the crew are dead. Lister finds a holographic projection device, but the only personality chip left intact is Rimmer. They find Kryten in the machine shop where he spent the past three million years reading the 'fire exit' sign. In the cargo hold is a creature who evolved from Lister's cat who is very protective of the piece of string he's been playing with.

Back in the control room, their future selves appear with a vital message. Rimmer is not among them, but Kochanski is — and she's alive! Before time runs out, Future-Lister tells them 'you gotta--' before they disappear again. Wondering what the full message might have been, present day Lister turns to the controls of the ship and, after pressing a few wrong buttons, shoots them off into space.

Before the end credits, Holly appears on-screen to explain some of the things the crew have been up to, such as learning to drive a Starbug and meeting a female mechanoid — all of which are illustrated with clips from the British *Red Dwarf*. She hasn't got time to explain everything, she says, 'but you'll get the details later'.

The Promo Tape
(The Second Red Dwarf USA Pilot)

Written, Directed and Produced by... Rob Grant and Doug Naylor

<u>CAST</u>
Lister... Craig Bierko
Rimmer... Anthony Fuscle
Cat... Terry Farrell

Background

This fifteen-minute promotional video was an internal project for NBC and is more of a trailer for a potential series than an episode. It opens with clips from *Red Dwarf V* and the caption: 'once there was *Red Dwarf* UK. And now — *Red Dwarf USA!*'.

Lister leans into camera as he records a message to send back to Earth, outlining his situation on Red Dwarf. This is illustrated with clips of new and archive material. In one new scene, Lister catches up with the Cat in the corridor and they spar over the difference between the lives and sex lives of cats and humans. Another scene is a re-recording of part of *Marooned*. Other clips are from the British show — mostly featuring Kryten — and from the first American pilot.

Red Dwarf USA
Behind the Scenes

In 1992, an attempt to make an American version of *Red Dwarf* was launched by NBC, following approval from Creators Rob Grant and Doug Naylor. It would be based on the British show, but go in its own direction — it would have no choice, as a typical series (or 'season') in America lasts twenty-two episodes, compared to *Red Dwarf*'s usual six. But before that was possible, a pilot had to be made. Almost every show in the USA began life as a pilot. Every year, far more pilots are made than are ever turned into series because the studios use them as a trial run and cherry-pick the ones they want to go into production.

The pilot for the American version of *Red Dwarf* (which has since become known as *Red Dwarf USA*) was produced by Linwood Boomer, a former actor who had previously written for the TV series *Night Court* and *Silver Spoons*. The American stars were Craig Bierko, who played Lister, and Chris Eigeman as Rimmer. Jane Leeves — who later pretended to be from Manchester in the hit comedy *Frasier* — kept her English Home Counties accent as Holly. The one member of the British cast to make the transition was Robert Llewellyn as Kryten.

It was a big decision for Robert to sign up to *Red Dwarf USA*, as it meant signing a five or six year contract. He stalled the producers by asking to have specific clauses added — such as having the same make-up artist from the British show, Andrea Pennell — all of which they agreed to. He worried for a long time about whether he should do it or not, until one night when he was lying awake in bed worrying about it, his other half Judy Pascoe told him to 'sign the fucking contract' so she could get some sleep! His decision was made.

All this was happening during the filming of *Red Dwarf V* and Robert was sworn to secrecy. He couldn't even tell the rest of the British cast, which caused him some considerable discomfort.

After *Red Dwarf V* finished, Rob Grant and Doug Naylor flew to Los Angeles to sit in on the read-through of the script. It was not as they had hoped it would be. "The implication over there is not 'let's make good television', it's 'let's get rich,'" said Rob. "They all gave each other high fives after the reading and said 'let's get rich, we're all gonna get rich, this is going to be a truly rich-making programme'. And Doug and I were looking at each other and thinking, 'er… it's shit!'"

Rob and Doug discovered they were part of a whole team of writers being asked to contribute one-liners to beef up the comedy, which is a fairly common practice for American sitcoms. But the problem — to their minds — wasn't so much the individual gags, but some of the basic elements of the show. They asked Linwood Boomer if they could re-write the script and present their version in the morning. Although he agreed to the re-write, he decided against handing out the script to the cast. So Rob and Doug took it upon themselves to slip it under the cast's doors to get their reaction. The cast preferred the new version.

The pilot was completed, but it was not enough for NBC to commission a series. However, they were still interested and called Rob and Doug back to do a promotional trailer which would give the studio an idea of what *Red Dwarf USA* could really be like. The writers had four days and very little cash to work with.

They thought Craig Bierko could be a good Lister if the part was moulded to suit him, so he stayed. They were much less keen on the original Rimmer and set about re-casting. They asked Chris Barrie to do it, but he was advised against signing up by his agent, and Anthony Fuscle was cast. As for the Cat, hopes of getting Danny John-Jules across on the plane were soon dashed because he was otherwise engaged, in the musical *Carmen Jones* in London. So, as the Americans were keen to have a woman on the series, they decided to turn the Cat into a woman, and cast Terry Ferrell. The female version of the Cat (dressed, appropriately, in a catsuit) was not only supremely good looking, but also supremely confident because she has nine lives and isn't scared of losing a few of them.

One day was allocated to filming in a space the writers described as a 'garage' and a few scenes were quickly shot. Terry Farrell told the *Smegazine*: "It took place very fast; we didn't even have time to rehearse. It was just that suddenly we were there. It would have been nice if we had had more time to rehearse."

NBC passed on this version of *Red Dwarf USA* as well and the project was officially dead.

Robert Llewellyn came home to discover his plumbing was broken and wrote a book about his experiences, *The Man in the Rubber Mask*. "It was an extraordinary experience," he later told *TV Zone Magazine*. "They spent a fortune on it, probably as much money on that pilot as we do on a whole series. What we actually came up with was a very good American-style rendition of a British sitcom. The pilot was very good considering the time it was done in and the acting was great."

Linwood Boomer went on to create the hugely successful sitcom *Malcolm in the Middle*, which also featured Chris Eigeman in eight episodes. The Tony Award-winning Hinton Battle already had a successful career in musicals which he was able to continue. Terry Farrell stayed in space to join *Star Trek: Deep Space Nine* as Jadzia Dax and later returned to comedy with the sitcom *Becker*.

Craig Bierko continued to work extensively in television, although not in a regular lead role. Some fifteen years later, the actor was asked on the internet programme, *Kevin Pollak's Chatshow*, what he thought of *Red Dwarf USA*. He seemed genuinely angry at the way the whole thing turned out. "Oh *Red Dwarf*, that was a disaster! Just horrible, horrible. A horrible Americanisation of a truly brilliant British show," said Craig Bierko. "America brought it over here and boy did America crap on it! It was just so un-funny. Casting me was a huge mistake, by the way — which you hear a lot of actors say — but it should have been a John Belushi-type guy, but America went 'well, we'll do like a Han Solo thing'. I was like 'I wanna pay rent, so great!', but it's instantly not funny, because it should be the opposite of what you've seen in *Star Wars*... I'm a huge *Red Dwarf* fan and *Red Dwarf* fans hate the Americanised version, with good reason, it was just terrible."

Red Dwarf USA
The Interview

This interview with Rob Grant and Doug Naylor took place in 1992, after the writers had come back from making the American pilot and promo. It is reprinted here in its original form.

Early in 1992, hopes were high that *Red Dwarf* would follow in the footsteps of many other British sitcoms by getting its own American version. The Americans had had their eyes on the show for some time. But the creators and writers of the series, Rob Grant and Doug Naylor, weren't prepared to let just anyone get their grubby little paws on the series.

"We'd had offers for years from America," Rob Grant explained, "and they usually were of the ilk where they say, 'hey, we really love the idea, does it have to be set on a space ship?'. Usually, they'd come over and take us out for extravagant lunches and say, 'we really think the American audiences won't relate to a dead guy and the Cat's too weird' and that stuff."

After years of sending TV executives back on the Boeing, NBC came up with an attractive deal that seemed to be in the spirit of the original series.

Rob Grant and Doug Naylor were invited over to the States as creative consultants on the show. "We expected to go over there this January and see it being made and just basically say, 'we think Lister's hair should be parted on the left,'" said Rob. "In fact we got off the plane in Hollywood and we started work the instant we hit the hotel... we were doing re-writes all week and he [the producer] was working us like a dog and we had jet-lag and it was horrible."

Rob and Doug had a lot of input at script level, but optimism began to fade when it came to recording the show. "*Red Dwarf* is a very difficult TV show to make in terms of the effects and you do need experience in shooting science fiction," explained Rob. "You can't use wide shots, for instance. If you look at *Alien* there is not a single shot of people's feet because the instant you see it's a set you've blown it. And so the rule is: shoot it as tight as you can and cut as quick as you can, and all this stuff. The director's experience came from *Night Court* and he was kind of shooting *Night Court* in space and we were saying, 'no, light it *nice*, there's no need to turn all the lights on, turn some of them *off!*'"

One of the tricks used a lot in *Red Dwarf* is split screen where two parallel parts of a scene are shot at different times using the same camera then merged together so it looks like there are, for example, two Rimmers on the ship at the same time. Rob remembered the American assistant director didn't really understand the concept. "We were going around saying things like — trying to be polite, but also trying to make sure they do it right — 'you do realise you have to lock the camera off with the split and sort of put armed guards round it so people don't knock the camera?' And she said, 'oh no we were going to use two cameras to do the split screen' and I was thinking, 'oh my God they've got a whole new technology over here that I know nothing about, what a wonderful idea!'"

It turned out they intended separating the two halves of the screen with some sort of blue line. "They simply had no experience of shooting special effects or anything like that," said Rob. "The day of recording was just a complete nightmare. They'd gone along with the dictum of wanting to play-down the science fiction... They knew nothing about science fiction and didn't think it mattered. In the pilot script when Lister picks up Rimmer's lightbee and throws it in the air, the lightbee's described as a 'gizmo' and that's when the chills started going up my spine and I thought this has no chance."

Rob and Doug were also unhappy about the casting and would have re-cast if they had had the power to do so. Craig Bierko's Lister obviously didn't fit the part as it was originally written, and Rob remembered trying to explain this to the producer. "We said, 'look, Craig Bierko is too good-looking to play the part of this guy who can't get a date with this girl [Kochanski]'. And everybody, all the crew were saying it. And all the women on the crew were gog-like about Craig Bierko... And the network executives took us into this little room at the end of the show and said 'Craig Bierko doesn't work, he's too good-looking'... We had the weekend to rewrite the show and make it so he wasn't just a loser and it's kind of hard to completely re-create the character over the weekend and I think a lot of the rest of the show suffered because of it. In fact the whole opening scenes, up until the first sleeping quarters scene were never rehearsed, they just went on in front of the camera and did the best they could. So that explains part of why it's a bit flat at the beginning."

Doug said it seemed to him that the American team didn't have anything new to bring to the show other than American actors. "It's really like they didn't have an original thought," he said. "We began to get seriously worried about whether the show could sustain at all. It was born out, really, because when we got the next four scripts they'd just crossed out Rob Grant and Doug Naylor and put Linwood Boomer on them."

"We couldn't believe it when we first went out there that they had actually copied the entire set," said Rob. "They had the same ashtrays! God knows how they got them. They bought these special space-age ashtrays in. I tell you, going round with jet-lag and worked out of your nuts and listening to the same dialogue from American voices on the same set was a very unreal experience."

"Also Rimmer was played by a guy called Chris Eigeman, Lister was played by a guy called Craig Bierko," added Doug. "So you got 'Craig' and 'Chris' going, then you see Robert [Llewellyn] there and you think, 'oh we're back in England'. And then you go, 'I can't cope with this, I'm gonna have a cup of coffee'. And I went to have a cup of coffee and the Mars bars were called Milky Ways and the Milky

Ways were called Mars bars. And you just think, 'oh, it's just a parallel universe!'"

After the disappointing pilot was completed, Rob Grant and Doug Naylor decided to make a short promo film which they had control of and would hopefully lead to a series being commissioned. "NBC really wanted a female Cat and they really wanted to recast Rimmer," said Doug. "We didn't want a female Cat... We felt we couldn't just change Danny's part and give it to a woman and it would be the same... I'm not sure there'd be any comedy there going 'hey, aren't I fabulous looking?' because she is!"

The clash of the American and British cultures were very much evident while they were recasting. "When we were trying to recast Rimmer," said Rob, "the number of actors who came in and did such phony British accents to try and — I don't know — it's so curious. A lot of them treat you like you're from Moldavia."

Doug thought one actor who auditioned had a speech impediment. "He sat there and started to say, 'hi, how are you? How's it going? How long have you been in town?' — all this. His accent was just so extraordinary, like a cross between Dick Van Dyke doing his cockney accent and I thought, 'oh the poor guy, there's something wrong with him' and the American casting woman was going, 'oh wow, oh neat, oh wow, that's just so terrific!' and it turns out he was doing what he thought was a very, very good British accent. And suddenly he started speaking in an American accent, and it was like, 'oh you're *not* an idiot!'"

Despite the many faults in the American pilot, Doug thought it could have worked if it had gone into production. "All we needed was six shows and it would have made it... Craig Bierko would have been a star. Robert would have been a mega-star. We could have always changed Rimmer. Terry Farrell [the female Cat], although it doesn't really come across in the promo, is a very very funny comedienne, really really funny. I wasn't crazy about Holly, but not offensive, certainly anybody over there who speaks with an English accent they just fall around at."

Although NBC chickened out of making the series, CBS expressed an interest and suggested a series of six American episodes to Rob and Doug. "We got a two-page fax from these two writers in Los Angeles," said Rob. "They weren't going to make it three million years in the future, they were going to make it like a couple of hundred years so that people weren't too worried and so that Earth was still there and they were going to have contact with Earth and the basic mission was for Lister to get 'babes' was how they described it. They weren't going to have a Cat at all, they were going to have a character called Veronica. Her plus point was that she was what do they call it? — 'issue orientated' — so that she would bring issues to it. And they asked for a reply and we said 'fuck off and die', basically."

The project never went into production. But when Rob Grant and Doug Naylor left the States in 1992, there was still very much a buzz about *Red Dwarf* and a feeling that something similar could be made. "I wouldn't be shocked if Universal come up with *Dudes in Space*," he commented dismissively.

Red Dwarf Movie

The Film That Never Was

There had long been rumblings about the possibility of making a *Red Dwarf* movie, but attempts to get the project underway really got started after *Red Dwarf VI*. Executive producer Doug Naylor was determined on two points: that it would star the original British cast; and he would not be bullied into making creative decisions he didn't agree with. There was just one problem — he needed to find someone to pay for it.

Work on the movie was interrupted for *Red Dwarf VII*, although Doug Naylor's decision to bring a woman into the main cast — Kochanski — was taken partly with the movie in mind. It was likely to be made with some American money, and US executives wanted to see a main female role.

By 1997, Doug was determined it was going to happen. "Yeah, I keep saying there's going to be a movie," he said at the launch of the *Red Dwarf Re-mastered* DVD project. "We'll start making the movie after we've done series eight. People are constantly cynical [saying things like] 'you're only doing this [re-mastering old episodes] to appeal to the American market because you want to have the movie made'. We don't need to appeal to the American market, we've already got the money, so we have the money, the film will be made even if every single person in the States hates the series, it has no effect on whether the movie's made. Obviously, if the movie's successful there, it will be a more successful movie, but primarily we don't do anything to appeal to the States, we do it because we want to do it."

Even the cast were prepared for the movie to go ahead. Craig Charles, in 1997, said he was going to film "a *Red Dwarf* movie later on next year. It's going to happen. You heard it here first!"

The movie didn't happen in 1998. The filming of *Red Dwarf VIII* was a little later than Craig thought, although plans for the movie remained very much alive. Director Ed Bye, while in post-production for the eighth series, was actively on board. "I have a plan of how to shoot it," he said, with confidence. "Doug and I are working on a plan for the best way to shoot the *Red Dwarf* film to make sure that it's the best it can possibly be, to avoid the pitfalls of TV spinoffs going belly up. We have a secret plan, we know how to make this, nobody else can do it — that's official! We'll probably shoot in the year 2000. These things, particularly with movies, there are loads of negotiations and bits of paper to be signed before it comes off and being a British film, you have to make sure you can get the people you want, the budget you want and all of that, but it'll happen."

Ed was looking forward to doing all the technical things he hadn't been able to do on a TV budget. "Absolutely!" he said. Then thought about it for a moment. "No, probably not, we'll probably be struggling for money. I can never imagine a situation with somebody going 'Ed, spend what you like' — except possibly in an advert... If you're shooting a movie, obviously everything's going to be more expensive and the thing that would be great about it would be to spend a bit more time on things, because time is money. But we won't, we'll be racing against time and we'll always be going, 'oh God, why can't we afford all that?'"

At this point, there was no script, although some story ideas had been discussed. Doug Naylor was planning to write it in 1999, after post-production for *Red Dwarf VIII*. "We're going to do a movie," he confirmed at the time. "It will be with the British cast, it will be shot over here, with location work wherever — if there's a desert sequence, Tunisia or wherever. And it will be with money primarily from Europe, some money from Japan. Maybe there'll be some Americans in it, but it won't be, 'oh, here's the American Lister'. That's what they're talking about at the moment, but they're saying the baddies should be American.

"I think that's no bad thing, actually, because I hate all that, that the English are always these uptight baddies. But in the end, it's about making the film that's as good as we can get it. I'm sure we're not going to get Will Smith or anyone like that and I don't particularly want to go, 'oh, this guy was a movie star in 1973, but we can get him' because that won't bring anything to the party either. So it's really about trying to get creative control over the thing and getting it made."

At the time, Doug was looking to shoot it in the spring or summer of 2000, and he was considering bringing in an audience. It would have been a bold move, and one that had not been done by any other movie. "No, it hasn't," said Doug. "[But] I'd really like to test the material. Obviously you can't do huge great action sequences — well, you can, they can be edited and shown to the audience like we do with the location stuff — but in terms of the dialogue, the funny dialogue sequences, I don't see why you can't shoot those in front of an audience and throw the tape away and go and do it again, or whatever. Rather than shooting the whole movie and going to the preview audience, 'what do you think of this?'… I think it's very important that the *Red Dwarf* movie is a comedy movie first and special effects and science fiction second because people can do special effects better than we can and we can't compete with Industrial Light and Magic, but I think we can compete with people if we go for the comedy."

At this point, the writing partnership of Rob Grant and Doug Naylor, which had created *Red Dwarf*, had been over for some years, but Doug contacted Rob to ask if he wanted to be involved. "I think I've spoken to him once in the past year," said Rob in 2000. "I spoke to him in March. He wanted to talk to me about the *Red Dwarf* movie." But Rob had moved on and didn't want to do it. "I don't think so, I don't think I'll have the time to be honest."

In August 2000, it looked like it was really going to happen, with the cast officially pencilled in to start shooting in the spring of 2001. All the main players were involved — Craig Charles, Chris Barrie, Robert Llewellyn and Danny John-Jules; with Norman Lovett as Holly, Chloë Annett as Kochanski and Mac McDonald as Captain Hollister.

March 2001 and the cast gathered at Shepperton Studios for a read-through of the script. To assist with the read-through, additional parts were played by Richard O'Callaghan, Angela Pleasance and Rupert Bates. This prompted some re-writes and a new version of the script arrived in time for rehearsals in May. Those rehearsals featured all of the main cast apart from Danny John-Jules who was working on another film in Prague at the time. From the outside, signs looked good that the movie would be made later that year. Sadly, that didn't happen.

The movie never went into production because the money fell through. This happened on several occasions, and each time, Doug Naylor went out to raise the money again, only to be disappointed.

Everyone involved in the project signed a non-disclosure agreement, so details of the script are sketchy. But it appears the movie would have been what the industry has come to call a 'reboot'. It would have starred the original cast, but the plot would go back to the beginning, to tell the story of how they were stranded on Red Dwarf in the first place. But, rather than re-hash *Red Dwarf*'s first episode, *The End*, it would be an entirely new story.

Red Dwarf Movie Timeline

- **The late nineties:** Doug Naylor secures £10 million funding from a film company to make a *Red Dwarf* movie with a projected budget of £15 million.
- **1999**: Doug Naylor writes the script over the course of nine months.
- **August 2000**: All the main cast are pencilled in to start work in May 2001, with production slated for the spring.
- **c.2000**: The film company's share price collapses and they can no longer fund the project.
- **c.2000**: Doug Naylor re-finances the project with a tax-incentive scheme. Those involved sign contracts.
- **March 2001**: A script read-through takes place at Shepperton Studios with all the main cast.
- It is announced that Doug Naylor will co-direct with Ed Bye. Other members of the crew are confirmed — all of them *Red Dwarf* regulars: Editor Mark Wybourn, sound supervisor Jem Whippey, casting director Linda Glover, make-up artist Andrea Finch (nee Pennell) and costume designer Howard Burden. A storyboard artist, Jim Cornish, is hired; as is line producer Patricia Carr and production designer Allan Cameron.
- Production slips to September for a planned three-month shoot.
- **May 2001**: The cast return to Shepperton Studios to rehearse a new draft of the script, all except Danny John-Jules who is busy filming *Blade 2*. Another actor stands in for Danny, while other roles are read by Andy Taylor, Carole Nimmons and Richard O'Callaghan.
- Harvey Harrison enters into talks to become director of photography. A second storyboard artist, Denis Rich, is hired.
- Robert Llewellyn has his whole body and face cast in preparation for a new Kryten mask and costume, overseen by make-up designer Andrea Finch.

• **July 2001**: Doug Naylor tells the *Red Dwarf* Fan Club that Ed Bye has left the project and that he will be directing solo. He also reveals the movie budget to be in the region of £18-£19 million.

• **Summer/Autumn 2001**: Those involved with funding the movie via a tax incentive scheme get cold feet and pull out. Funding for the movie collapses. Again.

• Behind the scenes, Doug begins flying all over the world to meet people who might be able to save the day.

• **September 2001**: The date when production was due to start comes and goes and nothing happens. There is no official announcement.

• **October 2001**: Grant Naylor Productions releases some of the storyboards for the movie on their official *Red Dwarf* website. They show familiar characters in impressive sets, but give away nothing of the story.

• **January 2002**: More storyboards are released as the *Red Dwarf* movie "approaches production".

• Doug Naylor is still trying to secure financing. Several promising avenues fall through.

• **September 2002**: *Red Dwarf* movie producer Charles Armitage announces that a new period of pre-production will begin in November, with the movie due to go into production in March 2003.

• **April 2003**: Doug Naylor goes to Australia to investigate filming at studios and locations over there. A funding deal still hasn't been secured.

• **2004**: Doug Naylor writes an open letter to *Red Dwarf* fans apologising for the delay in the movie and cataloguing his frustrating journey to get the money to make it. However, he also reveals that he met some American investors at the Cannes Film Festival and, on the eve of further talks with them, was hopeful the movie would finally get the green light.

• **2005 - 2007**: All goes quiet.

• **2008**: Grant Naylor Productions talk to digital channel Dave about a *Red Dwarf* TV special. The movie is mothballed.

Red Dwarf Oddities

Children In Need

The BBC's annual telethon raises money for good causes through its *Children In Need* charity. The accompanying programme features guest spots from various TV celebrities and BBC shows as the audience are asked to ring in and pledge money. In 1993, during the filming of *Red Dwarf VI*, the crew of Starbug sang a version of Queen's *Bohemian Rhapsody*, with Lister miming on his guitar. A little snippet of this was compiled with snippets from other programmes and presenters to form the entire song which included everyone from TV weathermen to children's presenters. The result was somewhat bizarre, but it was for charity.

During 1998, while filming *Red Dwarf VIII*, the main cast filmed a sketch — in character — for that year's *Children in Need*. It features everyone in the cockpit of Blue Midget with Rimmer squeezed into the middle wearing his hard light hologram outfit (so as not to reveal he would be alive in the yet-to-be-broadcast series). Holly finds some old broadcasts from Earth, which turn out to be clips of *Children in Need*. They proceed to make fun of jovial host Terry Wogan and discuss the merits of giving to charity, an idea which is anathema to Rimmer. They then send a message back to Earth with Kochanski urging people to give some money. The sketch includes good gags and is actually pretty funny.

Can't Smeg, Won't Smeg

In 1998, on the tenth anniversary of *Red Dwarf*, BBC2 put on an evening of programming to celebrate, calling it *Red Dwarf Night*. This included a documentary, a showing of *Gunmen of the Apocalypse* and two specially produced programmes, the strangest of which was *Can't Smeg, Won't Smeg*.

Can't Cook, Won't Cook was a popular cookery programme

at the time, with members of the public cooking meals under the instruction of the host chef, with the winner decided via blind taste-test. This chef was usually Ainsley Harriott, who had appeared in an episode of *Red Dwarf VI* as a GELF. In the *Red Dwarf Night* special, Lister and Kryten 'cooked-off' against Rimmer and Duane Dibbley with Kochanski as the taste-tester. All the cast acted more-or-less in character for what was a non-scripted show in front of a studio audience. This led to a lot of fooling around and a certain amount of cheating. "[It was] disastrous, quite honestly," said Ainsley Harriott on the night of the recording. "It was pretty messy, especially with Lister and Kryten. I think they had a right old session down there!"

Universe Challenge

Another programme made for *Red Dwarf Night*, was a spin on the famous TV quiz *University Challenge*. Rather than pitting two teams of students from different universities against each other, this had a team of *Red Dwarf* fans against the cast (Craig, Chris, Robert, Danny and Chloë). The Quiz Master was Bamber Gascoigne and the questions were all linked, in some way, to *Red Dwarf*. The result was a narrow win for the fans.

* * *

Acknowledgements

My thanks to all members of cast and crew who took part in various interviews over the years. I'd also like to thank the magazine editors who kept asking me to write about *Red Dwarf* when each new series came out, especially Mike Butcher at the *Red Dwarf Smegazine*.

Finally, a thank you to my first readers, Julia Daly and Jacqui Collier, whose valuable advice on the original manuscript was much appreciated.

www.ellybooks.co.uk

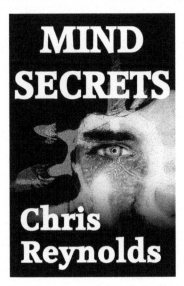

Lightning Source UK Ltd.
Milton Keynes UK
UKOW04f0838090118
315805UK00001B/103/P

9 781908 340061